Between pulpit and pew

Folk religion in a North Yorkshire fishing village

Between pulpit and pew

Folk religion in a
North Yorkshire fishing village

DAVID CLARK
Institute of Medical Sociology, Aberdeen

CAMBRIDGE UNIVERSITY PRESS
Cambridge
London   New York   New Rochelle
Melbourne   Sydney

CAMBRIDGE UNIVERSITY PRESS
Cambridge, New York, Melbourne, Madrid, Cape Town, Singapore,
São Paulo, Delhi, Dubai, Tokyo

Cambridge University Press
The Edinburgh Building, Cambridge CB2 8RU, UK

Published in the United States of America by Cambridge University Press, New York

www.cambridge.org
Information on this title: www.cambridge.org/9780521125017

© Cambridge University Press 1982

First published 1982
This digitally printed version 2009

A catalogue record for this publication is available from the British Library

Library of Congress Catalogue Card Number: 81-18166

ISBN 978-0-521-24071-0 Hardback
ISBN 978-0-521-12501-7 Paperback

Contents

Illustrations

Preface

This book is an invitation to enter the world of religion in a small fishing community. It deals with the historical and sociological development of religion in the North Yorkshire fishing village of Staithes and provides a detailed account of religious life there during the mid-1970s. I hope that it will not be read solely by academics, for I believe that its interests extend beyond those of the seminar room or lecture hall to anyone with a curiosity about village life in general or religion in particular. In Staithes the two are often curiously intertwined and the local religious culture continues to have a pervasive influence upon other aspects of life in the village. Without its particular form of religion, Staithes would be a very different place. Indeed, I hope to show that religion not only provides a means whereby Staithes people make sense of their individual lives but also contributes to the way in which they create a sense of communal identity in relation to the rest of society.

Some readers might immediately be sceptical about such a claim for, like other villages of its type, Staithes has been vulnerable to the attentions of writers eager to indulge a romantic streak. From the mid-Victorian period onwards, in fact, a number of commentators have provided us with exaggerated accounts of the village's quaint and parochial qualities. In writing about Staithes today it would be relatively easy to continue in similar vein for, despite its proximity to an industrial conurbation of considerable economic and administrative importance, the village retains a sense of isolation and detachment, which, though hard to define, is none the less tangible. In providing a detailed description of day to day events in Staithes I have therefore borne this in mind, seeking to convey something of the 'flavour' of the place, whilst trying at all times to scratch below the surface gloss which frequently dazzles outsiders. My success in this must be for others to judge and I hope that those interested enough to pursue the argument will find adequate validation in due course. Meanwhile, if we are to reach destinations beyond academe alone, a few signposts are necessary.

The popular aphorism which maintains that 'you don't have to go to church in order to be religious' has considerable importance for an understanding of religion in Staithes, where, as we shall see, a large amount of religious activity takes place outside of church or chapel. To some extent, of course, this is a matter of definition: 'it depends what you mean by religion'. Here I take religion to mean many things, preferring in the first instance an inclusive rather than an exclusive approach. By casting a wide net it is then possible to include in the category religion, at least for purposes of argument, numerous examples of popular belief, local custom, superstition and ritual; these, despite an apparent persistence in many communities, have so far largely been ignored by sociologists. In other words, I am trying here to get at the underlife of religion in Staithes, as well as its more public face. In order to do this it is helpful to distinguish between two categories of religion: 'official' and 'folk'. The term 'official religion' I use to refer to all aspects of religious belief and practice which find a warrant in the formal teachings of any church, denomination or sect. 'Folk religion', on the other hand, refers to beliefs and practices outside the church, as well as to unofficial aspects of doctrine, theology, organisation or worship which may be found within it. If official religion represents a particular religious persuasion in the abstract, then folk religion is the way that it may be translated in a specific setting. I do not wish to imply, however, that the two are in any way exclusive categories, indeed it is the inter-relationships between them which are of particular interest. At times we see folk and official religion in conflict, on other occasions they appear in symbiosis, each deriving mutual benefit from the other. It is when viewed in terms of combined effect, however, that the distinction is most telling, since it provides a useful means for assessing the totality of religion in the village rather than simply its more visible aspects.

Of course, to look at religion in these terms raises certain problems of method. How can folk religion – an essentially diverse and fragmented subject – be adequately studied? In this case, I have opted for the method first employed by anthropologists studying alien cultures, but which has subsequently been used to such good effect in more familiar settings. Between April 1975 and July 1976 I lived in Staithes as a fieldworker, deeply immersed in the minutiae of village life. In addition to attending and observing religious services and meetings of all kinds, including funerals, baptisms, harvest festivals and anniversaries, I was also able to talk to people in their homes, at their work and in a variety of other settings conducive to *ad hoc* questioning as well as more formal interviewing. From these several vantage points it was possible to build up a picture of religion in the village, uncovering not only its diversity but also its tensions and inconsistencies. I also sought to reconstruct Staithes's religious past, at first through the oral testimonies of elderly villagers and later through a systematic analysis of documentary archival evidence, along with letters, diaries, newspaper articles and a variety of published sources. In presenting the findings of the study I have largely reversed the order of its execution since, logically, any discussion of the historical development of religion in the village should precede an analysis of religion in Staithes today. 'Today' refers to the 'anthropological present', for at no point do I discuss events or circumstances after 1976. This time-lag is regrettable, but whilst changes have occurred in the village since the period of fieldwork I doubt if these would invalidate the general argument presented here.

As I have already implied, the book has two possible audiences. On the one hand it is aimed at professional students of religion and addresses a number of recent debates in the sociology of religion; alternatively the general reader may find interest in the work as an account of the place of religion (especially Methodism) within a small fishing community. With this distinction in mind some may wish to skip the introductory chapter as relevant only to the deliberations of specialists. Parts of Chapter 3 may also be omitted on the same grounds, save the section on 'Fieldwork' which deals with my research activities in the village and is therefore important to an overall understanding of the study. Naturally I hope that most people will feel inclined to read the whole work and in so doing find there some of the excitement and the frustration which I have had in writing it.

To the memory of Alan Pigott

Acknowledgements

A book which is entirely devoted to religious life in a single village must begin with acknowledgement of the many adults and children living there who so generously gave of their time and interest to help me in my enquiries. Without the co-operation and helpfulness of the people of Staithes, the research could never have been brought to fruition. I hope that they will find interest in my account of their village, though, as they will no doubt recognise, it remains but one possible version among several. To all those I met and talked with, my warmest thanks.

Since 1974, when the study began, I have drawn considerable support, criticism and encouragement from friends and colleagues at the University of Newcastle-upon-Tyne. At our numerous meetings Mike Stant, Séan Carey, Tony Archer and Maurice Staton have all commented extensively on earlier drafts. Above all, Bill Pickering, as tutor and friend, has been unstinting in his support and guidance. A number of others have given help and supplied useful information, including Steve Cornish, Stephanie Jones, Peter Frank and John Howard. Members of the B.S.A. Sociology of Religion Group, as well as the various participants at Edward Bailey's Implicit Religion Consultations, have all motivated my endeavours. It was their interest which led directly to the appearance of an earlier draft of Chapter 8 in the *Research Bulletin* of Birmingham University Institute for the Study of Worship and Religious Architecture. Since 1977, and our collaboration on another research project, Jackie Burgoyne has contributed enormously to my understanding of sociology. Reflecting a similar zeal, Rex Taylor read and commented exhaustively on the penultimate draft of the manuscript.

Many have assisted in the process of data collection. I would like to thank in particular members of staff and librarians at Cleveland County Archives Department, North Yorkshire County Record Office, the Borthwick Institute, the Public Record Office, the John Rylands Library, Middlesbrough Reference Library, the *Whitby Gazette* and the *Evening Gazette*. I am extremely grateful to the Whitby Literary and Philosophical Society for permission to reproduce photographs (nos. 1, 2, 7, 12 and 14) from the Tom Watson collection, which were efficiently and speedily printed by Kenneth Baird. Tom Watson (1863–1957), a joiner turned photographer, lived for most of his life at Lythe, near Whitby, and worked extensively in the area between Staithes and Robin Hood's Bay on the coast and Westerdale inland. The examples of his work reproduced here provide us with a valuable naturalistic record of the physical characteristics of Staithes in the early 1900s. I am also indebted to Richard Cale for the recent photographs of Staithes (nos. 4, 5, 8–11, 13 and 15, taken early in 1981) and also for continuing to hold my sociological arguments in such healthy contempt. Graham Normington produced the early versions of the sketch maps. From 1974–5 the project was supported by a Social Science Research Council postgraduate studentship; I should like to express my thanks to the Council for its help at that time. Mies Rule typed the manuscript expeditiously and suffered my late alterations without complaint.

More generally, I owe a deep debt of gratitude to my parents, who have never failed to encourage me in my work and who will, I hope, recognise much that I have written. Lastly, I thank Diane Clark, who has lived with the study since its inception and endured its vicissitudes with forbearance and enormous encouragement.

New Deer, Aberdeenshire
March 1981

1

Introduction: some preliminaries concerning folk religion

Only in recent years has sociology begun to show much interest in religious life outside the institutional churches. It is something of a paradox therefore that whereas a central task within the discipline as a whole has been to question official versions of 'reality' wherever they are found, the sociological study of religion has generally displayed a slavish and uncritical acceptance of officially constituted definitions of religious phenomena. In preference to any more general attempt at defining religion in a particular society, a number of conservatively 'denominational' sociologies, which first emerged in the 1950s and 1960s, have each been concerned with some narrow slice of visible and institutionalised religiosity. As some critics have pointed out, an area of social existence which was once fundamental to the issues raised by the founding fathers of sociology has subsequently become little more than the object of a marketing enterprise, plotting the relative fortunes of the various churches, denominations and sects.[1] The approach has led inevitably to a preoccupation with the measurement, conceptualisation and evaluation of the process of secularisation, depicted in terms of the diminution of institutional religion and portrayed increasingly as a global phenomenon. The present work may seem remote from such a task, being concerned only with religion in one small community. Yet it has been conducted in the belief that it is only through detailed examination of religious life in specific settings that we can develop an understanding of the manifold processes of secularisation. To achieve this however we must first shed those blinkers which so frequently detract from our view of religion and embark upon a study which does not confound the religious institution with the religious *tout court*.

The idea of folk religion

Thomas Luckmann is now acknowledged as the most vocal critic of theory and method in the sociological study of religion and in a classic essay has sought to provide a framework for new departures in research (Luckmann 1967). Luckmann seeks to overcome a situation in which 'religion is

1

amenable to scientific analysis only to the extent that it becomes organized and institutionalized' (*ibid.*: 22) and where 'religion becomes a social fact either as *ritual* (institutionalized religious conduct) or *doctrine* (institutionalized religious ideas)' (*ibid.*). The question is then one of identifying 'symbolic universes' (*ibid.*: 43), some of which have congealed into specialised religious institutions. This 'official religion', as Luckmann conveniently labels it (*ibid.*: 72), is of course currently being subjected to successive crises of plausibility wherein its relevance to individual experience becomes increasingly selective and fragmented. Indeed, the official model is required to compete pluralistically with other ideologies and systems of meaning. Luckmann therefore postulates the end of institutional specialisation in religion and the emergence of new systems of non-trascendent 'ultimate meaning'. These he confidently locates in the private sphere of social relations – home and family – and in the sense of autonomy which characterises the individual in modern society. The examples, unfortunately, are tenuous – 'familism', 'the mobility ethos', 'sexuality'; remote indeed from conventional definitions of religion – and rightly so – but to what extent validated in the meanings attached to the beliefs by the actors themselves? Surprisingly, little empirical research has yet been undertaken to test the notion of 'invisible religion'.[2]

Certainly other writers have been sceptical (Berger 1973: Appendix 1; Weigart 1974) and there is a suggestion that Luckmann's prototypical religious form may be no more than an expression of the intellectual angst and generalised identity crisis of certain sections of the American intelligentsia. Indeed, some social critics have explored the same phenomenon from rather different viewpoints (Lasch 1978; Sennett 1977). More helpfully for our purposes, Robert Towler has argued that Luckmann's polarisation of religion into the official and the natural, or non-transcendent, runs the risk of excluding an important intermediary area. This middle ground is taken up with something Towler calls 'common religion', defined as: 'those beliefs and practices of an overtly religious nature which are not under the domination of a prevailing religious institution' (1974: 148). In an earlier article, written with Audrey Chamberlain and on the basis of some, albeit limited, empirical data, he has been able to suggest some of the forms which 'common religion' might take. These include: the necessity to believe 'something', beliefs in the efficacy of prayer and the rites of passage, the provision of an ethical code, religion as a means of making sense of personal experience, etc. Common religion may therefore include beliefs in luck, fate, chance, astrology and so on. For Towler and Chamberlain it represents a 'large grey area' which has frequently been hidden from empirical studies of religion. On the one hand it 'bears little reference to the beliefs and practices of any recognized religious denomination', and on the other 'it is highly thematic in form, and does not occur as a systematically elaborated set of codes and beliefs' (Towler and Chamberlain 1973: 24).

Towler's concept of common religion is crucial in drawing our attention to religiosity outside the churches.[3] The empirical chapters which follow here are therefore an attempt to tease out some of the forms which this religiosity may take. However, as we shall also try to demonstrate, contrary to Towler's implication, many of the relevant beliefs and practices may also be found within the life of the institutional church, though frequently subject to disapproval and criticism. Certainly much of that which Towler calls common religion is alien to the church, but it may also be the case that many popularly held beliefs can coexist *alongside* official ones in a relationship of considerable complexity. In the present work we shall try to examine this relationship in terms of the cross-fertilisations which ensue when two markedly different cultural forms come into contact with one another. Popular beliefs and practices may, of course, be viewed by the church as superstitious or pagan relics whose anachronistic persistence is irrelevant to religion in the modern world. It would be dangerous for the sociologist to subscribe to such a view of what may turn out to be a genuine and full-blown system of popular religiosity.

Given some *a priori* notion of this 'unofficial religion' it is logical that we should ask questions both about its historical origins and its contemporary persistence. Two recent historical studies may be used to illustrate the first of these problems. In a foreword to his study of popular beliefs in sixteenth- and seventeenth-century England, Thomas writes:

As my work progressed, I became conscious of the close relationship which many of these beliefs bore to the religious ideas of the period. In offering an explanation for misfortune, and a means of redress at times of adversity, they seemed to be discharging a role very close to that of the established Church and its rivals. Sometimes they were parasitic upon Christian teaching; sometimes they were in sharp rivalry to it. I therefore widened my scope, so as to make room for a fuller consideration of this aspect of contemporary religion. By juxtaposing it to the other, less esteemed systems of belief, I hope to have thrown more light on both, and to have contributed to our knowledge of the mental climate of early modern England. I have also tried to explore the relationship between this climate and the material environment more generally. (1973: ix)

Similarly, Obelkevich states in a preface to his work on religion in nineteenth-century Lincolnshire:

It is not in any case the religion of the professionals, religion in its doctrinal purity, that I have sought to recover, but rather concrete phenomena with all the impurities of a specific social context . . . to attempt a social history of religion is not therefore to ascend to a realm beyond experience – but to return to men's 'common thoughts on common things'. (1976: vii, ix-x)

Thus both writers are concerned with the social bases of religion, not in any crude epiphenomenal sense, but at an interactive level where religion and society can be seen moulding and shaping one another. In so doing they allow us a fascinating opportunity to view 'religion from below'; the religious ideas, feelings, practices and sentiments of the common people, expressed not in terms of their degree of incongruence with institutional religion, but depicted instead as an autonomous religious system juxtaposed with the official one.

From Thomas we learn that the relationship between official and popular religion in England can be traced back to the time of the early church, whose missionaries frequently found it expedient to graft 'pagan' beliefs onto Christian rootstock. Throughout the middle ages a dialectical process then developed in which officially sponsored magical items were acquired by the people and turned to their own purposes, only for them to be then in turn denounced by the church. The boundaries between popular and official were never absolute, however:

the legitimacy of any magical ritual depended upon the official view taken of it by the church. So long as the theologians permitted the use of, say, holy water or consecrated bells to dispel storms, there was nothing 'superstitious' about such activity; the Church . . . had no compunction about licensing its own brand of magical remedies.   (Thomas 1973: 303)

The Reformation, Thomas argues, saw attacks on both levels of magic – official and lay – and taught that solutions to the practical problems of everyday life were to be found in self-help, hard work and prayer, rather than in attempts to harness the supernatural for instrumental ends. Yet, as he points out, the Reformation did not prevent extensive recourse to magic, witchcraft and astrology, which continued as alternatives or supplements to institutional religion. Therefore, even in the sixteenth and seventeenth centuries, many men and women remained ignorant of basic Christian dogma or were sceptical and unsympathetic to teachings which seemed to offer little redress to the practical concerns and problems of everyday life.

Obelkevich's detailed study of religion in South Lindsey in the period 1825–75 echoes similar themes. Even in an age of religious revivalism and, indeed, 'an optimum environment for organized religion' (1976: viii), a rich fusion of official and unofficial beliefs seems to have existed. In a chapter entitled 'Popular religion' the author describes the various elements which accompanied the life cycle rites as well as the progression of the ecclesiastical and agricultural calendars. Magical practices abounded and a plethora of superstitions provided predictions and portents of good or bad luck. Moreover, these forms of religiosity were not restricted to a 'pagan' few who shunned the teaching of the churches and chapels which abounded in the area. Obelkevich writes,

Never had the churches shown more energy and expansiveness than in the nineteenth century, and never perhaps had they attracted more of the village population, yet they were by no means the sole expression of rural religious life. Villagers might attend both church and chapel, but their religious realm extended beyond the churches, indeed beyond Christianity, to encompass an abundance of pagan magic and superstition. (1976: 259)

Historical evidence of this kind compels sociologists to reappraise their understanding of institutional religion. It is clearly no longer possible or desirable to conflate religion with the institutional churches when even in periods of apparent ecclesiastical hegemony such a variety of unofficial religious elements can be seen to have persisted. A broader conception of religion is certainly required which can incorporate both the systematic and the fragmentary, the formal and the informal. Only then will we be in a position to go on to examine unofficial religion in contemporary society and its relationship to other social factors.

Since the present study restricts itself to religious life in one community, it is proposed to label the phenomenon in question 'folk religion' and to use the term as a vehicle for the understanding of non-institutional religious beliefs and practices as well as variants or reformulations of official religion.[4] It should be made clear at this point that we are not concerned with postulating hierarchical theories of cultural and religious development; the idea of folk religion does not refer to a primitive form of religion which has generally been superseded by a more sophisticated one. Nevertheless, it may be that folk religion is extremely localised and particularistic and that its beliefs and practices vary between different communities. In the empirical chapters that follow, some of the items described are clearly peculiar to the local area of study; others however will be recognised as having a much broader basis within contemporary culture where they form a persistent complex of hitherto largely ignored religious elements.

The elements of folk religion

Is it possible at this early stage to isolate the distinguishing features of folk religion and say something about their extent? A preliminary discussion may be useful in breaking-up the ground prior to a reading of empirical findings and may indeed help to locate these in a more general theoretical context. The theoretical framework here *preferred* – the word is used advisedly – is one deriving from the separate and joint writings of Berger and Luckmann, from which it is possible to suggest a relationship between folk and official religion, individual, community and society.

The central thrust of Berger and Luckmann's argument in their well known work *The Social Construction of Reality* (1971) is the conception of society as a product of on-going human activity. In an unending process we both create the social world, only to be in turn shaped and constrained by the 'objects' of our creation. The theory is used by Berger (1973) as a point of departure for the sociological analysis of religion. Within this process of 'world-building', humans are 'congenitally compelled to impose a meaningful order upon reality' (*ibid.*: 31). It is a search for meaning precipitated by the omnipresent forces of anomie, chaos and destruction, which continually threaten the existence of social reality. Legitimations, defined as 'socially objectivated knowledge that serve(s) to explain and justify the social order' (*ibid.*: 30), are a vital source of support for this swaying societal edifice. Berger distinguishes two types of legitimation. The first, that of 'self-legitimating facticity' (*ibid.*: 40), represents the legitimation of society through the very 'facticity' which it possesses as an object (*ibid.*). Secondary legitimations, however, derive from challenges to this facticity; they may vary considerably in degree of theoretical sophistication, from the simplest of aphorisms to the all-embracing *Weltanschauung*. Berger asserts that historically the most effective forms of legitimation have been religious, since religion possesses the unique potentiality for grounding the things of this world within a cosmic frame of reference. The concept of religious legitimation is clearly relevant to the idea of folk religion, since it posits the notion of beliefs which may exist at various levels of theoretical and organisational development, whilst addressing themselves to common themes of 'world maintenance' (*ibid.*: Chapter 2).

The idea is most strikingly illustrated, as Berger points out, in the problem of theodicy, a term generally accredited to Leibniz and posed by the theologian, Hick, as follows: 'Can the presence of evil in the world be reconciled with the existence of a God who is unlimited both in goodness and in power?' (Hick 1966: 6). Whilst this classical formulation of the problem is located within a framework of ethical monotheism, Weber (1965) has used the term to advantage within his comparative sociology of religion. Indeed, for Parsons, one of the main themes of Weber's entire thought is 'the integrations and discrepancies between expectation systems which are institutionalized in normative orders and the actual experiences people undergo' (Parsons 1965: xlvi). Theodicy, at its most general level, may be seen as the problem of legitimation which arises out of the existence of suffering in the world. Like legitimations in general, theodicies may vary in complexity and sophistication. Weber (1965) and Berger (1973) both discuss them in terms of a continuum of rationality–irrationality, though Berger is critical of Weber for failing to include the Christological solution to the problem of evil, wherein human suffering is negated through the enduring pain and ignominy of the crucifixion: 'it is crucial that the incarnate God is also the God who suffers' (Berger 1973: 84). Nevertheless, we might add that the Christological solution is merely one among several in the Christian tradition and a theologically rarified one at that. Predestination, as well as beliefs found in various millennial and messianic eschatologies and in the 'born again' movement, are others; so too, at a more fundamental level, are beliefs in life after death and the existence of heaven, since all serve to ameliorate present misfortune by reference to a future state of bliss.

As we shall see in Chapter 8, a number of other theodicies seem to be available within folk religion, where they are often localised, individualistic and subject to modification and accretion. Berger notes that 'large masses of people continue to conceive of society in essentially archaic terms down to our own time and regardless of the transformations in the "official" definitions of reality' (1973: 44). This suggests that popular beliefs may tend to lag behind changes in official doctrine or that 'theoretically' crude forms of legitimation may continue to validate personal experience long after religious experts have formulated more sophisticated 'solutions'. We might speculate, for example, as to the degree of influence which debates on the 'Death of God' or the 'Myth of God Incarnate', or even, indeed, more recent discussion of changes in the liturgy, have had upon the person in the pew or the occasional church attender. We shall argue that the laity not only lag behind their spiritual – and often liberal, reformist – leaders but that at times they may ignore them completely, in favour of folk constructs made available through traditional beliefs and the norms of family and community.

It is a frequent claim that science has 'demystified the world' and that the 'cognitive function' of religion has now been largely superseded. But whilst it is a truism that science may attempt to explain how events occur in the natural world, the explanation of *why* they occur remains highly problematic. 'How' and 'why' questions seem therefore to keep alive the distinction between science and religion. When related to some condition of human misfortune – say sickness – they may be posed as the opposition between two problems: 'how is my condition caused?' and 'why is this happening to me?'[5] Where does the individual find answers to these 'why' questions? A limited amount of existing data allows us to begin to consider this, though comparison between findings is difficult where a variety of methodological styles and a spread of time periods are in evidence. Towler maintains that the answers are found within common religion itself; moreover, its very survival is dependent upon its ability 'to bestow meaning on that which would otherwise be perplexing' (1974: 149). Though Towler fails to indicate just how common religion provides answers, we may assume that in many cases the official church is not perceived as having any worthwhile solutions. As David Martin states:

It would seem that vast numbers of people work on the assumption of two basic principles: one is the rule of fate or chance, conceived as rooted in a kind of symmetry (such as that disasters occur in threes), and the other is a 'moral balance', rooted in a universal homeostasis whereby wicked deeds eventually catch up on those who perpetrate them. (1967: 76)

Beliefs of this nature may be more extensive than is recognised; as Martin comments elsewhere, to adopt the label 'Christian' to describe English society may be to 'obscure the luxuriance of contemporary metaphysic and superstition' (1969: 108).

Beliefs in luck, fate or chance are referred to in a number of empirical studies. Richard Hoggart's observations in working class Leeds include reference to the pervasiveness of luck-related beliefs. 'The world of experience is mapped at every point, particularly closely at the great nodes, in two colours, into those things which "mean good luck" and those things which "mean bad luck". These divisions are invoked daily and automatically' (1958: 29). Gorer's (1955) survey of English character has pointed to the widespread practice of possessing mascots, lucky charms and amulets of various descriptions as well as to beliefs in lucky numbers, lucky days, and so on. More recent evidence for beliefs in luck comes from Abercrombie *et al.*'s Islington survey (1970) and from Jahoda (1970). Occupational superstitions are also fairly well documented in the literature on miners (Dennis *et al.* 1969; Gouldner 1955), fishermen (Poggie and Gersuny 1972) and footballers (Gowling 1973). The notions of good and bad luck which these superstitions contain may hold an important place in folk religion, where they provide a loose framework in which experiences can be given some meaning or rationale; they may even hang together, as Martin suggests, in an 'underground stream of primitive pragmatism, half hope and half fatalistic despair' (1978: 52). The beliefs will naturally be tempered however by the social situation of those who adhere to them. As a member of the Islington team has pointed out: 'Luck is socially patterned ... People are "lucky" to be born with ability or to money, but their good or ill fortune depends on their social position. The better-off have more opportunities. They have more resources to exploit and more protection against misfortune' (Baker 1975: 199). Thus Abercrombie *et al.* report 'One in five working class men rated luck as more important [to success] to only one in twenty of the men in non-manual occupations' (1970: 104). As Hoggart puts it: 'to working class people, luck figures as importantly as steady endeavour or brains' (1958: 138).

Sparse though the evidence is, and despite obvious problems of interpretation and comparison, it does suggest that such beliefs may make up a folk religious theodicy. A sequence of unfortunate events may thus become 'a run of bad luck'; disasters 'come in threes'; 'the wicked flourish, but the good die young'. By these means suffering and misfortune are located in a broader explanatory and mitigatory framework.

If we assume with Berger that all religion has its roots in a generalised propensity to ascribe meaning to reality, this does not, of course, imply that religion manifests itself only at times of great crisis or anomie. As Geertz has pointed out, religion is an integral component in the cognitive apparatus which a culture provides for making sense of the whole of a people's experience (1966). Equally important therefore are the ways in which religious legitimations may serve to integrate the stages of the personal life cycle, the major events of the calendar and the routines, interludes and changes of family and community life: situations characterised by periodicity, transition and tension, rather than catastrophe. We shall argue that in all of these settings it is possible to observe folk and official legitimations, of belief and action, frequently juxtaposed and intermingled and giving rise to a fascinatingly complex religious culture. It is interesting to note, for example, that official religion (which in the present study is predominantly Methodist) does not have a monopoly on the form and content of life cycle rituals. Many elements of these rites in our society originate outside the sphere of institutional religion and are often the object of criticism and disapprobation by clergy and ministers who are prone to regard them as unnecessary 'trimmings' which obscure the rites' 'true' religious significance. Sociologists should avoid such judgements since, as we shall try to argue, many of the accretions are regarded by those concerned as absolute prerequisites to the successful completion of a particular ritual. Moreover, folk elements in the rites of passage may, against a more general backdrop of decline in institutional religiosity, prove a vital area of religious persistence, for which even the church itself may in time prove thankful. Similarly, in the case of the annual cycle, where we find an overall diminution in the significance of the ecclesiastical calendar for secular pursuits, certain crucial festivals may retain observance amongst an otherwise dilatory worshipping population: Christmas and Easter are obvious examples. Yet the significance which they have may also be powerfully maintained in unofficial practices of one sort or another – gift and card exchange, Christmas trees and Easter eggs, family reunions, and so on. In still other cases – the social practices surrounding the celebration of the New Year, for example – folk elements may predominate in the virtual absence of any official religious recognition of the festival. It is important that we understand the meanings which attach to the observances in particular settings, for they may yet give some clue to the very warp and weft of social existence.

Methodological problems[6]

By abandoning the assumption that it is official religion and the churches which determine the totality of religious life in a society, we allow ourselves a broader conception of religious belief and practice and begin to see the possibility of religious items existing at a number of theoretical and organisational levels. The present study attempts to uncover these in a single community, where religious rites, symbols, beliefs, attitudes and meanings punctuate a considerable range of human activity and experience. Yet to tap such a range and to attempt an enquiry into a form of religiosity which may be fragmented and inchoate raises certain methodological difficulties. We shall try here to fuse insights and techniques from three disciplines: sociology, anthropology and history. Only by such eclectic means may a comprehensive picture of religious life in Staithes be produced. The picture we present is by no means complete however and contains many omissions and discrepancies. Where relevant, these have been linked to problems of interpretation arising from the different sources used. The organising principle of the study is sociological: an attempt to explore religious life in terms of its relationship to other aspects of social structure and culture. The primary method employed is the fieldwork technique which originated in anthropology. The data derived in this way have in turn inevitably raised questions about historical antecedents and social change which have been explored through the examination of oral testimonies and a variety of primary and secondary sources. The fusion must be judged on its merits as one possible entrée into a hitherto largely uncharted religious world. For the moment however we turn to an examination of the study area.

2

The village

... a fishing village, situated upon the coast, in a rugged creek, surrounded by
lofty hills, and so completely is it secluded from the eye of the traveller, that he
looks in vain for the town till he arrives at the summit of the craggy hills by
which it is immediately encompassed. The inhabitants live almost wholly by
fishing . . .   (Baines 1823: 547)

... a remarkable village, situated in a deep, narrow, creek, surmounted by
high, overhanging rocks, ranging from 200 to 600 feet in height. A scene more
impressive could scarcely be imagined: the tall rocks shrouded with luminous
mists; the pale glimmering radiance of the murmuring billows; the white
rustling sails gleaming in the distance; the cottages of the weary fishermen
bathed in the lovely light of the moon!   (Ord 1846: 298)

Many aspects of life in the village have changed since these vivid
descriptions of Staithes were written, but their powerful evocation of the
visual impact which the place makes upon any visitor remains as relevant
today as in the first half of the nineteenth century. It is important to grasp
something of the village's physical and geographical location before
proceeding to an examination of its sociological characteristics. The men
and women who first occupied the site towards the end of the fourteenth
century clearly had two important criteria in mind when choosing a place of
settlement – requiring a constant supply of fresh water and some degree of
shelter from the dangerous northerly winds, both for themselves and their
fishing craft. Accordingly, Staithes grew up adjacent to the mouth of a
stream, Colburn Beck, which flows into the sea beneath the protective mass
of Cowbar Nab, the high cliff which curls round to shelter the seaward side
of the village from the north. To the east, across the small bay, the view is
dominated by Penny Nab. Between the two cliffs stretch the wide scaurs,
exposed at low tide, and the shingle beach.

The village lies on the north-east coast of England, some ten miles north-
west of the port of Whitby and eighteen miles east of the Cleveland
industrial conurbation. Formerly a part of the North Riding of Yorkshire,
since the reorganisation of local government in 1974 Staithes stands on the
northern edge of the County of North Yorkshire, which is divided from
Cleveland County by the beck.[1] More locally, the village forms a part of the
parish of Hinderwell, which also includes the villages of Hinderwell,

11

1. Staithes from the south. Early settlers required protection from the northerly winds and a supply of fresh water from the beck. In the left foreground is the staith.
Photograph by Tom Watson, early 1900s.

Runswick and Port Mulgrave, along with the hamlets of Dalehouse, Roxby and Borrowby.

Access to Staithes is gained by the A174 motor road, the main coastal route between Middlesbrough and Whitby. Two minor roads, branching off the A174, lead into the village. The most important of these is Staithes Lane, which runs north from the main road and then down a steep hill where it becomes Staithes High Street and terminates on the sea-front. The other minor road, formerly known as Colburn Road (Ord 1846: 300), which gives access to the northern edge of the village, leaves the principal route one third of a mile to the west of Staithes and descends into the village on its north-western edge, ending in a slipway at the mouth of the beck. These two minor roads are not linked for motor vehicles and pedestrian access between them is by way of the small Abraham footbridge, which crosses the beck.

In 1971 the population of the parish was 2551; Table 1 lists parish populations since 1801. It is possible to estimate the present population of Staithes itself by aggregating the figures for the relevant Census Ennumeration Districts, which again for 1971 give a population of approximately 1500 persons.[2] Atkinson's *History of Cleveland Ancient and Modern* (1874) lists the population of Staithes in 1871 as 1306, at a time when the total for the parish was 2599. The parish population, with the exception of a fall[3] between the years 1881 and 1901, which was principally caused by migration due to economic depression in the region, has therefore remained

2. The view to the east with houses by the beckside. *Photograph by Tom Watson, early 1900s.*

relatively stable for the past century, whilst the population of Staithes itself has increased by about one sixth.

'Steeas' and 'Lane End'

Physically and culturally, Staithes is not one, but two communities. The old village consists of a jumble of cottages and small houses hemmed in by cliffs. Settlement is on the small area of flat land adjacent to the harbour and also in the valleys of Colburn Beck and a small subterranean stream,

Table 1. *Population of parish of Hinderwell*

Date	Population	Date	Population
1801	1224	1891	2021
1811	1397	1901	1937
1821	1483	1911	2491
1831	1698	1921	2608
1841	1970	1931	2146
1851	1736	1951	2386
1861	2571	1961	2412
1871	2599	1971	2551
1881	2467		

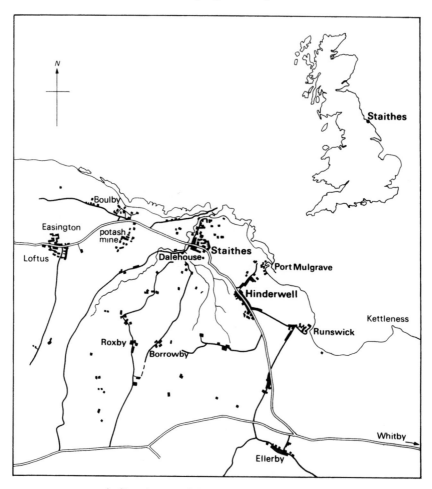

3. Sketch map of the parish of Hinderwell.

slightly to the east. The 'Old Stubble', a hilly mound which protrudes between these valleys, is unsettled. Two rows of dwellings, known as Cowbar Cottages, are situated on the cliff top to the west of the beck, and houses are also found on each side of Church Street, which is a no-through-road leading up from the sea-front to the cliff top. To enter the old part of Staithes, from the cliffs or by road, one must descend, as the local people say, into 'the hole', where the combination of high cliffs, hills and sea which surround it, produce an effect of remarkable physical isolation. The location of the dwellings is explained in part by their method of occupancy, which appears to have been based on 'squatters rights'. John Graves, a visitor to Staithes in the early 1800s, makes the following remarks:

the sea reaches many of the houses at high water. But this is not the only precarious tenure, to which the inhabitants are exposed. The ground, upon which the houses are built, is the property of Lord Mulgrave; to whom the occupiers pay only a trifling acknowledgement, which leaves his Lordship at liberty at any time to dispossess them of their habitations. (Graves 1808: 322)

Housing in the old village is largely made up of narrow cottages, having two, three or even four storeys. Many of these are built into the cliffs and rocks and are reached by a labyrinthine network of passages and innumerable steps, linking small yards or 'garths'. The apparent farrago has been a source of concern to more than one visitor. The late A.S. Umpleby, a former stationmaster at Staithes and a distinguished dialect poet, wrote these lines in a long ballad concerning the fortunes of a man on his first visit to the village, who is about to be deserted by his 'guides'.

> 'Away', ah sez, 'deean't leave ma ere,' –
> I'Jane Wade yard they ed ma –
> 'Ah's nivver finnd mi rooad oot ere!'
> Seea oot i t'street they gat ma.
> Yance oot Ah sez: 'A'en't ye neea leets?
> Ah deean't knaw hoo ye mannish;
> Ah lay ye gi yesens sum freets,
> Theeas neets as black as Spanish.'
> 'Leets? Leets?' they sez, 'ye want ni leets,
> Them's nobbut for awd women;
> Beeath t'meean and stars cums oot at neets,
> An nowther wants ni trimmin.'

(Umpleby 1934: 43)

The more recently developed part of Staithes, situated at the top of the hill in the area between the junction of the A174 and Staithes Lane and the point where the road begins to descend steeply into the old village, contains a variety of housing types. These include villa-style private residences built before the First World War and smaller inter-war semi-detached houses, as well as other individual private homes built more recently. In addition there are two estates of post-1945 public housing, one of which is situated in the area west of Staithes Lane and north of the A174 and the other, a group of recently completed houses, on the opposite side of the main road, to the south. Housing types form an immediate contrast between the original nucleus of the village and the newer areas. In addition, the dwellings enjoy markedly different levels of amenity. The 1971 census records, for example, that out of a total of 260 dwellings in the old village, 15% had no hot water, 26% had no bath and 16% had no inside toilet facilities. The corresponding figure for the bank-top area were 4%, 2% and 4%.

Whilst, for administrative purposes, Staithes is made up of both the old village adjacent to the sea and the newer developments at the top of the

4. 'Steeas' today, with Cowbar Cottages, built to house the incoming ironstone
miners of the 1850s and 1860s. *Photograph by Richard Cale, 1981.*

bank, for villagers the two constitute quite distinct areas of social space.
Whilst the old village is generally referred to in the local dialect as 'Steeas'
and is considered by most to be the 'real' community, the bank-top
settlement, by contrast, is typically regarded as a mere accretion to the
original. 'Lane End', as it is called, is considered, at least by older villagers,
to be populated largely by 'foreigners' who have moved into the modern
housing there from the surrounding district, or else by Staithes folk who
have somehow turned their backs upon the old community. 'Lane End'
therefore represents, for all practical purposes, another village, having its
own shops and post office, as well as a pub and social club. The Roman
Catholic Church, along with almost the entire population of about 100
Staithes Catholics is also situated there. Indeed, the population of this area
has considerably outgrown that of 'Steeas' and in 1971, 1000 people, or
approximately two-thirds of the population of the whole village, were living
at 'Lane End'.

The steep hill dividing the two parts of the village separates them at a
number of levels. For the young in particular, to move to 'Lane End' upon
marriage represents a significant change of lifestyle, particularly in terms of
physical living arrangements and amenities. Much of this stems from
discontentment with the cramped accommodation in the cottages of the old
village. As one woman put it, summing up a widespread viewpoint: 'Some of
the young 'uns won't stay down here now, they want bathrooms and fitted

5. Council houses at 'Lane End'. *Photograph by Richard Cale, 1981.*

carpets and a toilet inside.' For these young people, a modern council house at the bank top represents a vast improvement on a small, ancient, dark and frequently damp stone cottage. 'Lane End' has also carried a certain kudos historically and was once the destination of the upwardly socially mobile. Sea captains and successful retired fishermen, for example, built their large brick villas there in the early 1900s. The difference is not simply a matter of social class however and whilst for some young people a removal to 'Lane End' may represent a real improvement in living standards, the houses available there are usually owned by the local authority. Thus, many parents feel that to rent a cottage in the old village is preferable to life in a council house at the bank top. The older of the two council estates is undoubtedly regarded as a 'rough' place by many villagers, who are often critical of the behaviour of those children and youths living there, particularly when they spend their free time hanging about in the old village.

It is important to make this 'Steeas'/'Lane End' distinction clear since it represents a powerful disjuncture in the minds of villagers and serves to divide the population into separate and distinct communities. A fieldwork observation may illustrate this more effectively. It concerns an occasion when I heard two middle-aged women discussing one of their friends, who had moved on the previous day into a new council house, after living in the old village. One of the women remarking on the move with a sense of

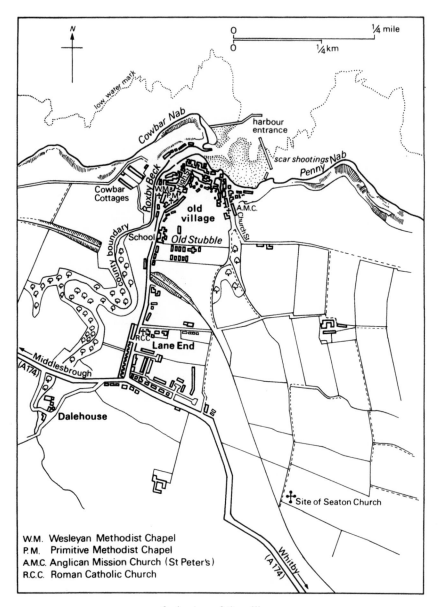

W.M. Wesleyan Methodist Chapel
P.M. Primitive Methodist Chapel
A.M.C. Anglican Mission Church (St Peter's)
R.C.C. Roman Catholic Church

6. A plan of the village.

resignation and regret, sighed, 'aye, she's a Lane-Ender now'. Seemingly, their friend had, in consequence of a removal to 'Lane End', undergone an immediate social reclassification. Likewise, villagers refer habitually to 'going up to Lane End', or 'going down to Steeas' in a way which signifies more than the physical distance separating the two areas and involves a set of implicit assumptions about the nature of social life in them. Perhaps the best way to conceptualise the dichotomous nature of village life is through the use of a traditional/modern distinction. Life in the old village continues to embody many of the hallmarks of traditionalism – social and geographical immobility, the pre-eminence of familial and communal norms, the continued importance of religion, and so on. Here we find that fishing, gossip, chapel events and drinking in the pubs remain the dominant concerns of villagers and, as we shall see later, there is a sense in which these aspects of communal existence are defended against the encroachment of the wider society. Many continue to shun the creature comforts to be found in the expensive council houses at the 'Lane End' and bewail the building programme which has brought newcomers into the village. Their traditionalism is rooted in a strong desire to preserve a certain style of life from erosion by outside forces.

By contrast, 'Lane-Enders', some of whom were themselves born in the old village, have tended to repudiate certain aspects of its community life. Many of these, especially the women, wish to escape the inquisitiveness of neighbours and the limited privacy to be found at the foot of the hill. Likewise some men and women also seek to spend their leisure in different ways to those of the old village. At 'Lane End' the centre of social life is the Staithes Athletic and Social Club which, with a membership of almost 2000, attracts people from a wide radius as well as from Staithes itself. Entertainment here revolves around cabarets, bingo-sessions and discos, rather than the hymn-singing and story telling which form the basis of an evening in one of the old village pubs. This is not to say, however, that Staithes-born 'Lane-Enders' disassociate themselves completely from matters to do with the old village. Most still retain an allegiance to one or other of the chapels there, continue to send their children to Sunday School and are eager to offer support at important annual events. Similarly, several men from 'Lane End' are still actively involved in part-time fishing, spending most of their free time in the old village and giving their services to the manning of the local lifeboat. For these men, living in a council house reflects the weakness of their position in the housing market – most would prefer to live in a cottage by the sea, but are prevented by the high costs of purchase and renovation – rather than any desire to escape the old village. The traditional/modern comparison is thus in no sense an absolute one, but merely serves to indicate an important community division; that it is purely a relative distinction will become apparent when we observe the high degree of traditionalism which pervades the *entire* village.

It should be made clear at this point that throughout the period of fieldwork (1975–6) I lived solely in the old village; it was among the people there that the greatest amount of my time was spent and it was religious

belief and practice there which formed the main focus of my attention. In so
far as 'Lane-Enders' impinged upon events in the old village, they formed a
part of my research interest. As a lone fieldworker, and in the time allowed,
it would have been virtually impossible to have carried out equal and
adequate proportions of participant observation in the two areas of the
village. Virtually impossible, but not entirely so, and I confess that the
richness and diversity of religious life in 'Steeas' seduced me so completely
that little time was left for investigations at 'Lane End'. There lies another
study; meantime, the present work, whilst containing frequent reference to
'Lane End', should be regarded essentially as an account of religious culture
in the old village of Staithes.

Historical development and economic life

Earliest references to Staithes are found in Domesday Book, wherein is
mentioned a settlement, including a church, at Seaton Hall, about three-
quarters of a mile to the south-west of the present village. Russell states that
in 1284–5 Seaton was one of the ninety-seven vills in the wapentake of
Langbaurgh 'and, although now always described as "lost" may have been
the present Staithes, which was not in that list of vills, for in 1450–1 and
1461–2 the hamlet of Seaton Staithes (i.e. Seaton, landing-place) lay within
the manor of Seaton' (Russell 1923: 366). It seems likely therefore that in
the intervening period the original settlement had been largely abandoned in
favour of the present site at the foot of the cliffs adjacent to the sea. Quite
who the populace of the manor of Seaton were at this time is largely
unknown, but speculation is rife, both among villagers and local historians.
Many villagers aver to the slightly romantic notion that their forbears were
Scandinavians who came in from the sea and settled in the area. In this they
are supported by a noted Cleveland antiquarian of the last century.
'Certainly Staithes . . . is designated by nature and position to be made
available by men who, if not originally sea-rovers themselves, which they
probably were, were yet descended from them at no distant interval'
(Atkinson 1874: 224). Place-name evidence in support of this view is open
to some dispute. In 1817 the Rev. George Young argued that both Staithes
and the nearby village of Runswick were exceptions to the general rule that
'by far the greater of the names of the towns, villages and hamlets in the
district are more than 750 years old' (Young 1817: 86), and went on to say
that 'the name of Staiths [*sic*] is derived from the numerous staiths erected
to secure the houses against the sea' (Young 1817: 650). Young clearly felt
that the settlement was comparatively recent in origin and took its name
from the wooden and stone constructions erected to prevent marine erosion
and to consolidate the area adjacent to the shore.[4] However, since sites
requiring staiths for protection were, by definition, already likely to have

been occupied, it is reasonable to assume that they were already named. Atkinson makes this point in a footnote and therefore claims Young to be in error in assuming the comparatively recent origin of the village. He suggests that Staithes is almost certainly the old Norse *stöd*, meaning landing-place (1874: 224). A solution to the problem lies well beyond the scope of the present work, though the Scandinavian influence is well attested by Lawson's (1948: 1949) linguistic study of dialect in the village. It seems likely that the early population of Staithes was composed of a mixture of sea-borne settlers and indigenes, who came together in the period of relative stability following the Viking raids of the ninth and tenth centuries and the Norman conquest of the eleventh, and established a more or less peaceful settlement somewhere around the early fifteenth century.

For the period before this, the recorded history is concerned entirely with Seaton and its manor, rather than Staithes. Before the Norman conquest, three carucates[5] of land in the parish were held by Richard de Surdeval; during the thirteenth century these passed to the Brus family. The under tenants were the Seaton family who were Lords of the manor up to the end of the thirteenth century, after which Edward I granted the lands to Peter de Mauley (Russell 1923: 369–70). The de Mauleys were a powerful land-owning family in Yorkshire and were later to build Mulgrave Castle, between Whitby and Staithes. The manor at Seaton along with others held by the de Mauleys passed to the Bigod family in 1415, when Peter de Mauley (the seventh) died leaving his sister Constance, who some time before 1410 had married Sir John Bigod, as co-heiress. When Constance died in 1451 her share of the de Mauley lands, which included a large area of land in the East Riding near Settrington as well as Mulgrave Castle and the manors at Hinderwell and Seaton, passed to her son Ralph Bigod (Dickens 1959: 54). The religious enthusiasms of Ralph's son, Francis, are discussed in Chapter 4.

After the movement away from the original settlement at Seaton and the establishment of a community close to the sea at Staithes, fishing must have quickly emerged as an important source of livelihood. By 1539 fishermen were being called to the musters of Henry VIII for service in the King's Navy (Russell 1923: 365) and Fox, writing in his journal, expresses concern over the exploitation of the fisherfolk in the village by the local clergy (1952: 80). Other forms of economic life were also beginning to develop. From the early seventeenth century until almost the middle of the nineteenth, North Yorkshire was an important area for the manufacture of alum, which was used as a mordant in dyes and employed in the paper making and leather tanning processes. In the Staithes district, shale was quarried at Mulgrave and Sandsend from 1613 (Turton 1938: 114) and Boulby and Easington from the 1670s (*ibid.*: 191). Alum was prepared by burning the shale in heaps; the charred substance which remained was then leached by steeping in pans, which dissolved out the crude sulphate and produced a thick liquor. This was purified by boiling with urine or burnt kelp, and further concentration was obtained by crystallisation. Staithes played an important part in this process through the production of large quantities of burnt kelp. Women and children gathered seaweed from the scaurs at low tide, after which it was left to smoulder in heaps on the beach for long periods. This activity, combined with the storage of urine in wooden casks, must undoubtedly have contributed to the name 'stinkin' Steeas', which the village enjoyed at the time. The manufacture of alum continued until about 1816 at Boulby, Kettleness and Sandsend (Raistrick 1950: 92) when a more successful process was devised for manufacturing the product from coalfield shales.

By the early 1800s Staithes had established itself as one of the primary fishing ports along the Yorkshire coast and its fishermen were said to have been known from Aberdeen to Lowestoft.[6] Young states that in 1816 Staithes had fourteen large fishing 'cobles', each manned by a crew of five. He describes them as, 'forty-six feet long, sixteen feet eight inches broad, six feet three inches deep, clinker built and sharp bottomed; they have one deck, with a large hatchway in the middle; measure about fifty-eight tons; have three masts, carry four sails, and are generally swift sailers' (Young 1817: 820). Every coble was attended by two smaller vessels, each with a crew of three. These were, 'twenty-five or twenty-six feet long, and five feet broad, with a bottom nearly flat, and a very sharp stern. They are between one and two tons burthen; and have a mast, occasionally "stepped" with a "lug sail" ' (*ibid.*: 820). In addition to these there were some thirty other three-man cobles and eight small lobster boats (*ibid.*: 823). Towards the middle of the century another local historian, Ord, lists 'upwards of eighty boats' working out of the village (1846: 298).

In 1885 a correspondent of *The Times* paid a visit to the village and in an article entitled 'The fishers of Yorkshire' listed the Staithes fishing fleet as comprising 'smacks and cobles of different sizes . . . over 120 in number'. The smacks referred to carried a crew of ten, along with as many as sixty nets, and when fully equipped were considered to have a value 'very little under £1,000'. This period appears to mark the high point of the fishing industry in the village for in subsequent years the increasing problems of selling the catch, along with mounting competition from large steam trawlers, seem to have taken a heavy toll. By 1906, according to Lawson, there were only 100 men still involved in fishing (1949: 3). Shortly afterwards, the First World War had further adverse effects, naval vessels were said to have driven away the herring shoals and it was claimed that German U-boats destroyed several Staithes cobles. By the end of the war, the number of fishing boats was reduced to four (Lawson 1949: 3).

A variety of fishing methods were used throughout the period described.

7. By the beginning of the twentieth century the fishing industry at Staithes had already started to decline. *Photograph by Tom Watson, early 1900s.*

Each year from March until late July and from early October until the following spring, the fishermen concentrated on long-lining for cod, haddock, ling and turbot. The lines, each about 500 fathoms in length and carrying forty to fifty score hooks, were weighted at either end and left on the sea bed for two or three hours before lifting. Depending on the size of the craft, each boat worked anywhere between three and eight lines. During the summer months, attention turned away from lining to the southward travelling shoals of herring which were caught in drift nets. Some of the bigger boats would sail north to Aberdeen in June and July, following the shoals south throughout the summer and finishing in Lowestoft in the autumn. During the same period a certain amount of crab and lobster fishing was done locally, using special 'pots' or creels made from hazel rods and twine and weighted with stones. Against a general background of decline, this particular form of fishing increased during the late nineteenth and early twentieth centuries as home and foreign markets expanded.

Whilst the business of catching the fish was overwhelmingly a male activity and, as we shall see in Chapter 8, the prevailing sexual division of labour gave rise to a number of ritual injunctions and magical beliefs, much of the essential ancillary work, such as repairing and tanning nets, was done by women. Despite its arduousness, the daily preparation of the long lines was generally considered to be 'women's work'. Lines were kept coiled on oval wicker trays, known as 'skeps', with the hook 'snoods' heaped carefully in the centre. These had first to be cleaned and fragments of seaweed and old bait removed before the hooks could be re-baited in preparation for the next day's fishing. The most unpleasant aspect of the whole process, and also the one requiring the most dexterity, was the job of 'skaening' the mussels from their shells. They were then allowed to stand in fresh water before being deftly attached to the hooks in twos and threes. The numerous lines and vast numbers of hooks required enormous quantities of bait and dwindling local supplies had to be supplemented increasingly from outside the area – a costly and intermittent source. Accordingly, a growing reliance was placed upon limpets – known along the coast as 'flithers' – which were gathered from the scaurs at low tide. It was the wives and daughters of the fishermen who followed the ebbing tide out to engage in the operose and backbreaking task of 'flither-gathering' among the bladder-wrack and in the rock pools. Whenever the weather permitted the women's routine was therefore a continual and exhausting round of 'flither-picking', 'skaening' and baiting.[7]

The fishing economy was based upon long-established village families, between which fierce rivalries existed. Capital was usually provided to finance family ventures and often came from kinsfolk who were shop and innkeepers, or in some cases, the owners of Whitby merchant vessels.[8] Boats were divided into sixty-fourth shares and each week, whatever the size of the catch, the ritualised 'reckoning', or 'dole', took place, with proportional shares going to the various parties. In addition to individual men and boy crew members, the 'boat' also took its share, with money allotted to the repayment of the loan as well as to the purchase of new gear. The transaction was traditionally sealed by the taking of a 'reckoning jug' of ale and the 'reckonings' often served to heighten jealousies and competition between crews. However, a fine balance existed between competition and co-operation, since the fishermen relied on each other heavily for assistance in the crucial task of launching boats 'up' and 'down' and dragging them ashore out of the reach of bad weather. Without the help of others, any individual crew would have found it impossible to work effectively.

The fishing trade also spawned numerous secondary activities, and approximately 300 men and women were variously employed as boat-builders, sail-makers, coopers, fish-buyers, curers, hawkers and so on. The latter took fish along a network of pannier ways into the moorland villages of the region and to towns as far away as York. Large amounts of fish were also sent out of the village by horse and cart to the nearest railway station at Grosmont. In addition to the expense which this incurred the quality of the catch frequently suffered as a result of the journey. The railway came to Staithes in 1865 and from then on fish trains left the village three times a week. The service also improved the regularity of bait supplies bought in from outside.

Whilst, as we have seen, the alum industry had gone into a steep decline by the early decades of the nineteenth century, it was soon to be superseded by a new and more profitable local industry. Bands of ironstone were discovered in the area around Staithes in the 1820s (Chapman 1976: 5) and exploitation of the resources first began in 1838, when the Wylam Iron Company started working on the beach about a mile to the west of the village. Ironstone was removed in difficult tidal conditions which permitted activity only at low water and even then only in the summer months, since winter storms and high seas denied cargo vessels access for loading. The ore was shipped to the Tyne and thence inland to Wylam where it was smelted. Some evidence of the iron workings can still be seen today, including the tracks of the rails along which tubs of ore were pushed or hauled and, just outside the present harbour, the post holes of the wooden loading jetty.

The Wylam Iron Company's interest at Staithes was short lived however, for in 1847 a superior source of ironstone was located further inland at Grosmont on the River Esk (Chapman 1976: 6). Nevertheless, work was later resumed, by Thomas Seymour and Cox, who began extracting ore from the cliffs in the early 1850s. About 1854 the interest was taken over by Palmers of Jarrow who were eager to locate sources of ore for their smelting and shipbuilding concerns on the Tyne. Soon afterwards Palmers constructed a harbour, consisting of two stone jetties, in a small inlet about one and a half miles to the south-west of Staithes. The harbour was initially called Rosedale Docks, but when the Rosedale Abbey district further inland began producing ore in the late 1850s, the name was changed to Port Mulgrave in order to avoid confusion. From here the company was able to transport ironstone to Jarrow, initially in sailing vessels, and later in barges towed by paddle steamers.

In 1875 the Grinkle Park Mining Company, a subsidiary of Palmers, opened up a new mine at Grinkle about two miles to the south-east of Staithes. This ore was transported by a narrow-gauge railway which passed through two tunnels and across three bridges spanning Roxby Beck before reaching Port Mulgrave. The Grinkle pit continued operations into this century and in the 1920s was linked up to the Whitby–Middlesbrough railway line. This signalled the abandonment of the narrow-gauge line to Port Mulgrave and the ultimate demise of the harbour, which is now used only by a few part-time fishermen. Mining at Grinkle continued until 1934, when flooding finally led to its abandonment (Chapman 1976: 12).

The extraction of iron ore was also carried out five miles away at Loftus where the mine became the third largest in Cleveland. Opened by the Quaker firm of Pease and Partners in 1865, it remained in their hands until 1947, when taken over by the Skinningrove Iron Company who owned it until its closure in 1958 (*ibid.*: 18). In 1903 the Skinningrove Iron Company also began mining at Boulby, on the high cliff above Staithes.

Nearby, corrugated iron huts were constructed to accommodate the miners and these came to be known locally as the 'tin city'. Mining operations at Boulby ceased in 1934 (*ibid.*: 4).

The development of the ironstone mines had a number of important consequences for social life in Staithes and the surrounding area, bringing in a large influx of new workers and leading to the growth of new communities. Between the years 1851 and 1861 the population of the parish increased by the unprecedented figure of 835 persons. Many of these came from the contracting tin mines of Cornwall and Devon and brought with them a strong brand of religious nonconformity; elsewhere in Cleveland they formed Bible Christian (or Bryanite) groups, whilst in Staithes some of them appear to have become involved in the life of the Primitive Methodist chapel. New workers placed increasing pressure on local housing and new accommodation had to be built. At Staithes a terrace was built for the miners at the top of the bank on the road leading into the village, and two more terraces were constructed on the cliff top at Cowbar. In all some sixty homes were provided. Mining also created other new needs; accidents were frequent occurrences and a small miners' cottage hospital (now a dwelling house) was established. The new industry gradually usurped the pre-eminence of fishing along the coast and had a considerable, though mainly undocumented, effect on the social structure of the whole district.[9]

Economic life in the twentieth century

During the twentieth century a number of important economic changes have taken place in Staithes and the surrounding area. Some old industries have disappeared and others have replaced them, whilst in the village itself the local fishing industry has seen both slump and revival. After 1918 the coastal fishing trade was unable to recover from the state of recession brought on by the war. Four ten-man mules continued to be worked by Staithes fishermen out of Port Mulgrave, but these were sold up in the mid-1920s when competition from deep sea, distant water vessels began to increase. From this period onwards only a few cobles continued to work full time. After the Second World War their crews began to fish almost all the year round for crabs and lobsters, working long lines for only two or three months in the winter when the weather made lobster 'potting' impossible. This work became increasingly lucrative as overseas outlets for the catch were developed and the market price of lobster steadily rose. During the 1960s the government began to encourage the redevelopment of inshore fishing through White Fish Authority loans, which stimulated the buying of new fishing craft. Amidst a general mood of expansion, some men who had only fished on a part-time basis for a few months in summer now turned full-time, whilst others took a new interest in part-time lobster potting.

During the period of fieldwork the fishing industry in Staithes was in a healthier condition than it had been for over half a century. Seven boats were engaged in full-time work throughout the year, each crewed by two or three men, whilst during the summer, some ten to fifteen smaller craft were involved in part-time fishing. Catches are bought by a national fish-buying and wholesale company which took over the business of the Staithes fish-buyer during the 1960s. Crabs and fish are sold entirely to the home market, but lobsters are kept alive in large sea-water tanks before being collected for export onto the Continent.

The fisherman's income fluctuates drastically. One man showed me his account book for the year 1975, which revealed a range of weekly takings varying from £34 to £200. Each week one quarter of the earnings was deducted for repayment of a White Fish Authority grant and the remainder divided between him and his crew member. Part-time fishermen, working only in the summer months and at the height of the lobster season, frequently earn large sums of money. Unlike their full-time counterparts, many of these men go to their lobster pots, of which they might have between sixty and one hundred, both in the morning before leaving for work and then again in the evening. In this way they are able to secure good catches, earning up to £100 per week. Whilst today's lobster fishing is lucrative, the number of jobs which it is able to support are few when compared with the nineteenth century. Almost all of the ancillary occupations have now disappeared and only one Staithes man continues to sell fish in the markets at Teesside. Boat-building, fish curing and barrel-making have disappeared completely as village industries. As we shall see in subsequent chapters, however, the social and cultural significance of fishing and sea-faring continue to have an importance which entirely belies the smallness of the local fishing industry.

The middle part of the twentieth century also saw the final working out and closures of the ironstone mines in North Yorkshire and Cleveland. Soon afterwards, however, new and more valuable subterranean deposits were located in the area. Towards the beginning of the 1960s considerable quantities of potassium carbonate, believed to have extensive commercial potential, were discovered in the eastern area of North Yorkshire. By the end of the decade planning permission had been obtained for a potash mine at Boulby, overlooking Staithes from about a mile away to the north-west. A few years later construction work started at the mine, owned by the Cleveland Potash Company. Operating at considerable depths, potash is pumped from the underlying strata in solution and is then processed on site. The disused railway line, which formerly ran from Middlesbrough to Whitby has been redeployed to transport the product to Teesside. Liquid waste is dumped at sea by means of a pipeline; none the less a number of accidents have occurred, resulting in spillage into the beck and the killing of

8. New developments in local industry: the potash mine beyond the houses at 'Lane End'. *Photograph by Richard Cale, 1981.*

large numbers of fish. Despite legal action, the problem appears to be one which will remain.

Whilst villagers are naturally concerned and annoyed by the spillages, the potash mine provides a welcome source of local employment. Over seventy villagers, nearly all men, were working at the mine during fieldwork.[10] Approximately two-thirds of these were unskilled manual workers, with the remaining third divided equally between skilled manual and non-manual occupations. Work at the mine, for which travelling time is minimal, conveniently complements involvement in part-time fishing. These worker/fishermen, some of whom also serve on the crew of the Runswick and Staithes lifeboat, form an important subcultural and occupational group within the village and, along with the full-time fishermen, express in their behaviour and values the most developed form of the traditionalism alluded to earlier. For these men, economic and social life is essentially village-based and is accompanied by a general mistrust concerning the wider society. The remainder of this core group is made up of men who work approximately seven miles away in the rolling mills of British Steel at Skinningrove. Almost all shift-workers, they are likewise heavily involved in village-based activities.

Of the remainder of the male working population, about seventy are employed in the Teesside steel and chemical industries and a further fifty in building and construction work in Teesside and Cleveland. For these men a lengthy journey to work, either by private or public transport, or alternatively in one of the special work buses, is an essential feature of the daily routine. The time thus taken up frequently limits their involvement in the local fishing and also reduces their opportunities for standing about with other men on the sea-front during the day or in the early evening. Men working away from Staithes are, therefore, noticeably less involved in the dominant male culture of the village. Other employment in the area – especially that of a non-manual kind, is found in shops and offices in Whitby and Loftus as well as the shops in Staithes. Several women and girls work in offices in Middlesbrough, and some are employed on public transport. In addition, during the fieldwork period there were some ten teachers living in the village.

Community life

As the twin bases of village society in the nineteenth and early twentieth centuries, the fishing and mining industries had an important influence on the nature of social life in Staithes, which appears to have had many of the hallmarks of a traditional working class culture. The harshness of physical conditions and the material uncertainties and dangers of work-life were accompanied by well-developed extended family and social networks. Family life was inextricably intertwined with the fishing economy; fathers and sons manned the cobles and smacks, whilst mothers, daughters and younger children assisted in the various related tasks. Homes frequently stank with the appalling smell of mussels and 'flithers' and the tiny cottage kitchens served not only as places to eat and relax when the work was done, but were also used for drying and repairing gear and clothing. Life oscillated between times of lean and plenty. A fall in the price of fish could frequently render a whole day's work profitless and if the catch could not be sold off at rock-bottom prices for conversion into fish meal, it was frequently dumped back into the sea – a waste of both resources and effort. Alternatively, when prices were good, especially in winter, bad weather might result in enforced periods of idleness and consequent loss of income. At such times, families were forced to scrape by on meagre resources; to be thrown back on the poor relief was beneath the contempt of many villagers, though from the mid-1830s the Staithes fishermen organised their own scheme of mutual support.

The precariousness of the family budget merely reflected the dangers associated with wresting a living from the sea in small boats. Numerous examples exist in the annals of village life concerning tragic and fatal fishing accidents. One of the worst of these took place on Friday 14 April 1815, when a total of twenty-nine men from Staithes and Runswick were drowned during a storm (Young 1817: 822). Another equally tragic and illustrative example of the dangers of the fishing trade is depicted in the following passage from the *Whitby Gazette*:

STAITHES FISHERMEN DROWNED – This place has been visited with one of those calamities so common to the coast population of our island engaged in fishing. Whilst pursuing their occupation on the Doggar Bank, on Friday week, there was a heavy sea, rendering the work of overhauling their lines very dangerous, and several of the men in the cobles had a very narrow escape. The two cobles (which the large boats always take with them) belonging to the *Racehorse*, Capt. John Theaker, had both left the boat, each with three men, leaving three boys, the oldest only 16 or 17 years of age, to manage the boat. A heavy sea unfortunately overrun and filled one of the cobles, having on board two brothers named James and William Harrison, and their brother-in-law, Thomas Shippey, who had charge of the coble. Expecting the coble was going down, Shippey seized an oar and jumped out, but finding that it was not sufficient to buoy him up, and the boat, although full, not sinking, he swam back and got into it again. In the meantime, the boys, seeing the accident, run the boat as near to them as they could, and making a line fast to a timber head, they threw it to the men. The brothers Harrison got hold of the line, and were pulled out of the coble, but the boat was going so swiftly through the water that it was impossible for them to retain their hold, and it was dragged out of their hands. James immediately sunk, and his brother floated a short time, and then waved his hand and disappeared. The boys continued to use their utmost efforts again to get near the coble, where Shippey still remained, and, after making three or four boards, succeeded in bringing the boat so near as to throw him a line and pull him on board. The brothers who were drowned, were both married, the oldest James, has left a wife and four children with the probability of another, and William, a wife and one child.

(*Whitby Gazette* 4 April 1868)

These dangers and uncertainties caused numerous men to leave the sea in the middle of the nineteenth century, when the opening of the Cleveland and North Yorkshire iron mines got under way. Attracted by the prospect of economic security via a regular income, the men soon found, however, that they had not escaped the perils of physical danger at work, and were constantly over-shadowed by the spectre of death and misadventure underground. Some indeed were unable to stand 'shore work', and soon returned to the sea once again.

The physical conditions of home life did little to mitigate the harshness of the world of work and the tiny cottages made privacy an expensive luxury. Sanitary conditions were equally poor, since many houses were without even earth closets and waste had to be emptied into the sea. The Ordnance Survey six inch map of the village has recorded for posterity the very spot where such activities took place and names an area on the scaur adjacent to the harbour as 'scar shootings'. A certain modesty appears to have been exercised by the cartographer however, since villagers continue to refer to the place in question as 'scaur *shitings*'. Harking back to this era, people in the surrounding villages still remark on the 'Staithes bum' and a popular local joke maintains that it is possible to tell someone from Staithes 'by the ring round his arse'. Until the mid-1920s, water was only available from about five taps located in various parts of the village; all domestic supplies for washing and cooking had either to be carried from these or from the beck. Cooking itself was done entirely on open fires and in side-ovens, until the late 1930s when electricity was first installed.[11]

Various activities made up a 'hidden economy' which supplemented and often compensated for the vagaries of the official one. Throughout the eighteenth and into the nineteenth centuries smuggling took place along the coast (Ord 1846: 302). Less dramatic, though also important, were the compensations brought by storms and gales in the form of driftwood and other flotsam. Sea coal, washed out of sea-bed seams, could also be collected at low tide. Shipwrecks occurring nearby likewise provided opportunities for gain through salvaging. The diary of the village school-master in 1886 records, for example, how few children attended school on the morning of 3 February, due to considerable involvement of both children and adults in gathering up the disgorged cargo of a coal-carrying vessel which had been wrecked under the cliffs near the village. On another occasion, 20 September 1907, when the steamship *Whitewood* had run aground on the rocks known as 'Cowbar Steel', just to the north of Staithes, fishermen from the village successfully saved the ship from total wreckage and claimed over £450 in salvage money.[12] Many families also kept allotments, frequently with a pig and some chickens. Poaching seems also to have been widespread, both of salmon and sea trout from the beck and of rabbits and hares from the nearby fields. The activities may often have been of vital importance to the family budget, providing not mere extras, but fundamental provisions necessary for survival.

Such conditions are likely to produce certain types of social network and, in common with similar working class communities elsewhere, the village was characterised by mutual bonds of interdependence and support. It was a face-to-face society, based upon a mere handful of families with extensive inter-marriage between them. As one man put it, 'you *were* your brother's keeper, because if he wasn't your brother he was your cousin'. Parish records reveal a baffling duplication of the same christian and surnames and in consequence villagers seem to have abandoned conventional names completely, in favour of nicknames based on individual characteristics. Familiarity was thus a hallmark of personal relations. The community was one in which 'everyone knew everyone else', and where typical forms of address were 'Thou' and 'Thee'. Village social life was by no means entirely rooted in harmony however and we must beware the danger of romanticising the past. Conflict between rival fishermen appears to have been rife, as the crews of the different cobles competed with each other for the largest catches. Likewise, family feuds were legion and were often carried over into other areas of social life, such as religious affiliation. In such a society, privacy was severely restricted, both in the home and in the community. Where everyone did know everyone else, private affairs quickly became public property. Yet this was not without its advantages in certain situations. Many older villagers still recall how in their childhood, doors were never locked at night or even when a whole family went away from the village for a day. That some of these communal traits were found to persist during the period of fieldwork was to be of profound importance for our study of religion in Staithes.

Staithes and the wider society

We will conclude this chapter with a discussion of Staithes' relationship as a community with the wider society of which it forms a part. It is necessary to preface any remarks by emphasising the village's continued geographical isolation. Staithes is located in a part of north-eastern England which remains virtually unserved by major arterial roadways. Whilst the first trains arrived in the village in 1865 their services came to an abrupt end in the late 1950s, when the branch line connecting Staithes to Whitby and Middlesbrough was closed. Similarly, the village's extreme easterly location makes it remote from major north–south lines of communication. To the west there lies a forty miles wide expanse of moorland which even now remains a barrier to easy lateral movement. Consequently, the village has never been exposed to the stream of new ideas and influences which characterise life in communities on major trade and communication routes. One possible exception to this might stem from its coastal location. Many Staithes men have in the past been employed in the Merchant Navy, and its most famous adoptive son, Cook, the explorer, spent a few years there, but the smallness of the local harbour has always restricted its growth as a commercial port.

It would naturally be unwise to overestimate the factor of geographical isolation today, when many villagers own cars and there is a regular bus service to neighbouring towns and villages, but Staithes, in common with many other parts of rural Britain, continues to suffer from limited access to services which are taken for granted by the urbanite. For example, the village bank is open only once during the week and there is no library (readers must select books during the bi-weekly, fifteen minute calls made by a North Yorkshire County Council library vehicle). The nearest hospital is ten miles away, the nearest airport thirty miles, and so on.

Staithes' physical and geographical isolation also brings with it a degree of social isolation, even at a local level. Hemmed in by cliffs on three sides, and facing the sea on the fourth, the village is squeezed into two valleys with little room for expansion, except at 'Lane End'. Consequently, the tightly packed cottages of the old community have an insular and introverted aspect, which the stranger is immediately able to sense. New development at the top of the bank, by contrast, bears fewer marks of insularity and contains a larger proportion of families originating from outside the village. Neighbouring communities therefore view the old village as a place inhabited by strange and slightly different folk. People from Hinderwell and Runswick, for example, often refer to 'the funny lot' in Staithes who are generally considered as fair game for derision and mocking. Thus, references are made to the prevalence of madness in the village – 'You've heard of a village idiot? Well Staithes has got six'; or even incest – 'They say that a young couple moved into one cottage and there was a strange smell in it. They eventually found a baby's body wrapped up in a blanket in the attic' (a reference to the child of an incestuous union). Such anecdotes may, of course, be erroneous, but they do serve to highlight some of the attitudes which exist in the surrounding area. Another is the popular notion that until recently it was impossible for a man born outside the village to marry a Staithes woman and that 'foreigners' who had attempted courtship were summarily run out of the village.

Staithes people are in turn aware of their reputation in the surrounding area and therefore reciprocate with their own stereotypes of outsiders. Suspicion of neighbouring communities might be expressed, for example, in terms of a deep affection for Staithes' values and customs, which are felt to have disappeared elsewhere. This attitude remains remarkably prevalent even among the young people, many of whom are fiercely proud of their village and glorify life in it. For many of these young people leisure-time pursuits are essentially village-centred; for example, dabbling in part-time lobster potting, helping full-time fishermen, setting lines on the scaurs at low tide or the occasional poaching expedition, whilst for males and females in their late teens, and early twenties, the highlight of the week's social events may frequently be nothing more grand than a visit to 'the club' at 'Lane End'.

Even the annual arrival of tourists and the weekend presence of cottage owners do little to erode traditional village life. Whilst artists are no longer drummed out of Staithes for painting on the Sabbath, and the 'foreigner' is no longer the blatant object of suspicion of former times, there remains a sense in which 'real Steeas folk' still form an identifiable group whose depths are difficult to plumb. Week-enders who take to messing about in boats, or for that matter research students who seek to enter into the life of the village in order to study it, may be tolerated to a degree, but can never achieve the position of group integration enjoyed by the man or woman born in the village. Indeed, in the case of weekend cottage owners, local views retain a healthy contempt. It remains a paradox, for example, that those middle class people who have bought holiday cottages, of which there are forty to fifty in the village, have been attracted to those properties which many of the villagers regard as uninhabitable. A significant difference, of course, is the considerable financial means available to week-enders for effecting property modernisation – the very factor which frequently proves a barrier to young couples from the village who wish to buy their own homes. In recent years, as in many other parts of the country, dilapidated cottages have fetched high prices, the like of which, as villagers put it, 'you could have bought all Steeas for once upon a time'. Week-enders are in consequence regarded with a mixture of irony and bitterness; as one young man put it, 'They come down here with their cheque books, and leave their brains at home.'

Clearly Staithes' economic and social development has had important consequences for the nature of social relationships within the village. Nowadays however it is the semblance rather than the reality of geographical and cultural isolation which characterises local society. Nevertheless, villagers often work hard to maintain a set of self-images which can be juxtaposed in a favourable light with images of other types of community. Distinctions between 'Steeas' and 'Lane End' represent merely the tip of an iceberg of communal sentiment which forcefully separates a local way of life from that existing in the wider society. Naturally, to gain entry to such a setting in order to study religious life within it is a task fraught with difficulties. Let us therefore consider the techniques and research strategies by which this was attempted.

3

Studying folk religion

Whilst the research interests here described first emerged when I began postgraduate work in the sociology of religion in 1974, I hope nevertheless that this book will not be read entirely as a sociological one. Indeed, the overriding experience in writing it has turned on an attempt to somehow integrate the perspectives of sociology, anthropology and history. My dilemma in essaying this however has derived not so much from any intellectual identity crisis as from a continuing uncertainty about the various methodological techniques which such an exercise might require. In placing on record how the study has developed I therefore wish to give most attention to the practical, empirical aspects of the research, believing that these cannot be divorced from any subsequent generalisations or theorising which might be necessary.

The majority of my empirical findings relating to religious life in Staithes derive from an intensive period of fieldwork carried out whilst living in the village between April 1975 and July 1976. During that time 'participant observation' was the main research instrument employed and it is the consequences of this method, for my data, my respondents and also myself, which I wish to spell out here. As a technique for studying folk religion, participant observation is felt to have certain advantages over other methods. When successfully managed, it can provide unparalleled opportunities for examining the relationship between religious beliefs and practices and everyday and life-critical experiences. Through both the development of understanding and rapport between researcher and community, as well as the potentiality for unobtrusive observation in a variety of settings, participant observation furnishes an opportunity to study religious life 'in the raw', unconstrained by theological and institutional limits. As we saw in Chapter 1, such a methodology appears vital for any enquiry into religious elements which are deemed *a priori* inchoate, fragmentary and particularistic. Yet in practice a number of factors may contrive to frustrate one's ideals.

The criticisms of participant observation as a method are familiar enough.[1] Studies carried out in this manner are deemed impressionistic, unscientific, idiosyncratic and non-replicable. Success or failure therefore seems to hinge as much upon the individual researcher's personality and ability to interact with informants as upon the canons of scientific enquiry. Data yielded are concomitantly 'soft' (i.e. non-quantifiable), frequently biased and so diverse as to pre-empt anything but the most personalised form of analysis. Social enquiry in this context, it has been argued, becomes more akin to an art form and loses any stamp of scientific credibility. Sociology is reduced to good journalism, or as Glass described the community study: 'The poor sociologist's substitute for the novel' (1966: 148).

The methodological literature which has grown up in response to comments of this kind has by and large sought to answer these charges through an attempt to formalise the techniques and strategies of fieldwork. A typical example of this consists in separating out the constituent elements of participant observation through concentration on the researcher's role in order that discrete aspects of impression management can be identified: 'complete observer', 'observer as participant', 'participant as observer' and 'complete observer' (Junker, quoted in Cicourel 1964: 43). Likewise, Cicourel himself, in the context of a more general ethnomethodological quest for the basic rules which govern interaction, has proposed a set of ideal practical and theoretical 'recipes' for doing field research (1964: Chapter 2). These are concerned, for example, with negotiating entry into the field setting, establishing a plausible justification for one's activities, acquiring different types of informant, sustaining the research and finally, negotiating a successful exit.

Needless to say, most of these experiences rarely find their way into the published outcomes of field research and despite Becker's (1970) advocacy of a 'natural history' approach to the construction of fieldwork reports, the enduring impression created by many monographs is one wherein methodology is largely assumed as given. In anthropology, for instance, where for many years fieldwork itself was regarded as something of a rite of professional socialisation, methodology seems to have been founded on little more than a gentleman's agreement between tutor and student. As Beattie puts it, when describing his own training, 'one rather got the impression that fieldwork was simply a matter of getting into the field and being there; once there one would absorb information by a kind of osmosis' (1965: 5). Indeed, despite the origins of the method within social anthropology, it is bewildering that the acknowledged 'great' ethnographers tell us so little of their research techniques. A related problem, discussed by Bell and Newby, is that of the 'timeless quality' which is so often a feature of community studies in which 'it is as if it all happened on the same day' (1971: 79). A method which seems ideally suited to documenting social *process* therefore frequently yields nothing more than a 'single snapshot' of social life in a particular setting. Readers are thus not only denied an explication of the dynamics of community life but are also deprived of any account of the interactions between researcher and subjects taking place within it.

In another work Bell and Newby (1977) have argued that if adequate assessment of the findings of field research (and empirical studies in general) is to be made, then it is vital that full, frank and explicit accounts of research strategies accompany published results.[2] Inevitably, naturalistic accounts of this type may draw the accusation of washing one's dirty linen in public and are ultimately limited by the strictures of the British libel laws. On the other hand, they are important in going some way towards bridging the gap between 'methodology' and 'findings'. Indeed, we might argue that in the case of participant observation, 'findings' can *only* become intelligible within the context of a detailed knowledge of the research process and the role(s) of the researcher in the field setting. With these points in mind, it is therefore proposed to give some account of the fieldwork period in Staithes, before going on to consider briefly the ways in which the study subsequently developed.

Fieldwork

The principal factors governing the decision to choose the North Yorkshire fishing village of Staithes as the setting for an enquiry into the phenomenon labelled 'folk religion' related to a prior knowledge of the community. As a child I had spent some time there and had subsequently paid occasional short visits whilst an undergraduate. It is true to say that my earliest feelings, prior to fieldwork (and which to some extent still remain intact), were of a village characterised by social isolation and insularity as well as a degree of hostility towards the wider society. The village therefore constituted both a challenge to the prospective fieldworker as well as a possible environment for the nurture of the kinds of folk elements which formed the object of the study. In retrospect, this latter assumption should not have commended Staithes to me, since, in the manner of the 'affluent worker' studies, a more justifiable strategy would have meant the selection of a research setting seeming *least* likely to sustain one's hypothesis (Goldthorpe *et al.* 1969). After several preliminary visits made early in 1975 I became convinced however that here was a community with much to interest the sociologist of religion and perhaps having certain cultural artefacts in need of documentation for posterity.

My next move, therefore, was to write to the rector of the parish, explaining my research interests and requesting a meeting. The rector proved a valuable informant, something of a marginal figure in the local community, both through the historical incumbencies of his role and his own personal political and theological viewpoints. He was consequently able to provide me with an insightful, if rather jaundiced, view of religious life in Staithes. He also warned me of the difficulty of my task and, sociologising himself, argued that the village was 'untypical' and therefore incapable of comparison with other communities. It was a viewpoint which I subsequently heard echoed in the statements of many of the villagers themselves.

Having decided upon Staithes as the study area, I then began seeking accommodation for the fieldwork period. My first enquiries took me to local shopkeepers, one of whom viewed me with some suspicion (I later discovered that despite my tidy appearance, one woman had thought I might be a 'hippy'). After drawing several blanks I therefore called upon a lady who owned a small flat in the basement of her house and in which my parents and I had stayed when I was a child. Once again, I was unsuccessful; the lady told me that she no longer rented the place. Disappointed, I continued my enquiries in another shop, where I was soon followed by the same lady, who explained that after I had left, she had tried to 'place' my face and had duly remembered me as a visitor from some time before. She had changed her mind about the flat and if her husband was agreeable, would be prepared to rent it to me. The following day I received a telephone call confirming the offer.

It is not without irony that as a naive student, I moved into my cottage on 1 April 1975: All Fools Day. It was to be the starting point in over a year of intense observation and participation in the life of the village. For the first week, very little happened; indeed my eagerness to collect data quickly produced acute anxieties as the anticipated richness of folk belief and practice failed to materialise. Nevertheless, those early days were highly instructive methodologically. Various sociological field studies refer to the manner in which communities of one sort or another label the presence and purpose of the researcher (Arensberg 1939; Harris 1974). My own experience is interesting and relevant. From the earliest stages, several people in the village made no attempt to disguise their curiosity about the young man who had moved into the cottage down in 'Steeas'. Consequently, I was quickly beset with solicitous questions and statements directed towards solving the mystery. 'Just down for a few weeks?'; 'I saw you'd moved in'; 'What brings you to these parts?', were typical examples. On these occasions a note of caution sounded in me which derived from the fear of introducing the word 'religion' in an ill prepared context. Whilst I had no intention of concealing my research interests – actively or otherwise – I felt, none the less, that a certain caution was necessary in first articulating these to people in the village. Accordingly, I simply explained that I was a student from Newcastle University, that I was in Staithes to do 'research' and would be living there for several months. To me, this seemed neutral enough; to my interlocutors it suggested different meanings. To my surprise I was subsequently asked both about my 'work at the potash mine' and my 'interest in fossils'. The unlikely interpretations that I was doing research at the mine or that I was a geologist[3] were therefore the first to be placed upon my presence. These did not last long, however, and soon a more permanent, though equally erroneous, explanation was quickly affixed to my purposes.

The early weeks of fieldwork were spent in acquainting myself with activities in the village's chapels and churches, a process which was initiated simply by attending services at each of them. At this point I indicated in conversation that my interests in this direction went beyond those of the lay Methodist, Congregationalist or whatever and sought to outline my concern with the whole of religious life in the village – the chapels, folklore, superstition, birth, death, etc. – from an academic viewpoint. Once again, my deliberate vagueness, in itself designed to obviate rigid classification, was interpreted in a highly specific manner. Henceforth I was incorrectly, though for some indelibly, stamped as a young man 'training for the ministry'.[4] Despite regular protestations to the contrary, the appellation proved difficult to remove. It was both a hindrance and a help.

Undoubtedly, the primary difficulty it imposed was that on a number of occasions it served to set the seal on conversations which I had with various men and women. In particular, it may have influenced the ways in which individuals who were not regular Sunday worshippers at any institution talked to me about their religious attitudes and feelings. At these times one felt that certain aspects of belief were glossed, subjugated or otherwise distorted in order to present a set of opinions on religious matters which accorded with that of the official model. In short, some people spoke to me in much the same way as they would have spoken to the minister or rector.

The idea that I was a trainee minister also had an impact at a purely subjective level. For some months, during which I immersed myself in all aspects of institutional religious life, I felt an increasing congruence between my role and villagers' perceptions of it. In short, the power of the label, as sociologists of deviance have often demonstrated, was such that I actually began to respond in a manner which positively reinforced it. Consequently, I thought deeply for a time about my own religious standpoint and found the position of outside, scientific observer at times difficult to maintain, especially when confronted with particular aspects of doctrine, or more general social comment, such as that found in sermons. Up to the time of fieldwork I had little direct personal experience of Methodism, especially in the semi-isolated rural areas; the effect which it had upon me must therefore be seen in terms of the novelty of the experience and insights which it engendered. A principal consequence of this, albeit temporary, situation was to impose certain undesirable constraints upon my movements. I became acutely aware that my behaviour was being watched with interest and that I must make every effort not to offend those connected with the chapels through any activity which they would have considered inappropriate or offensive. This related especially to the drinking of alcohol, a habit much frowned upon by local nonconformists. The result of this was that during the first six months of fieldwork, and to a lesser extent for the entire period, I found myself extremely reluctant to go into any of the pubs in the village. This must, of course, have had a deleterious effect on the number and range of individuals with whom I was able to talk and made it difficult to speak with the minority of individuals who appeared to have no allegiance whatsoever to a church or chapel in the village.

These difficulties undoubtedly diminished as time went on, and several people had occasion to alter their perceptions of me and my work. For example, I worked occasionally as a labourer for a local builder and also involved myself to a considerable extent in the part-time fishing and in both cases came to present an image which was not entirely in accordance with that of a young man training for the ministry. Consequently, towards the end of fieldwork, when rapport was highly developed, I felt increasingly that the data which I collected was genuinely representative of religious sentiments within the community and not merely a set of hollow platitudes based upon stereotypical forms of Methodist or Anglican dogma, the like of which would, under normal circumstances, only be trotted out to please the parson or minister. On the positive side, the misconception about my role also had a minor advantageous effect. To be labelled as a man training for the ministry immediately invested me with a certain significance and respectability; here was someone to be taken seriously and whom most villagers were eager to help if they could. In the early stages of fieldwork this attitude was therefore a help in so far as it facilitated contact-making and enabled me to enter more easily as a participant-observer in the religious life of the chapels and churches. It is clear, however, that such a slight advantage did not outweigh the various disadvantages which arose out of the misconception.

Fieldwork began on 1 April 1975; from then until the end of July I left the village only on those occasions when coach outings took the local Methodists on visits to other chapels in the area. The period was one of intensive participant-observation during which I acquainted myself with as many aspects of religion in Staithes as possible. Data collection progressed on two fronts. On the one hand I directed considerable attention to the situation within the religious institutions and in so doing was able to cast new light onto my early folk religion hypothesis. These investigations began by making contact with those who were actively involved in the upkeep and organisation of chapels and churches in the village – clergy, ministers, members – before gradually broadening out to encompass the wide basis of support and sympathy found among a large proportion of the village population, something like two-thirds of which I estimated to claim allegiance to one or other of the religious institutions. Data was collected

b

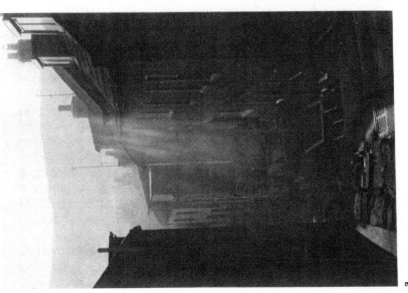

a

9a and b. The old village consists of numerous passages, steps and alleyways, linking small garths.
Photographs by Richard Cale, 1981.

through attendance at religious services of all kinds, meetings, special events and outings, followed, as time went on, by extended conversations and interviews with people in their own homes. At the same time, but on a different front, I spent periods in the presence of fishermen and workers from the potash mine with whom I began by collecting data relating to occupational belief and practice before progressing to an exploration of attitudes towards institutional religion. With these men, contacts and rapport were largely cultivated through hanging about on the sea-front, where they tended to congregate in groups at various times during the day. Later in the summer I was often called upon by part-time fishermen to assist with the lobster fishing, which was then in full swing. Hours spent in boats on fishing trips frequently provided opportunities for conversation in an easy, uncontrived atmosphere.

Such a procedure allowed me to execute, as it were, a pincer movement whereby I examined two apparently distinct groups – the religiously active on the one hand, and the relatively uncommitted group of young working men on the other. These groups in turn embodied the official religion of the church and the non-institutional beliefs and practices of folk religion. In so doing I hoped to overcome any bias which might be introduced by concentrating solely on either a search for folk religion within the church or for elements of religious belief and practice existing beyond it.

There was also a context in which the two groups could be observed in close proximity; both the regular attenders and the religiously less enthusiastic revealed high levels of involvement in the rites of passage. Large attendances were witnessed on these occasions and the detailed ritual preparations and outcomes which accompanied them, along with their related beliefs and observances, all provided valuable opportunities in which to document an important dimension of folk religion. The limited number of weddings taking place during the fieldwork period, however, created a serious omission in the documentation of life cycle rites. Initially, and in the belief that they exemplified the principles of the folk religion hypothesis, it had been proposed to study rites of passage intensively. Subsequently, it proved possible to identify numerous aspects of unofficial religiosity within the life of the nonconformist chapels in Staithes, and this discovery, coupled with the paucity of opportunities in which to observe marriage rituals,[5] accounts for the presentation of the empirical data which I have adopted.[6]

Towards the end of July 1975 I left Staithes for a period, returning at the beginning of September. Throughout the summer, social life in the village revolved predominantly around outdoor activities; with the advent of winter, life began to move indoors. Consequently, new research strategies were called for in a situation where participant observation became more restricted and the frequent conversational gatherings on the harbour side were prevented by the weather. In subsequent months it was therefore necessary to build upon the insights gained from participant observation, through the use of other research methods. By this time my interest in religious matters was well known in the village and I was able to talk freely to many people in their own homes. Much of the oral historical material presented below is based upon interviews carried out with old people during the winter of 1975/6. I found that retired people were both free and able to talk to me during the day and in many cases my desire to listen to their accounts of village life in earlier periods provided for them a welcome opportunity to pass away a few hours. The data gained in this manner, in the form of oral testimony, sometimes tape recorded, sometimes not, was invaluable. Through it, I was able to piece together a picture of religious life in the village at the turn of the century,[7] which could then be used for comparison with the contemporary situation and with data gathered from other sources.

In addition to interviewing, these months were also taken up with the collection of data from both primary and secondary documentary sources. Where available, church and chapel registers were consulted, as well as various diaries, minute books and newspaper cuttings. This was often time-consuming work, which brought little direct reward. Many of the documents which I sought had been lost or destroyed. In one case I discovered after much fruitless searching that certain records and registers of the two Methodist chapels had been destroyed in an air-raid which rased to the ground the Newton Memorial Wesleyan Church at Loftus, on 15 March 1941. Participant observation by no means came to a halt during this period however and I continued to use the method in order to collect data on various aspects of the life and annual cycles. Throughout the autumn and winter, baptisms and funerals were attended as well as Harvest Festivals, Christmas and New Year festivities and Sunday School Anniversaries. This work now benefited enormously from the steadily increasing level of acceptance which I began to enjoy among the villagers, particularly when the cold, dark months saw the almost complete disappearance of visitors and week-enders from the local scene. Several people at this time clearly understood that my researches, which kept me in the village for a lengthy period, went beyond those based on mere casual interest.

By the spring of 1976 I looked forward to a further period of participant observation. A number of key issues had by now crystallised – in particular the broad categories into which the elements of folk religion seemed to divide, and also, the surprising insight that much of the religiosity to be found in the chapels was better understood through the concept of folk religion than through denominational difference. Moreover, I became increasingly interested in the notion that folk religion could stem from a deeply felt, if only vaguely expressed, set of communal sympathies –

allegiance to local traditions, the chapel, and so on. The remaining months in Staithes were therefore directed towards further clarification of these questions and hypotheses.

In July 1976, almost fifteen months after I first moved to Staithes, full-time fieldwork came to an end, though I continued to live in the village for several months more and inevitably still noted useful material. I can only say that my own reaction to the formal cessation of data collection, and I suspect that of many villagers who had patiently answered my questions, was, in the words of the soldier in *Hamlet*, 'For this relief much thanks.' Fieldwork, one felt, had not been easy work. In my own case, initial anxiety about establishing a research role in the community had given way to furious activity during the summer, followed by a winter of at times claustrophobic interviewing. The frequently mentioned problems of sustaining the research had been particularly telling at this time. These stemmed principally from the simple difficulty of having a role in the community based largely upon one's activities as an asker of questions. Constant curiositiy is difficult to maintain and is frequently unwelcome to villagers who, if not actually threatened by one's questions, are often bored by them and are in consequence eager to pass on to other topics of conversation – the state of the fishing, the football results, etc. At the same time, I began to feel a certain personal ennui with the research process, which on occasions became an activity divorced from any apparent theoretical purpose. Such difficulties are not easily resolved, but occasional visits to my supervisor and discussion group in Newcastle were helpful in so far as, back within the confines of the University, one was able to re-establish the academic ends to which the fieldwork was initially directed. Such ends are easily lost sight of when one is immersed in the mechanics of data collection. Occasional retreats from the field are undoubtedly vital if the observational faculties of the researcher are not to be irreparably dulled, since under such circum- stances, those aspects of village life which in the early stages of research elicit curiosity and interest may easily become commonplace and mundane.

On the positive side, doing sociological fieldwork in Staithes had endless rewards. For the first time in my life I had been exposed at first hand and for a prolonged period to a religious subculture of fascinating richness and complexity. To explore religious life in the village was to discover something apparently undocumented in the sociological literature, a mode of religiosity only partly confined by church or denomination and containing a variety of unofficial elements. Through participant observation I came to explore this folk religion at close range. Without doubt, the overriding virtue of such a method is to force the student out of the library and into contact with human beings, where 'dirtying one's hands with research' is inevitable and essential. From a tangled web of conversations, interviews, acquaintances and friendships there emerges a research technique capable of producing what are hopefully worthwhile insights into the religious life of a community.

Postscript

Departure from the field setting and removal to another town did not signal the end of the research process. In 1978 my Master's thesis was duly submitted and, thankfully, 'satisfied the examiners'.[8] I then found, to my surprise, that others were interested in hearing my account of folk religion in Staithes. Papers delivered to sociology of religion conferences and seminars met with helpful reactions and I discovered that, contrary to anticipation, the successful completion of my postgraduate course of study did not signal the end of an interest in its subject matter.[9] Indeed, two kinds of distance, both from the village and later from the all-consuming task of thesis writing, brought beneficial consequences.

Certainly, the move away from Staithes, though determined principally by the exigencies of the labour market, proved vital in the emergence of a more considered attitude towards my findings. Whilst still living in the village and observing the local religious world continuously unfolding, I had found the task of data analysis hindered rather than helped. The events described in the case study (Chapter 5) of conflict between local Methodists, for example, were not circumscribed by the fieldwork period, so that it proved difficult, even with a concern for social process firmly in mind, to begin to make sense of them. More subjectively, I also felt that during fieldwork I had been 'too close' to life in Staithes and therefore needed to 'stand back' and view it, if not 'objectively', then at least from a more reflective distance. In retrospect, the process was one of recreating the naivety, freshness and freedom from distracting encumbrances which I believe had characterised my first encounters with religion in Staithes. In re-reading field notes and in discussing my findings with others I therefore began to discover once again the insight of the 'outsider'. My original documentation of this in the thesis has been retained here with little embellishment, save for some editing and changes in style. It would be a mistake, I feel, to attempt to write up ethnographic observations too long after they had first been recorded.

In other respects, the book contains much new material which is not found in the original work. This again appears to have resulted directly from the process of distancing. I found therefore that a removal from contemporary religious life in Staithes produced a concomitant fascination with its historical antecedents. In the period after the fieldwork ended I thus became increasingly involved, though by that time largely as a 'hobby', with the examination of primary historical sources, mainly in the form of Methodist records, minute books and correspondence of one sort or another.

Considerable time was spent in 1979–80 examining the records of the Loftus and Staithes Methodist Circuit, along with those of its Wesleyan and Primitive precursors; unfortunately, many of the subjective and cultural qualities of Methodist life which I was so eager to examine seemed to be missing from these sources, with their strong emphasis on the minutiae of chapel organisation and office. Other sources, such as obituaries and items in Methodist magazines and local newspapers were more insightful in this respect. Subsequently, I also found the various official histories and memoirs of nonconformity in the Cleveland and North Yorkshire area particularly illustrative of Methodism's preoccupation with its own cultural heritage and development. Against all of these I had to set both lengthy passages and short fragments of oral testimony collected during fieldwork.

Perhaps the most obvious approach to these historical data would have been one of piecing them together in order to arrive at some sort of composite picture of religion in the village in earlier periods. However, as I pondered the implications of this, it quickly became apparent that to do so would be to produce a set of 'findings' having their own internal logic and cohesion, but which relied for this upon a highly individualistic fusion of the relevant data. Some help seemed to be present in Denzin's (1970) principle of 'methodological triangulation', which advocates that a variety of perspectives be generated on a given phenomenon through the adoption of discrete methodological strategies, in order that, in the manner of a mosaic, a complete picture of the phenomenon in question may be arrived at. Thus, for the sociologist, this might mean the combined use of survey, interview and observational techniques within the same study. The most obvious consequence of this approach when applied to my own data, however, was not the degree of 'fit' between the different sources, but rather, the obvious discrepancies and contradictions. It then became apparent that these anomalies were in fact of the essence in evaluating the material. An *interpretative* exercise was called for in which 'triangulation' could be used to identify discrepancies between sources, which could then form the focus of subsequent explanation. My object in this was therefore to set different 'versions' of the development of religious life in the village against one another in order that elements of folk religion might be thrown into sharper relief through juxtaposition with 'official' items. I believe that such a technique (if I may so aggrandise it) is worthwhile wherever the concern is with the subjective and the weakly articulated. In my own case, it also proved a vital agency in helping to dispel a tendency which was becoming endemic to my analysis: that of finding 'folk religion' in every belief, practice and observance which fell to hand. Whilst I therefore hope that my account of religious life in Staithes is plausible and convincing, it is offered only as one 'version' among several, albeit one having some of the advantages which derive from a triangulation of sources and methodologies.

4

Institutional religion

Staithes people adopt a tripartite system for distinguishing between the different religious institutions in their village. The term 'chapel' is used to refer to either of the two Methodist chapels, as well as the former Congregational chapel. Correspondingly, the word 'church' denotes either the Anglican Mission Church in Staithes or the parish church itself, at Hinderwell. Worshippers and supporters therefore divide into 'chapel folk' and 'church folk' and the associated social divisions, familiar from elsewhere (Emmett 1964; Rees 1950), are also in evidence. Roman Catholics are referred to simply as 'Catholics', but the Roman Catholic Church in the village may also be referred to, not without irony, as 'Father's' or 'Father's place'.

In addition, within the chapels themselves distinctions are made between 'Primitive', 'Wesleyan' and 'Cong's.', or 'Bethel' (also known on occasion as 'high chapel', not because of any liturgical pretensions, but rather as a result of its location, on higher ground, at the foot of the hill leading out of the old village). Each of these terms may also be applied adjectively to individuals; for example, 'he is a Primitive' (or the shorter 'Prim.') or 'she's Cong's.' or alternatively, to the building itself – 'I was at the Wesleyan's last night'. For the sake of both accuracy and simplicity therefore we have adopted the local usages in the text and from henceforth the use of quotation marks will be discontinued.

Anglican neglect

As we have seen, the village forms a part of the parish of Hinderwell, which includes the parish church and rectory, the Chapel of St Nicholas at Roxby and the Mission Church of St Peter the Fisherman at Staithes. The parish takes its name from St Hilda (614–80), Abbess of Whitby. In the churchyard at Hinderwell can be found a spring or well, near to which Hilda is said to have had a retreat (Harrison 1973: 3) and whose water was once popularly ascribed with magical properties. Until the late nineteenth century the village was known by the name *Hilderwell*, being a corruption of 'Hilda's well'. I make no pretensions here to a thorough-going account of the ecclesiastical history of the parish and rely for the most part on secondary sources. My intention is merely to provide the information which is necessary and salient to an appreciation of the more general argument.

The earliest references to religion in Staithes itself are found in Domesday Book, which lists 'half a church' at Seaton, perhaps a church shared with the populace at Hinderwell. In the early thirteenth century – Harrison suggests a possible date of 1224 (1973: 23) – a church served by a rector was built at Hinderwell. This subsequently became the parish church. We have seen that during the course of the fifteenth century the inhabitants of Seaton seem to have moved down to the sea and it was about this time also that the church on the cliff fell into disuse, so that Hinderwell remained the only local church. It was a situation which was to continue for almost 400 years.

The development of reforming and anti-clerical ideas in the area during the sixteenth century is a subject which lies well beyond the scope of the present work. Nevertheless, in A.G. Dickens's (1959: 53–113) detailed biographical essay of Sir Francis Bigod we have an illuminating account of the life of the most important religious innovator to have been connected with the parish. Francis Bigod was born at Seaton on 4 October 1507; his father was killed soon afterwards in the Scottish War (*ibid.*: 55), whereupon Francis's wardship passed to Cardinal Wolsey (*ibid.*: 57). Later, whilst still ward of the Cardinal, he spent some time at Oxford where he was subjected to the influences of early Lutheran propagandists like Thomas Garret (*ibid.*: 58).

Bigod's life was to be distinguished by two main features: financial hardship, combined with zealous endeavour in the cause of religious reform. He supported a large household which frequently included various reforming clergy (*ibid.*: 65) and published *A Treatise Concernyng Impropriations of Benefices*, which contained a measured critique of the monasteries (*ibid.*: 69–74). Yet whilst Bigod gained considerable repute in London reforming circles, he failed to find agreement with other neighbouring landowners in Yorkshire (*ibid.*: 74–5). His overriding ambition, his marriage and knighthood notwithstanding, was to preach the word of God (*ibid.*: 77) and to this end he toured the north with a group of chaplains (*ibid.*: 107). Bigod emerges from Dickens's account as a zealous Protestant anti-clerical who in a curious way became involved in the Pilgrimage of Grace. The author argues that Bigod, always the rash eccentric, attempted to seize the leadership of the pilgrims in order to redirect the forces of popular, though conservative, discontent along more radical lines. The pilgrimage and Bigod's plans for it were a miserable failure, however, and after escaping to Cumberland, he was finally caught on 10 February 1537 and removed to London, where he was tried and subsequently executed on 2 June.

We can say little about religious life in the parish during the remaining years of the sixteenth century. It is apparent however that the community at Staithes was devoid of a church, though the extent to which this implies an absence of religious life at the time is arguable. Indeed, minority religious views appear to have been gaining a foothold in the area, for as Marchant points out, when George Fox, the Quaker, visited Cleveland in the early 1650s, 'his success depended in a large measure upon the existence of a considerable auditory who were already prepared to appreciate his particular religious outlook' (1960: 39). Marchant's comments are well borne out by Fox's visit to Staithes itself in 1651, of which Fox records in his Journal: 'It being very deep snow, I passed through the country to a place called Staithes, where I met with many professors and Ranters. Great meetings I had amongst them, and a great convincement there was' (1952: 80). Fox is quick to note the hardships endured by the fisherfolk at the hands of the local clergy.

And then I went to the steeplehouse, where was a high priest that did much oppress the people with tithes . . . For if the people went a hundred miles off a-fishing, he would make them pay the tithe money, though they catched the fish at such a distance and carried the fish to Yarmouth to sell. And the chief of the parish was very light and vain . . . (*Ibid.*: 80)

Even by the middle years of the eighteenth century little seems to have occurred to reduce the animus between church and people. Archbishop Herring's Visitation Returns for 1743 provide us with some insight into the place of established religion in the parish and its relationship to the community at Staithes.[1] The curate at the time, one Thomas Langstaff, records that there were 166 families in the parish, 'of which 7 are of the Sect commonly call'd Quakers'. Two of these families lived in Hinderwell, where the group held its meetings, and five others lived in Roxby. There were also three Catholic families, though their domicile is not stated. Religious services were held fortnightly at both Hinderwell and Roxby. Only one terse reference to Staithes appears in the return; it represents an interesting comment on the manner in which the fisherfolk may have been regarded by the local priest: '*Fornication.* – A.B. and C.D. (Staithes); he did penance; she excomd. and dencd.' When we consider the social background of the local incumbent, it is difficult to imagine what kind of rapport he would have had with the fisherfolk. Langstaff gained the degree of Bachelor of Arts at Trinity College, Cambridge in 1739 and served at Lincoln and Chester before coming to Hinderwell. His rector, a graduate of St John's, Cambridge and a fellow of Peterhouse, is unlikely to have had anything but the most fleeting contact with the parish at all, being simultaneously Dean of York, Rector of Folkton, Vicar of Hunmanby and Curate of Munston. In the absence of more complete evidence, therefore, plurality of office holding, the social distance of the clergy and the infliction of harsh tithes must be seen as joint causes of the gulf which existed between the people of Staithes and the religion of the establishment.

By contrast, Hinderwell progressively consolidated its position as the focus of Anglicanism in the parish. The local farming folk probably had good reason for overt displays of allegiance to their church, whose rector had an entitlement of forty-five acres of desirable glebeland and who also traditionally kept a bull to serve the cows of parish farmers. An instrumental desire to maintain good relations with the man to whom they tithed and paid rent may therefore have underpinned the apparent sympathy which the people of Hinderwell expressed towards established religion. Certainly, the material fabric of the church building underwent a steady improvement and the present edifice, which dates from 1773, was erected to replace an older, but apparently still sound, structure. Ord writes, 'The old church was a fine specimen of antiquity, the chancel being separated from the nave by a saxon arch, and the fabric so firm and compact that gunpowder was necessary to complete the work of demolition' (1846: 295). A tower was added in 1817 and further alterations carried out in 1895 (Russell 1923: 370). The rectory, which is older than the church, dates to the latter part of the seventeenth century (Harrison 1973: 13).

The obvious consolidation of Hinderwell as the seat of established religion in the parish may in turn have exaggerated the alienation of Staithes folk from the church in a situation where religious nurture in one community was matched by a corresponding negligence in the other. This process in itself probably had deeper origins. Certainly there has been a long-standing rivalry between the fishing villages along the Yorkshire coast and the neighbouring farming communities (see Chapter 8), which has often spilled over into such things as schoolyard fights among children and mutually held terms of abuse, like 'cod', or 'turnip-head'. Whilst those at Staithes have looked upon the farming people as middle class, Anglican and self-important, the people at Hinderwell have, in their turn, readily pointed to the 'quair' fishing folk living in semi-isolation below the steep cliffs in a 'rough' community hostile to both neighbours and strangers alike. These enduring stereotypes are certainly important to the task of disentangling the complex relationship between religion and communal life. Anglican neglect at Staithes, and its social correlates, must therefore be seen within the context of other patterns of relationships within the parish. For the people at Staithes, however, the absence of an established institutional religious presence in their village inevitably created a setting where nonconformity, and Methodism in particular, could gain a following and, eventually, exert a pervasive influence upon local society.

Nonconformist growth

Eighteenth-century England was a place of great religious contrast, wherein the declension and apathy of the early decades gave way to widespread and enthusiastic revival. The new nonconformity flourished and the fires of the old dissent were in many places rekindled; evangelism sought to transform the heart and, with it, the very conditions of social existence. Where it gained a purchase, there were important consequences. These have, of course, been interpreted in markedly different ways, typically, polarising into either critique or apologia. In many cases however, as E.P. Thompson has pointed out, writers have been relatively unsuccessful in recreating the experience and texture of the revival, other than in purely institutional terms, such as rates of growth or changes in organisational structure (1968: 91–8). The *meaning* which evangelical religion had for those who professed to it is largely missing from these accounts, masked behind descriptions of such things as wholesale conversion or, later, the humdrum of chapel office. And yet where glimpses of the underlife emerge, the scepticism, the doubt, the hypocrisy and the rivalry all reveal a religious world fragmented by official objectives and lay motivations. Accordingly, it would be a mistake to accept uncritically the notion that the evangelists transformed human existence wherever they encountered it, however briefly; we must also be alert to changes which took place within evangelism itself. As we shall see shortly, this is a consideration which official historians of nonconformity have often overlooked. For our purposes, and with a concern for the underlife in mind, we must be open to different interpretations deriving from different sources. Such an exercise may in turn enable us to uncover previously hidden aspects of an important period of religious growth.

The arrival of the evangelists along the Yorkshire coast, as elsewhere, was accompanied by the adoption of a particular stance *vis-à-vis* the local populace. The Methodists, for example, diagnosed a malaise for which they claimed a unique and powerful cure. Spiritual and moral turpitude were endemic; their accompaniments were superstitiousness, worldliness, baseness and depravity, to which alcoholic indulgence and Anglican laxity were frequent enough additions. The coastal towns and villages were clearly seen as mission territory, long since abandoned by the Established Church and requiring zealous and dedicated proselytisation. Consequently, we find in the writings of Methodist local historians frequent references to the graphic changes wrought by their faith, along with detailed description of the emancipation of entire communities from darkness into light. Whilst such accounts require careful treatment and raise important issues of interpretation and method when assessing the 'impact' of Methodism in any one localised setting, they do, nevertheless, present us with one version of the community's religious development, which can be set alongside other versions derived from elsewhere.

Evangelists of all persuasions seem to have faced common problems; first the Wesleyans and Congregationalists and later the Primitive Methodists all found it difficult to gain admission into a local social world which was apparently inimical to any form of institutional religion. Thus Patterson states that before the arrival of the first preachers in Staithes 'Gross ignorance, superstition and godlessness had . . . prevailed' (1909: 37). Social life was concomitantly base and the typical pursuits of folk in the region, according to another Methodist writer, were 'low and vulgar' and marked by a fondness for 'rude sports and pastimes' (Woodcock 1889: 24). Obituaries of early converts echo similar themes. For example, Sarah Smith, referred to by Patterson as a 'notorious character' (1909: 37), born in Staithes in 1779, upon her death at the age of fifty was eulogised in the *Primitive Methodist Magazine*: 'Prior to preachers visiting this place she was valiant in sin, and Staithes was noted for immoralities' (1829: 388). Indeed, it seems that the fisherfolk of the North Yorkshire coast regarded the arrival of the first Methodists with feelings varying from bemusement in some cases to outright hostility in others. So Patterson condescendingly describes how in Staithes 'when they first heard that the "Ranters" were coming, the young men of the village turned out to meet them, not knowing whether they were men or something else' (1909: 37). In Lythe, near Whitby, another early evangelist, Rogers, appears to have battled against considerable enmity towards himself and his fellow-converts. Writing of his experiences in the early 1770s, he states:

The enemy had often strove to prevent the Gospel from taking root in that wicked place; but now, seeing the word mightily prevail . . . he raged with redoubled fury. Some ruffians combined to prevent my preaching; and were determined, some way or other, to carry their point . . . After they had often disturbed us in our preaching-house, one night these sons of Belial collected all their forces, and assembled at the door to attack us as we came out.   (Rogers 1872: 294)

Even by 1824, the plan-maker for the Whitby and Guisborough Union Circuit thought it necessary to include the terse warning, 'beware of imposters'. Likewise, in Filey, a village further down the coast and sharing many similarities with Staithes, the evangelists were said to have 'tried again and again to establish a cause, but had been shouted, mobbed and pelted out of the place' (Woodcock 1889: 35). The 'victory' in this case fell to one Johnny Oxtoby, who 'entered the village and sung along the streets to the beach, where he preached to a rough and rude audience. Presently, backs straightened, cheeks flushed, hearts softened, tears began to flow, and numbers were convinced of the wickedness of their lives' (*ibid.*: 35). Patterson describes a similar victory at Staithes where despite initial hostility the fishermen 'were quickly susceptible to the methods of worship and evangelisation pursued by the early Primitive Methodist missionaries' and as the people 'responded to the hearty singing and preaching', 'a transformation took place in the village' (1909: 37–8). Woodcock, again writing of Filey, can be still more explicit: 'Many of the fisher-folk became as exemplary for virtue as they had been for vice' (1889: 36).

Whether or not these descriptions accurately portray the initial hostility of resistance and its subsequent evaporation, or, as seems more likely, represent suitably exaggerated and romanticised accounts of the behaviour of high-spirited youths, eager to capitalise on the preachers as objects of amusement, they do none the less supply us with interestingly stylised official portrayals of the spread of the faith. They are redolent of Methodism's concern with its own history and constitute the very wellspring of an imagery upon which the established and respectable denomination later fed with relish. In subsequent chapters we shall have the opportunity to explore the varied cultural outcomes and mutations of the evangelical revival; for the moment, however, we may briefly turn to the mechanics of nonconformist growth in the village, and one of its important concomitants, sabbatarianism.

The initial stirrings of nonconformity in Staithes did not congeal into institutional form until the early decades of the nineteenth century. Before that time it is likely that the faithful had congregated in *ad hoc* groups of one sort or another, gathering together both spiritual and material resources. Meetings of the first Wesleyans in the village were held in the schoolroom of a teacher named John Garbutt, and by 1817 a Sunday School was in existence with sixty scholars and four teachers (Howard 1966: 5). Classes were held in a building in Granary Yard, close to the beck and near to the site of the present chapel. In 1821, a chapel at Staithes, with a membership of thirteen, appears on a Guisborough Circuit List for the first time.[2] Two years later, at a cost of £190 and with money borrowed from Mr Thomas Parks of Staithes, a warehouse was purchased in Granary Yard. The building was converted into a chapel and opened for worship in the following year.[3] By 1830, membership had increased to fifty-six.

One common feature of Methodism's expansion was an attendant revival in older established dissenting groups, where, as at nearby Whitby, for example, doctrinal disputes and secessions gave rise to new congregations ascribing to slightly modified theology and practice (Edwards 1906: 7–8). The opening of the Congregational chapel in Staithes on 3 September 1823 may have resulted from such a process and certainly must be seen in terms of more general religious developments taking place in the village at the time. 'Bethel', as the chapel was named, formed a part of the local Congregational County Association until 1832, when this organisation united with a number of similar bodies to form the Congregational Union of England and Wales. In its earliest years the chapel was 'taken under the charge of the congregation at Whitby' (Miall 1868: 368) before, in 1827, obtaining its first resident pastor, the Rev. R. Henderson. Though little survives in the way of primary source material from this period in Bethel's history, it is apparent that it was a time of growth and expansion, culminating in the building of a new place of worship in 1835.

Though a later development within the revival as a whole, Primitive Methodism makes its appearance in Staithes at about the same time as Wesleyanism and Congregationalism. During the period 1819–20, and prior to the first Primitive Methodist Conference at Hull, William Clowes, the movement's joint founder, preached his way through the North Riding of Yorkshire with a number of followers (Kendall 1889: 52–3). His presence seems to have had a speedy effect and a Primitive Methodist preachers' plan for the Whitby and Scarborough Union Circuit for 1824–5 lists thirty-five places of worship, including a chapel at Staithes. Again, expansion seems to have been a keynote of the period and in 1838 a purpose-built chapel was opened in the village, with seating for 200 persons.

It is by now well recognised that the returns of the 1851 Ecclesiastical Census should be interpreted with extreme caution (Pickering 1967), but with this in mind, the results of the exercise do nevertheless provide us with a useful snapshot, albeit flawed and open to conjecture, showing the extent of religious practice in the village at mid-century. As we suggested in Chapter 1, practice is of course but one aspect of religiosity in a particular setting and should not be conflated with the religious *in toto*. None the less, the figures enable us to form some impression of the magnitude of religious affiliation in Staithes. The returns are listed in Table 2.[4] Even a cursory glance at these figures suggests that the numbers have been rounded out for convenience and probably in an upward direction. Yet even if we make due allowance for exaggeration, the figures remain high, especially so for the Primitive Methodists.[5] In 1851 the population of the parish was 1736 and that of Staithes itself, around 1200. On the morning of Sunday 30 March 1851, therefore, some 40% of the total village population were in the two Methodist chapels. When we add in the adult evening attenders at Bethel (and for reasons which will become clear in the next chapter, it is unlikely that any of these would have been in either of the Methodist chapels for morning worship), the figure rises to 57%. If we then append the average reported estimate of attendance at the Bethel Sunday School, we can speak, though with diminishing authority, of some 64% of the population attending chapel on a given Sunday.

Such attendances imply significant changes in village life during the first half of the nineteenth century. When we combine this kind of evidence for institutional growth and levels of allegiance with the accounts of non-conformist historians, cited above, we are forced to ask the question, to what extent did the incoming faith transform local social life and values? Perhaps the most effective way to answer this question is to conceptualise

Table 2. *1851 religious census returns for nonconformist chapels in Staithes*

	Morning	Afternoon	Evening
Wesleyan Methodist			
Adults	170	50	80
Sunday School	70	70	–
Primitive Methodist			
Adults	180	200	200
Sunday School	60	60	–
Congregationalist			
Adults	–	150	200
Sunday School	– [a]	–	–

[a] No Sunday School returns are listed for Census Sunday at Bethel, though the average attendance at the Sunday School in earlier months is listed as ninety scholars. It may have been that the school met only fortnightly.

the impact of nonconformity upon the village as an encounter between two cultures, one reflectively and self-consciously sacred and the other spontaneous and popular. In depicting the evangelising of the region as a process of spiritual and moral transformation, the Methodist historians, as we have seen, emphasise the inevitable and unequivocal establishment of the sacred culture and, despite some early difficulties, eventual supremacy over its popular antecedents. In the early days, as E.P. Thompson has pointed out, the relationship between the two was often adversarial: 'The Wesleyans first, and the Primitive Methodists after them, repeatedly sought for outright confrontation with the older, half-pagan popular culture, with its fairs, its sports, its drink, and its picaresque hedonism' (1968: 918). We should, however, employ a certain discretion in accepting the official version of the eradication of paganism and popular culture by the new faith and look instead for areas of overlap, tension and cross-fertilisation between the two.

What then were the distinguishing characteristics of the sacred culture? Undoubtedly it took shape and developed in the beliefs and practices which surrounded the chapel as a social institution. 'Chapel life' gave expression to the sacred culture and 'chapel folk' were those who, in varying degrees, identified themselves with it. From the earliest days, therefore, the new faith had an institutional guise, beginning with the open-air evangelistic gatherings, proceeding to the small groups of men and women who met in rented accommodation and progressing quickly to the development of a Society having formal links with the broader Methodist fellowship. Through the

Sunday and week-night preaching services, the class meeting and the bible readings, the sacred culture gained a foothold in the local community.

Sabbatarianism held a central and unifying place in the culture and represented one of its most graphic manifestations, imposing a pattern on human activity, at once interrupting and renewing the course of communal existence. It was an ethic affecting the world of work and home alike and was even capable, on occasion, of overriding the contingencies and material hardships of day to day survival. Nowhere is this better illustrated than in the victory which the Methodists claimed over the Sabbath-breaking of local fishermen. The obituary of George Jenkinson, of Filey, contains the following passage:

He quickly placed himself in opposition to some of the prevailing vices of his time. Prior to the revival visitation Sabbath-breaking was general, and shamefully open-faced; and his contemporaries were generally fishing, or preparing to fish during the whole of the sacred day. His brothers ... and a few others set their faces against the reprehensible practice; and the signal manner in which God owned and prospered them, led to its general abandonment, and to a reverential observance of the day of rest. *(Primitive Methodist Magazine* 1878: 307)

This strict sanction upon any form of work during the Lord's day along with other manifestations of sabbatarian observance were well attested by oral evidence collected from retired men and women during fieldwork. '[The fishermen] might leave it so late, but they allus made sure to get in afore midnight of a Saturday ... same as Sunday nights, they might be off straight after twelve, but never on a Sunday itself.' Similarly in the home, various kinds of work were impermissible, as was any form of leisure-time pursuit save that of bible reading or the singing of sacred songs: 'I can remember me mother wouldn't even wash up of a Sunday, she used to put t' dirty pots away in a cupboard rather than wash 'em. Same as kids, there was no playing about – you were in your Sunday best and that were it.' One story, still told in the village, though probably apocryphal, bitterly reveals the power of the sabbatarian ethos and its ability to transcend the most basic needs of the populace.

Me dad used to say how there was one time when a ship had gone down in 'pot-a-boilins' [a large and dangerous hole on the scaurs to the north of the village] and a great load of coal had washed up. But it were a Sunday and no-one would go down to carry it off. Next morning they got up and t' tide had taken it all.

It is likely that even by the time of the religious census such a sabbatarian ethos was already firmly established. In the decades which followed, however, significant transformations began to take place within the sacred culture. These are indicative in certain ways of a gradual process whereby religious movements with radical and iconoclastic origins either disintegrate or, alternatively, maintain themselves through an incipient conservatism (Niebuhr 1929). In this sense the period was one of consolidation wherein the chapels established their own congregations and reservoirs of support, often based on particular families whose allegiance had been inculcated in the Sunday Schools. It was also a time of visible entrenchment, particularly for the Methodists, where, in both cases, the chapels found themselves a part of circuits which were continually shrinking in their geographical extent as the number of chapels in the district as a whole increased. The Wesleyan chapel had at first been a part of the Guisborough Circuit, until 1829, when the Stokesley Circuit was formed, which contained some thirty rural churches. The circuit superintendent had been resident at Stokesley and preachers travelled considerable distances to conduct services in the village. In 1863 the circuit was split up and until 1871 Staithes Wesleyans were once again part of the Guisborough Circuit. In that year the circuit was narrowed down to a still more local level and the Loftus and Staithes Circuit, containing nine chapels in all, came into existence. From 1875 the circuit had two ministers, with the superintendent traditionally living in the manse at Loftus and his assistant at Staithes. The Primitive Methodists, too, became part of an increasingly localised structure, with circuit jurisdiction devolving from Whitby and Guisborough to Whitby (1823–4), and then to Staithes, in 1868. By the early 1890s there were seven chapels and a preaching room in the circuit, which were being served by over sixty local preachers. Both groups demonstrated their importance and establishment through the building of larger and more commodious chapels; the Wesleyans in 1866 and the Primitives in 1880. Indeed, in the case of the Wesleyans respectability was underlined in the choice of the Marquis of Normanby, a wealthy landowner and member of the establishment, as the dignitary who ceremonially laid the foundation stone for the building.

Yet in other ways this apparent consolidation was paralleled by important shifts within the sacred culture whereby the meaning which Methodism had for villagers began to take on local variations and diverge increasingly from the official beliefs, teachings and procedures of the wider fellowship. In a process which we shall explore in some detail in the next chapter, specific tensions arose within local nonconformity which buried the nuances of theological distinction beneath an avalanche of partisan allegiance coupled with a powerful desire for self-determination in religious matters. As we shall also see, the sacred culture took a part in the cycle of annual events and in the periods of transition within the personal biography. Most significantly of all it eventually spilled out beyond the chapel portals to find a fragile commensality with the beliefs and practices of the popular culture. Methodism was not a unidirectional force; in time its recipients seized, moulded and transformed it into a system which had a powerful legitimating presence at a local level, but which met with increasing disapproval from the official guardians of the faith.

Later developments and institutional religion today

The Anglican Church's response to the growth of nonconformity in Staithes, in common with many other areas, was too little and came too late. In 1846, one local historian was prompted to make the following outburst.

Although Staithes contains considerably more than a thousand inhabitants, no regular system of national religious instruction has ever been afforded them, and they are permitted to wallow in gross ignorance. Moreover, to accommodate this mass of human beings, no means of spiritual instruction in the principles of the Establishment are provided; and whilst the Hindoos, Africans, Chinese and other distant lands [sic], are liberally supplied with Christian ministers, twelve hundred of our own white bretheren, close at hand, in the centre of a wealthy diocese, and in the midst of civilization, are actually without a church. It is surely high time that the Archbishop, the Ecclesiastical Commissioners, and the British public, should look to it.
(Ord 1846: 300)

Three years later, and perhaps influenced by Ord's protest, the National School Room at Staithes, which had been in operation since 1816 (Young 1817: 878), was licensed for worship by the Archbishop. The circumstances of the consecration are described, as follows, under the appropriate section of the 1851 religious census return: 'In consequence of Staithes being so far from the Parish Church at Hinderwell and the bulk of the population being at Staithes, the Archbishop transferred the Sunday evening service: Hinderwell to Staithes.'[6] The average attendance at this service is listed as 130, but no exact return was made for census day itself, when eighty adults and thirty-five Sunday School scholars were present for morning worship at Hinderwell. From 1874 onwards, the National School Room was used regularly for services, following its re-dedication as the Mission Church of St Peter the Fisherman (Harrison 1973: 21). This tardy establishment of a place for Anglican devotion was quite unable to stem the floodtide of nonconformity which had already swept over the village and which, in the absence of a serious Anglican presence, had been greatly facilitated in its development. A correspondent of *The Times*, who visited Staithes in 1885, notes, 'Many of them – the majority indeed – have gone over to dissent, the primary cause for this inclination being, as in the case of the Durham pitmen, that the Church has left them greatly to themselves' (22 September 1885).

The neglect which we have described frequently gave rise to the view that Anglican clergy were generally rather distant, socially superior figures; 'gentlemen' being the loaded appellation. This view persists, although the rector present during the fieldwork period proved a glorious exception, and his contempt for protocol often met with approval from non-Anglicans in Staithes. Much amazement, for example, accompanied his decision to join the lifeboat crew, rather than merely serve as a committee member. This popularity notwithstanding, the contemporary view of Anglicanism combines indifference with institutional apathy and the church itself remains essentially on the periphery of communal religious life.

This can be demonstrated in a number of areas of religious practice and affiliation. Most obviously, it is seen in terms of church attendance, where we see only a handful of worshippers at the Sunday morning communion service, but it is also revealed in the limited number of extra-curricular activities organised by the church. A Mothers' Union meets fortnightly, but in contrast to the chapels, fund-raising events, such as jumble sales, coffee-mornings, and so on, are fairly infrequent. Coach trips and outings are similarly sporadic and a few local Anglicans regularly take advantage of excursions organised by chapel folk to attend sacred concerts, Harvest Festivals and anniversaries in the area. Even at the life crises, the role of the church is limited, at least within Staithes itself, since all funerals and marriages take place at Hinderwell, rather than in the Mission church. Whilst the Mission church contains a baptismal font, the parish registers reveal that only eight christenings have taken place there since 1874.

It may be argued, of course, that poor active support for the church may not be significant, in so far as a religious sub-stratum might persist beyond and independently of the life of the churches. We are particularly concerned here, for example, to reject the assumption, common within the sociology of religion, that institutional decline or weakness is *ipso facto* linked to secularisation. Writers such as Bryan Wilson (1966) have certainly acknowledged the existence of a nominal Anglicanism in which self-ascription to the Church of England is as much based upon a condition of Englishness as upon any strongly felt religious persuasion, but see this as in itself a product of secularising forces – in particular falling support for the Free Churches. Such a view fails to recognise nominal Anglicanism for what it is, namely a residual, but highly resistant form of folk religiosity. Yet arguments of this kind are of little relevance to an understanding of religious life in Staithes where nominal ascription to the Church of England is *low* precisely because the same form of allegiance to the nonconformist chapel is so widespread.

Roman Catholicism has had still less of an effect upon religious life in the village, indeed its influence upon the whole of the North Yorkshire coast is extremely limited. This is, however, in marked contrast to the situation further inland, where in many of the upland farming communities of the North Yorkshire moors there is a rich and historically self-conscious Catholic heritage which reaches back to before the time of the Reformation and which later persisted in recusant form. The martyr, the Venerable

(Father) Nicholas Postgate (1596–1679), whose canonisation is the ultimate goal of a flourishing Postgate Society, is the most potent symbol of this local underground Catholicism. In Staithes, however, where a Roman Catholic Church (the only place of worship at 'Lane End') was built in 1886, there is little sense of Catholic tradition and almost all of the village's Catholics are from families who are relatively recent incomers. In the old village itself there is only one Catholic family.

Indeed, current attitudes towards Catholics remain sceptical and confused, displaying in some cases a bewilderment almost akin to that of the westerner when confronted by aspects of a primitive religion. On Christmas Eve 1975, one lady in her late fifties told me the following story: 'When we were younger . . . lads and lasses . . . on a Christmas Eve . . . we used to go up t' Catholics for Midnight Mass. We didn't take the communion of course, but they used to say that Father used to ride around the church on a donkey . . . well, you know, we went lots o' times, but we never saw it!' Similarly, another favourite anecdote describes a young man who courted a Catholic girl and whose father, worrying that the relationship was becoming serious, is said to have warned him, 'if tha sticks wi' 'er much longer lad, they'll have thee ridin' t' donkey!'. Such attitudes frequently extend to the clergy themselves, who are sometimes known in the village as 'black men'. When in the 1930s, as a part of the fiftieth anniversary celebrations of the local Roman Catholic Church, a service was held in which the sea was blessed by a priest, fishermen are said to have claimed that the fishing was bad for months afterwards. As the present priest himself put it, 'there is still a lot of prejudice against us, some of them still seem to think we've got tails'. Some Methodists even showed concern when, during the fieldwork, I attended Mass at the Catholic Church; I was duly warned to beware the dangers of 'turning' or 'being caught'.

These attitudes reflect the alien qualities which Roman Catholicism appears to embody for most villagers. Among chapel folk, Catholics are acknowledged as having their own religion, albeit a false one, and are left to pursue it without interference, but with few efforts towards rapprochement. Ecumenical events, which have become such a commonplace aspect of national religious life, are largely unknown in Staithes, where clergy and laity alike appear to abstain from theological interchange or mutual discussion. There are some 300 Catholics in the parish as a whole, of which over two-thirds live in other villages, mainly in Hinderwell. Sunday morning attendances at the Mass average seventy to eighty persons, but the siting of the church in Staithes seems in many ways inappropriate and came about, I was informed by the priest, as a result of a suitable site being bequeathed by a land-owning Catholic. Prior to 1886, Catholics in the area worshipped at Ugthorpe, about six miles away, and many still feel that the church would have been more suitably sited at Hinderwell. Despite the church's dedication to 'Our Lady Star of the Sea', it has always looked to landsfolk, rather than fisherfolk, for its support.

In turning to the situation of nonconformity in the village during the present century, it might appear that decline has been the predominant tendency. A cursory glance at membership, attendance, and so on, would certainly support such a view and there are senses in which religious life in the chapels today represents the terminal morain of a once massive nonconformist sentiment. But this apparent institutional atrophy belies a persisting relevance in the community. We shall therefore close this chapter on institutional religion with a brief overview of the chapels today.

Throughout its entire existence Bethel seems to have undergone long periods without a resident pastor and various visitors' reports make reference to the need for a minister in the village. The last pastor to live and work in Staithes retired during the mid-1960s, and whilst still available to conduct the occasional funeral or baptismal service, he now plays little part in the life of the chapel. Since his retirement, a small number of prime movers, mainly members of one family, have worked hard to maintain the viability of the chapel and have, in turn, shifted its doctrinal emphasis. For example, in 1968 Bethel withdrew from the then Congregational Union of England and Wales and subsequently there has been staunch resistance to any suggestion that it should become a part of the United Reformed Church. When active members were questioned on this decision, explanations centred on an increasing dissatisfaction with the role of the church in the modern world coupled with a growing concern that the 'quality of fellowship' was being polluted by modernism and the activities of liberal thinkers. Bethel's supporters, by contrast, make an appeal to *biblical* knowledge as the basis of a Christian life and profess allegiance to a fundamentalist theology. Preaching in the chapel has in recent years taken a markedly eschatological turn, with great emphasis on the imminence of the millennium and the return of Christ into the world. Regular attendance at Bethel during fieldwork revealed that many of the sermons were drawn from texts in the Book of Revelations.

Weekly activities at Bethel follow a regular pattern. Two services are held each Sunday; a man from the village preaches in the mornings to a congregation which is often fewer than ten in number and an evening service, which attracts between twenty-five and thirty-five worshippers, is conducted by one of a number of regular visitors from the surrounding area. A Sunday School is held each week, in the afternoons. Every Saturday evening a Christian Endeavour meeting takes place and in addition a small number of sympathisers meet regularly in their own homes for bible study and prayer.

The future for Bethel remains uncertain. In recent years the most committed members have adopted a decision to eliminate almost all fund-raising activities and events of a secular nature. Revenue, therefore, derives only from Sunday offerings and the occasional sacred concert; all other activities, including those which, as we shall observe, are an important source of Methodist allegiance, have been discontinued. In consequence, several women, while continuing to attend services at Bethel each Sunday, have become increasingly involved in a number of interests and groups connected with the Methodist chapels. Apart from these women, the majority of regular attenders appear largely unmoved by recent developments within their chapel. Observation at services revealed a clear feeling of boredom on the part of several of the congregation, yet beneath this, a loyalty to the chapel remains. It is conceivable, however, that should the brand of religion offered prove too radical, or obviously sectarian, then a general drift away from the chapel, in favour of its theologically more comfortable counterparts, might result.

Since the First World War both the Wesleyans and the Primitives have suffered a gradual decline in membership, from, in each case, a total of around sixty members to the present thirty-four Wesleyan and thirty-two Primitive Methodists. Both chapels suffer from a top-heavy age structure in their membership, with the majority in each being middle-aged or retired. The longevity of women in comparison to men has also created a sex imbalance, especially for the Primitives, where women outnumber men by three to one. An ageing membership, coupled with only sporadic recruitment, inevitably creates a situation of multiple office-holding wherein administrative duties fall upon a few resolute shoulders. However, attendance at Sunday worship produces a more favourable impression than membership rolls might suggest; paradoxically, many members are not regular attenders, and vice versa. Wesleyans average around twenty worshippers on Sunday mornings and thirty in the evenings, with Primitives drawing respective attendances of fifteen and twenty-five.

Other weekly activities are well supported. Each chapel runs a Sunday School, in each case with the regular help of younger and middle-aged non-members. The Wesleyans have fifty children on their roll, about two-thirds of whom are regularly present for classes, where they are taught by six teachers. The Primitives have forty scholars and four teachers.

Women from both chapels have a 'Bright Hour' each week and it is a source of considerable dismay to the minister that these meetings frequently attract attendances well in excess of those at the Sunday services. The 'Bright Hours' are characterised by a relaxed informality and visiting speakers are advised to avoid weighty or controversial topics, the women apparently preferring to watch handicraft or needlework demonstrations, flower arranging, cake-icing, and so on. The sessions have only the most tenuous religious character in so far as they open and close with a short prayer. The minister's wife, who is chairperson of the Wesleyan 'Bright Hour', expressed her dissatisfaction at the lack of religious content in the meetings and had on one occasion attempted to offset this by inviting the rector of the parish along to speak to the ladies. She was appalled when,

instead of ministering the word to them – and to be quite honest, that's the one time in the week when some of them get any chance to hear about the Lord – all he did was tell a lot of funny stories. He said, 'it's the middle of January, let's cheer ourselves up a bit', and then just told a lot of jokes. It's not good enough really, is it?

Despite the chairperson's protestations to me, the rector's talk was remembered by most of the women as highly entertaining and further strengthened the conviction that, unlike his predecessors, he is a 'good sort'.

The 'Bright Hours' draw their support from a broad circle of women who consider themselves as either Wesleyans or Primitives, even though, as we shall see in the next chapter, this self-image may be rooted in the most limited ties to the chapel. Neither formal membership nor regular Sunday attendance are considered a prerequisite for the appellation 'Wesleyan' or 'Primitive'. Nevertheless, those who so define themselves can be relied upon to give support to a wide variety of events and fund-raising activities. Chapel and Sunday School Anniversaries, Harvest Festivals, coffee-mornings and Autumn Fairs are all well supported, in many cases by those who would be extremely loath to make a more self-consciously religious commitment to a particular institution.

Visits to other chapels in the area for concerts and special events are particularly popular among the Methodists and are seen largely in entertainment terms. Shortly after my arrival in Staithes I was invited to travel with the Primitives to a remote chapel on the North Yorkshire moors. At the time I was still ignorant of what took place on these outings and so one man explained, 'Well I can promise you this, you'll have a good night out. On t' bus we all have a lovely ride out through the countryside. When we get there there's a service. Then we all have supper – sandwiches, sausage rolls, cakes, everything. Then back to Steeas and a good sing in t' bus on t' way.' The trips also tell us something about popular images of community life in Staithes. This is exemplified in the case of the Wesleyan chapel's Male Voice Choir. Consisting of about twelve men, the choir is noted in the area for its programme of sacred songs. Drawn largely from the pages of such nineteenth-century hymnals as *Moody and Sankey* and *Redemption*, its repertoire is dominated by a mixture of rousing evangelical pieces, for example, 'Have a Little Talk with Jesus', 'Sailing Home' and 'Carry your Cross with a Smile', contrasted with slower renditions of 'The Habour Bell', 'Eternal Father' and 'Saviour! Lead Me'. The imagery of the sea is strongly to the fore in the choir's choice of material and throughout the summer months the singers travel, often considerable distances, to other churches and chapels in the north-east, where their performance is invariably advertised and introduced as that of 'The Staithes Fishermen's Choir'. Now, this is a name which is steadfastly avoided in Staithes, where other sections of the community, to wit representatives of the old popular culture itself, have a claim on the title. It is a curious facet of the cross-fertilisation of the two cultures that the singing of hymns, particularly those containing sea-faring themes, is an activity much beloved by the regulars of public houses in the village. On a number of occasions in recent years, film of this 'custom', as the Staithes people like to regard it, has been broadcast on local and national television. In consequence, the singers in one pub have come to regard themselves as 'The Staithes Fishermen's Choir'. Village Wesleyans, for their part, have vigorously dissociated themselves from such activities and are careful to avoid using the same name in Staithes itself, so that when each week a rehearsal is announced from the pulpit it is for members of the 'Male Voice Choir'.

Outside the village, however, they clearly enjoy the alternative title and ritualistically dress for each performance in the traditional serge trousers and dark blue guernsey. A further element of pretence underlies such occasions since none of the members are full-time fishermen, though three of them fish on a part-time basis in the summer. Nevertheless, the men are careful to preserve a romanticised image of the village which is projected to the wider society through their songs and appearance. This stylised picture of community life is further strengthened by the friends and relations who accompany the singers. A coach is hired for each trip and between twenty and thirty Wesleyans will travel to the concerts. On the coach, particularly on the homeward journey, there is much singing and talking and it is on such occasions (to the delight of the fieldworker!) that individuals feel free to recall past times, events and characters in the life of the chapel. The evenings, therefore, help to keep alive certain community norms and to consolidate an attitude of security and assurance as 'chapel folk'. Furthermore, the performance raises the morale of choir and supporters alike, so that the pressing matters of economic stringency or dwindling membership are swept away in a euphoric tide of emotionalism and sentiment which for a few hours briefly recaptures the heyday of the sacred culture.

Summary

Whilst, as we have argued in Chapter 1, institutional religion alone cannot be held to represent the sum of religious belief and action in a society, we are nevertheless aware that the institutional religious background will be relevant to a full understanding of folk religion. Staithes is clearly a community which has been exposed to long periods of neglect on the part of the Established Church. We have suggested that this state of affairs made the village a fertile seed bed for nonconformist ideas and influences and that the history of institutional religion in Staithes in the nineteenth century is largely a history of nonconformist growth and consolidation.

The impact of nonconformity upon local life has been portrayed as an encounter between two cultures: sacred and popular. The notion of a sacred culture is triggered off by the early evangelists' own self images. Other-worldly, ascetic and governed by a rigorous ethical code, the early Methodists, for example, attempted an outright confrontation with the popular, local culture. This latter, however, is difficult to recover from the historical record, and regrettably, does not appear strongly here, other than through the eyes of Methodist historiography. Yet glimpses of it are found in oral testimony and even in present day observation; I shall argue that the idiosyncratic elements of local nonconformity, described in the next chapter, make sense in terms of this relationship between a sacred culture which was (and is) essentially *imposed* from outside and a set of beliefs and practices relating to communal identity, which were (and are) village-based in origin. Despite the powerful influence of nonconformity on village life, it never won the 'battle' outright and a continuing state of tension persists between official and popular elements. Both cultures were transformed in the process and in some cases the resulting cross-fertilisations took on their own autonomy, so that 'sacred culture' and 'popular culture' became virtually indistinguishable.

5

Chapel life and chapel folk

The establishment of nonconformity in the village was accompanied by important shifts in the relationship between the two cultures. Indeed, during the later nineteenth century, distinctions between the sacred and the popular became increasingly blurred. Eventually they were visible only to the ministry, whose professional survival was dependent upon an ability to distinguish between what was and what was not 'religion'. For villagers, the two cultures became a seamless web. Methodist doctrine, superstitious observance or denominational prejudice were all 'religion' and were inextricably intertwined in symbol, rite and belief. The sacred culture may for a while have provided the leitmotif of religious life in the village, but the embellishments of harmony, counterpoint and, at times, discord quickly threatened to swamp the main theme. It was as if nonconformity had so captured the hearts and imagination of the villagers, that they wished to take it completely to themselves and make it their own.

Chapel rivalry and nominal affiliation

A considerable amount of rivalry continues to exist between certain religious groups in the village which, contrary to anticipation, is mainly intra- rather than inter-denominational. That is to say, there is no evidence of tension between Free Church groups, Anglicans or Catholics. Their institutional activities are carried out with only the slightest nod in the direction of ecumenism, and for the most part they are completely independent of each other. Where strain and antipathy exist, it is *within* and *between* the chapels, especially between Primitives and Wesleyans. Here a long history of rivalry maintains itself, even today, in an elaborate and protracted schism. Yet much of the rivalry seems to be explicable not in theological or doctrinal terms, but within the context of generalised nominal affiliation to a particular chapel which finds expression in a deep-seated empathy with its traditions, its sentiments and its customs.

Traditional Primitive–Wesleyan rivalry

The death of John Wesley, in 1791, precipitated various constitutional changes in Methodism associated with the twin strains of fragmentation and consolidation within the movement. In 1797 the Methodist New Connexion was the first group to secede from the parent body and the early years of the nineteenth century witnessed a proliferation of breakaway movements, such as the Band Room Methodists (1805), the Independent Methodists (1806), the Primitive Methodist Connexion (1811) and the Bible Christians (1815). In 1857 the United Methodist Free Churches were formed out of a union of Wesleyan Reformers and the Wesleyan Methodist Association. In 1906, three groups, the Methodist New Connexion, the Bible Christians and the United Methodist Free Churches, came together to form the United Methodist Church. Finally, in 1932, the United Methodist Church, the Primitive Methodists and the Wesleyans joined forces in Methodist Union to constitute the present Methodist Church. It was a sociological, organisational and theological development which was shot through with disputes, controversies and tensions, in which the rivalry between Wesleyans and Primitives was notoriously paramount.

Even so, the continuing use of such denominational distinctions might seem inappropriate when they have long since been formally abandoned by the Methodist Church as a whole. Yet in Staithes the terms 'Primitive' and 'Wesleyan' are still considered legitimate and over forty years after Methodist Union, chapels are referred to by their pre-1932 names instead of 'Staithes High Street' and 'Staithes Wesley', which are the official designations appearing on the circuit plan. The labels have become the source of an extensive fund of jokes and humorous stories, a folklore of Methodism. The following are two oft-recalled examples.

One time two chaps in a coble were lost in thick fog, in Skinnygrove Wyke [a nearby bay] – their engine had broken down. Then all on a sudden they hears another coble going by and starts shoutin' out. Blokes in t' other coble shouts back – 'Is thee Prims. or is thee Wesleyans?' They shouts back at 'em, 'We's Wesleyans'. T' other blokes shouts, 'Hang on then you can have a tow.'

They used to say about one young chap in t'aud days who went to work for a farmer up Roxby way who was a big Wesley man . . . Yah day he was working with another fellah on t' farm . . . they were working away on a fence and t'other chap says to him – 'pass us that Wesleyan hammer will tha?' 'Which yan's that?' he says. 'That two-faced 'un over there', t'other bloke says.

By such means detractors drew attention to the hypocrisy which a supposedly egalitarian faith might engender and telling the stories provided an opportunity for chastening any image which chapel folk might have of themselves.

Reference to religious affiliation is still a form of categorisation which falls readily to hand. So on one occasion during fieldwork I stood watching some fishermen loading lobster pots into their boat, when one man caught his smock on the side of another boat, tearing it. 'Bloody Wesleyans', he said to his friend, and laughed, since the offending vessel was owned by a family who supported the Wesleyan chapel. Likewise, others told me how some years ago the members of all three chapels would congregate on the sea-front early on Sunday evening for a session of community hymn-singing. As the time for the evening services drew near, they would all set off in procession up the High Street, with each denominational group peeling off from the main body as they reached their own chapel. Harmony might pervade the highly enjoyable singing of hymns in the open air, but was never allowed to enter in the chapel door.[1]

Jokes of a similar nature are reported elsewhere in Methodism. Probert's *Sociology of Cornish Methodism*, which deals with a social setting having many similarities to that in Staithes, contains the following observation: 'At Camelford the Wesleyan chapel was known as "High and Mighty" or "Pride and Prejudice" whilst the Free Methodist was nicknamed "Spite and Envy" and the Bible Christians as "The Old Folks at Home" ' (1971: 37–8). E.P. Thompson (1976) in a review of Moore's (1974) *Pit-men, Preachers and Politics* criticises the author for failing to come to grips with the reality of this kind of Methodist underlife and points to the important aspects of such humour. Drawing upon his own personal experiences of life in communities with well-developed nonconformist traditions, Thompson writes:

In all cases one came to realize, after a time, that there was a folk-lore of humour within the community. I think it unlikely that much of this humour originated from the committed nonconformists themselves. It appeared more as a defence by the uncommitted within the community, and one would hear it only in certain places, certain pubs, certain times of sociability . . . This humour – often particularized and personalized and often very funny – turned around traditional themes: above all, nonconformist hypocrisy.   (1976: 395)

For Thompson, the humour has a two-edged quality, representing both 'a kind of criticism [and] a kind of self-defence' (*ibid.*: 396). It operates in a similar way in Staithes; tellers of the stories are most likely to be irregular attenders at chapel, but occasionally, in a relaxed moment (when the advantages of participant observation are most clearly visible), a chapel member might recount one of the anecdotes in a way which suggests both levity and guilt. The jokes not only highlight tensions and conflicts within the group but also serve to demarcate the community from the wider society, where the nuances of the humour go undetected. Indeed, a self-mockery, appreciated only by the insider, is implied; for example, when, late in the evening, the hymn-singing strikes up in one of the village pubs, a wag might ask, 'Which shall we have: the Staithes tune or the Runswick tune?'

The continuing jokes about Primitives and Wesleyans refer to far more than a conflicting set of doctrinal positions. Indeed, for many, the religious differences out of which the distinction arose are unheard of and unquestioned. A functionalist might argue that the humour has none the less an enduring purpose in permitting the harmless release of tension between the two groups. But this would be to deny the meaning which the jokes have for villagers, who clearly see them as an expression of one aspect of local religious life. To joke in the pub about nonconformist duplicity is to fuse the two cultures together with great imagination and flair.

Changing forms of commitment

In the earliest days after the arrival of the evangelists, entry into the sacred culture was most typically *achieved* by way of some kind of conversion experience wherein the individual's life was said to have been radically transformed from the ways of the world to those of God. The atmosphere of the early meetings, at first held in the open air amidst great excitement and enthusiasm, must have been highly conducive to such dramatic biographical shifts, which the official historians and Methodist commentators were always eager to document. Obituaries of the first converts underline the potency of the new faith; for example, that of Sarah Smith which was noted in the previous chapter. But for later generations, consolidation blunted the edge of conversionist zeal and produced an increasing emphasis upon a nonconformist life which began with early childhood membership of the Sunday School and progressed, through successive anniversaries, to full-blown adult participation in chapel life as an active, office-holding member. Such an ideal might also include honourable service in other, more secular spheres. By the early decades of the twentieth century suitable remembrances of Methodist stalwarts reflected not so much the personal transformation of individual life which they had undergone, but rather a dogged devotion to chapel duties combined with some visible contribution to the general good. The obituary of John Brittain, of Staithes, provides a good example of this change of emphasis.

He had a record of service of which any man might be proud. The Board of Trade presented him with a certificate and silver medal for forty years' service with the 'Rocket Life Saving Brigade'. He held gold and silver medals and a roll of honour for fifty years' service in the Sunday School. For many years he was society steward and school superintendent . . . He loved his Church and was a liberal supporter of its interests.　　　　(*Primitive Methodist Magazine* 1913: 573)

The eulogies also provided an opportunity for enriching certain aspects of Methodist self-imagery by way of an appeal to popular elements within the sacred culture.

'Old Singing Isaac is dead', was the news that awoke the sympathy and sorrow of every inhabitant of the village of Staithes, on Nov. 21st 1909. Isaac Verrill was almost the last of the group who joined our church some 50 years ago, and gave their powers and service to the Church. Few communities can boast of a finer race of men. Isaac Verrill was a class leader for 21 years, but he will be remembered most for his work in the choir. For the almost unprecedented period of 40 years he held the post of singing leader.

The funds of the Church and circuit were enriched by the efforts of Isaac and his choir. The great event of the year was the Christmas Carol singing. One of the company carried the money box, a miniature ship, fully rigged. At hall and cottage they generously contributed to the ship's cargo of silver and gold.

One characteristic service he rendered the village was his constant attendance at all funerals. He sang at the home of the bereaved and at the grave of the departed ...

The people's tribute to his memory and the Church's recognition of his labours were seen on the day of his burial. The whole village turned out, and representatives from all over the circuit came to pay their homage to this departed servant of God.

(*Primitive Methodist Magazine* 1910: 236)

Through the propagation of such romanticised images, Methodism generated its own historical self-consciousness and underwrote the view which chapel folk had of themselves. In consequence, there grew up a sense of identity based upon shared allegiance to a particular religious institution and its traditions.

A concomitant of this was a certain pluralisation in the meaning which being a 'Wesleyan' or a 'Primitive' or a 'Congregationalist' might have for any one individual. 'Ascription' would be the most appropriate sociological concept by which to describe later forms of nonconformist recruitment. Religious socialisation, rather than the 'heart experience', became the basis of allegiance to one or other chapel. This might express itself in different ways. Again, we should avoid the notion of one culture superimposing itself upon another and think instead in terms of a gradual fusion which generated a continuum of commitment, all the way from religious zeal to apathy. The zealots would be unlikely to include *all* members, but would consist of those who worshipped and attended the class meeting regularly and who took up office in the chapel. Similarly, attendance at the Sunday services is not in itself a reliable guide to levels of religiosity, since many non-members may have been regular attenders.

At the opposite extreme there were those who rarely, if ever, set foot inside the chapel and who, in some cases, might even retain an active contempt for the sacred culture. Throughout the second half of the nineteenth century correspondents of the *Whitby Gazette* made continued reference to such local 'troublemakers' who, it was claimed, not only eschewed authority and respectability but at times even threatened the safety of honest Sunday worshippers. The following passage, written in tones not far removed from those of today's tabloids, is a typical example.

I saw in your paper last week, that on the 13th inst., the police had charged nine men . . . for obstructing a public footpath at Staithes. I was glad to see that the case was proved against them, for I am sure they have been really too bad, but I am glad to say they are now a little better in the village, and the police are praised by many for the change they have effected. Still, there is more for them to do, and the place where it should be done is on the highway leading from Staithes to Hinderwell. Here it is obstructed – here the people are insulted by the rebels – here the police ought to be on a Sunday night when the congregations are leaving the places of worship and the people . . . are returning home; for the rebels come from half a mile or more along the road, running to and fro and flushing them about, with all kinds of brutish and insulting language to what they call 'country folks',[2] and if there be any young females, they almost tear the clothes off their backs . . . surely it is a scandalous shame . . . yours obediently, ONE DISTURBED BY THE REBELS.

(*Whitby Gazette* 6 March 1858)

It is important not to lose sight of those who remained resistant to nonconformity, though their appearance in the historical record is frequently cast in negative tones. But as E.P. Thompson points out, the old culture was 'neither stupid nor animalistic' (1976: 400); to portray it as such would therefore be to compound the felonies of Methodist historiography.

A continuum embracing the extremes of piety and indifference is still observable in the village today, though the ratios and weightings may have changed. Certainly, generalised 'Primitive', 'Wesleyan' or 'Cong's' affiliation continues to be commonly recognised and is usually taken to refer, not so much to one who is a regular participant in the life of a chapel, but rather to a person who at various times of the year can be relied upon for support and who would be expected to look to his or her chapel when in need of religious offices at the rites of passage. Affiliation, then, is a much looser concept than membership, wherein is implied a more profound religious commitment, coupled with regular involvement in week by week chapel duties. Significantly, affiliation is the form of nonconformist allegiance which is now most prevalent in Staithes, yet contrary to the beliefs of some of the zealots, it may not necessarily imply either spiritual atrophy or institutional demise. This can be substantiated if we examine some of the determinants of affiliation.

One frequently cited historical influence upon varying patterns of nonconformist allegiance, and the differences between Wesleyan and Primitive Methodists in particular, is that of social class. As Currie puts it: 'Each Methodist denomination was situated in a carefully graded system, at the top end of which were the Wesleyans, and towards the bottom, the Primitive Methodists or "Ranters" ' (1968: 205). Wesleyan Methodism was held to be composed of bourgeois and petit bourgeois elements, the mill owners, shopkeepers and trades persons, whilst Primitive Methodism drew its support from the proletarian and labouring class (cf. Pickering 1961: 24). As E.R. Wickham has written, Primitive Methodist chapels were found 'largely in the rural and mining parts; in East Yorkshire and the Wolds, for example, they were the church of the people . . . Primitive Methodism reached further down into the lower social strata than any of the larger denominations' (1957: 132, 133). Differences of this sort persisted into the twentieth century and seem to have played a part in the discussions which led up to Methodist Union. Currie, in his *Methodism Divided*, quotes Sir Newbold Key, a Wesleyan: 'The only argument against Union was one that could not be stated in public, and that was sheer snobbery' (1968: 207).

The part played by social class in determining religious preference seems to have been more marked in the larger towns and cities than in the rural areas and it is well known, for example, that places such as Bristol, Birmingham and Sheffield contained large and influential Wesleyan 'aristocracies'. In these areas the powerful local middle class was represented in considerable numbers among congregations who worshipped in the ornate and extravagant tabernacles. The differences were also pronounced in the quiet and conservative backwaters of the residential coastal resorts; many south coast towns, for instance, as well as Scarborough and Whitby in the north (Currie 1968: 210–12). In the rural and less densely populated areas, however, class differences between Methodists took on a rather different character. For in these areas as E.P. Thompson points out, 'Methodism of *any* variety necessarily assumed a more class-conscious form . . . The chapel in the agricultural village was inevitably an affront to the vicar and the squire, and a centre in which the labourer gained independence and self respect' (1968: 437, original emphasis). In this sense both Primitive *and* Wesleyan Methodists might have been perceived in the same light by the local clergy and middle class, that is as members of the lower orders practising their own highly contentious brand of religion. This establishment view of nonconformity has clearly been present in Staithes and environs where, as we have seen, there is good historical evidence of Anglican neglect.

Membership rolls which might have cast some light on class divisions between the chapels are sadly absent from the archival sources examined, though these did contain frequent reference to the Primitive Methodist chapel as a place of worship much frequented by the fisherfolk of the village. Traditionally, the Wesleyans, by contrast, were said to have drawn their support from small business people and farmers, whilst the local Congregationalists, at least in the latter part of the nineteenth century, consisted mainly of ironstone miners. In recent years class has not been an important factor in distinguishing between the groups. Today all three chapels have congregations composed principally of men and women from the working and lower-middle class and, in fact, a vaguely recognised pecking order in the village tends to set apart chapel members of any denomination from other villagers. Even among their own chapel sympathisers, for example, members may be criticised for being 'snobbish' or 'social climbers'. Social class does not therefore present itself as a useful explanatory variable for a division which, as we shall see, may be better described in the context of long-standing inter-familial and communal conflicts.

Neither is it possible to view theological disagreement, once such a divisive force within nonconformity, as a relevant source of division between the chapels. Certainly, early village Methodists will have been divided in attitudes towards such issues as ritual, lay authority and styles of worship. The term 'Ranter Chapel', for example, is still used to describe the Primitive Methodists. Services there are remembered as being altogether more enthusiastic and ecstatic than those favoured by the Wesleyans, where such 'ritualistic' elements as the wearing of robes by ministers and the playing of solemn organ music during the collection were typical features of Sunday worship. Dame Laura Knight, in her book, *The Magic of a Line* makes the following observation, 'Every now and again they held a prayer meeting at the [Primitive Methodist] Chapel, "when them as is drunkards confess, and is saaved an' don't ever get drunk any more". This heated state of ecstasy, leading perhaps to revelation of mutual sin, did not always prove too wise' (Knight 1965: 113).

No major theological or liturgical differences are discernible between the chapels today, though, as we have seen in Chapter 4, certain members of Bethel have in recent years pursued a more radical doctrinal path. For the Methodists there is little in the form and content of services by which to distinguish the two, and both belong to the same Loftus and Staithes Circuit. As one woman put it, when seeking to play down chapel rivalry, 'we're all going the same way, after all'. But while religious ends might be shared, there is considerable disagreement over the means by which these might be attained. Accordingly, we shall want to argue that these rivalries can be seen as a part of folk religion, since they emerge from and persist in spite of a particular set of institutional doctrines and practices in which they no longer find any official warrant.

For the great majority of villagers religious preferences are shaped by such factors as family tradition, religious socialisation and even, in some cases, place of residence. Since these outweigh any more overtly theological or doctrinal considerations, it is appropriate to speak of allegiance to the chapels as a form of *nominal* affiliation. This is nowhere better illustrated than in the part played by family and kinship in determining allegiance to a particular chapel.

It is common in Staithes for individual families to have long-standing connections with one or other chapel, to which they traditionally lend their support. None the less, some remarkable volte-faces have occurred, even during this century, and family feuding constitutes an important part of local

10. The Wesleyan chapel to the left and Bethel above right, each with the Sunday Schoolroom below. *Photograph by Richard Cale, 1981.*

chapel history. For example, in the early 1920s a dispute arose between the Primitive Methodist junior organist and the chapel trustees concerning the use of the chapel organ for practice purposes. During 1922 and 1923 the minutes of the Trustees Meeting[3] record details of a complex argument between the two parties, which finally resulted in the junior organist and his entire family leaving the Primitives for the Wesleyans, to whom the family has given its support ever since. It is a disagreement that has not been forgotten in the village; as one man wittily put it:

11. The Primitive Methodist chapel in the High Street, with Bethel opposite. As in illustration 10, the proximity of the buildings is clearly apparent. *Photograph by Richard Cale, 1981.*

It makes you wonder about it all. Half o' them what's supposed to be Wesleyans now used to belong t' Primitives . . . there was a great argument over t' organ and a lot all left. I once said t' minister, 'it's a waste o' time sending missionaries off tiv Africa, tha' wants to get some down 'ere'.

Family alliances seem, on occasion, to be linked to the simple expedient of propinquity. The inhabitants of certain yards, streets or passages which are close to a chapel may therefore come to be identified with it through physical proximity. Accordingly, the families living in Chapel Yard, which gives access from the High Street to the Wesleyan chapel, are almost entirely Wesleyan in their affiliation. The force of propinquity is illustrated in the following conversation, which I had with a man who, as a child, had lived in the yard:

My mother really belongs High Chapel, but we [he and his brothers and sister] always went to Wesley.
Q. Why was that?
Because it was nearer I suppose.

The determination of an individual's religious affiliation by family tradition and place of residence is further fixed and enriched through a process of religious socialisation in the Sunday School. The importance of the chapel Sunday Schools is readily attested by their membership rolls; Wesley has fifty scholars, the Primitive Methodists have forty and Bethel has twenty. Each Sunday School has both a morning and an afternoon meeting and most of the children on the roll are regular attenders at each. During the fieldwork period, over 100 children were receiving some form of systematic religious instruction. This primary level of religious socialisation, wherein children become familiar with the basic tenets of the Christian faith, is of particular importance, in so far as the enthusiasm which many of them display in the early years frequently begins to cool with the changing preoccupations and autonomy of adolescence. Only a few make the transition to regular chapel attendance and a major factor in this situation seems to be the complete absence of any form of youth group within the chapels. A variety of such groups exist at circuit level, but no teenagers from Staithes were ever observed at the meetings. There is, therefore, a prounounced hiatus between the flourishing Sunday Schools and the ageing chapel membership, which is not entirely an historical effect. Indeed it is conceivable that active participation and full membership of the chapel are more typically aspects of mature and later life.

Thus, for the majority of children, week by week involvement with the chapel ceases at the age of twelve or thirteen; henceforth attendance is usually restricted to the important events of the life and annual cycles. Despite its apparent arbitrariness, this form of chapel affiliation is likely to be lifelong. Thus on several occasions following the death of a villager, my enquiries as to the whereabouts of the funeral would be met with a reply such as, 'oh yes, he was an old Wesleyan. He used to go to the Sunday School, you know.' In this way even those men and women who had perhaps not attended 'their' chapel for many years, other than for special events, retained their religious identity, even in death.

The religious affiliation which we have described is therefore *nominal* since it derives from factors which do not form a relevant part of the officially constituted teachings and practices of the chapels. As we have seen, the labels are not an expression of regular religious practice or involvement, but derive from a set of associations of an entirely different order. For adults, nominal affiliation, grounded in the Sunday Schools, means attendance at the main events of the chapel year, such as Harvest Festivals, and anniversaries (though not, as we shall see in the next chapter, the main events of the Christian calendar). Undoubtedly it presupposes the baptism of one's children in the chapel and the expectation that one's funeral will eventually take place there. Nominal affiliation elicits support for coffee-mornings, bazaars, jumble sales and even, in some cases, extends to making monetary gifts to chapel funds in lieu of Sunday attendance. Above all, it signifies a deeply felt identification with the traditions of both village and chapel alike.

Robert Moore, in his study of Methodism in the Deerness Valley, in County Durham, alludes indirectly to the phenomenon of nominal affiliation when referring to 'sympathisers' who, though never active in the chapel, are still drawn into it at times and can be relied upon for sympathetic support. This 'penumbra of membership', he suggests, may in fact be an area in which Methodist culture is upheld as much as in 'the active centre of chapel life' (1974: 69). The point is echoed by Pickering, in his study of Scunthorpe and Rawmarsh, where he describes 'irregular' members, who attend perhaps once or twice per year for festivals and special occasions (1958: II. 15–21). The evidence from Staithes, where the 'irregular penumbra' is clearly visible, undoubtedly supports these viewpoints and, we would suggest, is indicative of a persisting form of religious identification which is all too often overlooked by those sociologists of religion who confine themselves to more obviously quantifiable measures of allegiance.

Tensions between ministry and laity

The more closely we examine the transformations which occurred within official Methodism, or the sacred culture, as we have preferred to call it, the more apparent it becomes that the people of Staithes have devoted considerable energy to the task of elaborating a religious system congruent with other, more broadly based communal norms and values. On many occasions this has brought them into conflict with the guardians of Methodism, in a way which has not gone unnoticed by commentators on religious life in the village. As a writer in the *Methodist Recorder* put it, when describing the 'long struggle' which preceded 'home rule' in the Loftus and Staithes Circuit, 'it looks as though the Methodists of Cleveland were as fickle in their allegiance as the Galatians' (*Methodist Recorder* 2 Jan. 1908). The judgement is one with which past ministers in Staithes might well agree.

In common with other dissenting and nonconformist movements, Methodism encountered numerous problems over the relationship between ministerial and lay authority. These difficulties were frequently compounded by increasing levels of organisational entrenchment as the denomination developed. Subsequent schisms highlighted the issue of authority, so that whilst in Wesleyanism, the role and expectations attaching to the minister frequently produced a feeling of social distance between him and his flock, the more radical secessionists were wont to regard the local minister as one among equals, or even, in some cases, as a paid employee (Davies 1961: 63). Feelings of this type were reinforced by differing organisational structures and systems of representation. Thus Wesleyanism invested authority in minister, circuit and district and was ultimately dominated by Conference, whilst Primitive Methodism espoused a more democratic ethic and always sought to decentralise power and authority. It is fairly clear, however, that in both cases considerable potential existed for local congregations to work out their own position in relation to their ministers.

In Staithes, scepticism about the ministry has a long history in the life of all three chapels, stemming back to the time when each had its own resident minister and when there seems to have been a conscious desire to regulate ministers' activities. As an older member of the Primitive Methodists told me, 'The old men always used to say to us, "don't take any notice of ministers, don't let them get a whip hand over you, because they're only ships that pass in the night".' Late-nineteenth-century visitors' reports for the Bethel chapel reflect, from the opposite viewpoint, similar sentiments. Thus the entry for 1889 includes the following remarks: 'Amongst some of the people, there appeared to be a feeling of depression and discontent its real cause I was unable to discover.'[4] The following year this becomes clearer: 'So far as I could make out the people are not all very hearty and co-operative in their attitude to the place and the minister. The reasons for the position they take I am not quite able to give.'[5] Ten years later the observations are still more explicit: 'Ministers generally are not credited with much zeal for visitation, or ability in preaching.'[6] About the same period, a more graphic illustration of the same phenomenon was taking place among the village's Wesleyans. The following is an extract from a letter written to the *Whitby Gazette* by a casual visitor to the Wesleyan Methodist chapel in Staithes:

being accustomed to attend a certain place of worship I accordingly wended my steps thither on a certain Sabbath morning. It was very cold and bleak outside – in fact it was a storm – and as I took my seat I could not help thinking there was not much contrast between the coldness without the chapel and the cold, heartless influence that prevailed within the sacred edifice. The preacher was in his place, and I may say he was a pleasant, kind and genial looking individual. The pews were many, but the worshippers few – few indeed. The minister proceeded in the usual way, by giving out the first hymn; when I found to my surprise that there was no organist. But thinking that illness or some such cause was the reason for the absence of that worthy official my surprise was somewhat lessened. However a few days after I had made the acquaintance of one of the officers of the chapel, and I casually remarked how unfortunate it was for the organist at a place of worship to be absent, and it was then that he did a tale unfold. I cannot pretend to give you word for word what he told me, but he gave me to understand that lately there has been as good almost as a play enacted whenever that person occupied the pulpit. The reason the organist was absent, and the reason for the coldness inside the hallowed walls was none other than that a certain few, headed by the organist, had taken completely against their head pastor . . . Well, being somewhat interested in the affair I made myself acquainted with the unfortunate minister of the Gospel, and he laid the case more fully before me than the previous person had done. He told me how the 'select few' had tried at the general meeting to vote him out of the Circuit. How they spoke of him in the most unkind, unfeeling manner, and then, not content with that, they absented themselves on the Sabbath day from the place of worship whenever he occupied the pulpit, and not only absented themselves, but did their best to keep others away also, and if a fair-minded individual tried to lay such things aside and do his duty he would be boycotted . . .

Is this the Christianity that will win the world for Christ?

Yours, A WESLEYAN.[7]

Ministers were, and are, frequently perceived as interfering 'foreigners', who, unacquainted with local conditions and attitudes, attempt to assert their will over that of the village populace. As one woman said of the minister in 1975: 'There's a lot in the village don't like him. When he came he wanted us to build a new church at the Lane End and for all three [chapels] to get together. That's when the trouble started. Before that we all used to get on fine.' Whilst, as we shall see below, the latter comment is hardly attested by the long-standing chapel rivalry in Staithes, it is nevertheless indicative of a general feeling of suspicion, mistrust and dubiety held in relation to the ministry.

A parallel situation is vividly portrayed in a scene from Leo Walmsley's novel, *Master Mariner*, set in the fishing village of 'Bramblewick' – actually Robin Hood's Bay, some fifteen miles from Staithes. In the novel, the Methodist Minister, a Mr Jones, has been endeavouring, without success, to convince his flock of the wisdom of building a new chapel in the 'upbank' area of the village (the equivalent of 'Lane End' in Staithes). One evening, when inclement weather keeps several 'upbankers' away from chapel, he stresses the urgency of his proposal to a stalwart member, but meets with the following rebuttal.

What's wrong with awd chapel eh? It was good enough for our fathers. Good enough for theirs. Good enough for John Wesley. And open air was good enough for him afore it was built. So long as its [*sic*] Gospel and the Lord's Word, it doesn't matter where it's preached. There'll be no flitting chapels in my time, Mr Jones. Get that straight. (Walmsley 1948: 44)

Two specific organisational factors, one a national characteristic and the other a local incidental, have provided a framework within which attitudes of this sort have emerged in Staithes. It was long the practice in Methodism for ministers to move automatically to a different circuit every three years (Wesley's original intention had been that they should move on annually). Later, the period of stay was extended to five years and now, under certain circumstances, chiefly mutual agreement between the parties, it is extensible indefinitely. Nevertheless, ministers remain comparatively itinerant, in contrast, for example, to Anglican incumbents. It is a Methodist convention which may have generated certain unintended consequences. Under a set of arrangements whereby a minister stays only a relatively short time in any one locality, a specific set of perceptions of the 'typical parson' is likely to develop. He may come to be regarded as one who arrives, often as a stranger to the area, perhaps unfamiliar with local habits and viewpoints and who stays for only a short time before being replaced by someone else. During his stay he may wish to innovate or modify existing arrangements to suit his own tastes and preferences. In short, he may be the agency of unwelcome change, whose relationship with the laity has the potential to develop into a conflict of interests.[8]

In Staithes itself this predisposition has been reinforced by another significant factor. Until 1972 it had been the practice in the circuit for the junior minister to live in the village, whilst the superintendent lived four miles away in Loftus. For many years these junior ministers were in fact, as we pointed out in Chapter 3, newly out of college and sometimes still unordained. This raises two points. Firstly, as newly trained men, it is reasonable to assume that they would have been eager and enthusiastic and that in some cases, perhaps fired by idealism and spiritual ambition, they may have had new schemes in mind. Again, they would have typified the image of the uninformed outsider. Additionally, as young and inexperienced individuals, they would inevitably have been vulnerable to manipulation and pressure from older chapel members. As one old man put it, some young ministers were 'scared to death' by chapel leaders who were determined to defend their interests. Even today, the prickliness of some of the Staithes Methodists is said to call for prudence and discretion; as one lay preacher remarked, recalling his period of training in the 1950s, 'we were always told: "go careful in Staithes" '.

A state of tension between ministry and laity presupposes some degree of disapprobation on both sides and in fact it is apparent that criticism is not simply from laity to ministry, but can also flow the opposite way. A conversation with the superintendent, concerning the chapels in Staithes and their supporters, produced the following comments.

I doubt whether some of them [the people] have any faith at all. They're worshipping the building, that's all – the bricks and mortar. If someone came to Staithes and wanted to go to church, I couldn't recommend them to come here. If they went here they'd just be trying to get money out of them to keep their 'chapill' [here he imitated the local accent] going. It's pathetic really.

The feeling was echoed by his junior minister, who in a conversation about Primitive–Wesleyan rivalry, stated: 'there are only two people who are mature enough Christians to agree to them [the chapels] coming together; one of them is an outsider and the other told me that if he went to the other chapel, his family would turn against him'. Similarly, and perhaps more expectedly in view of the small number of Anglicans in the village, the rector remarked, 'you'll find all sorts of things in Staithes, but not much religion'. Over a year later, when it had been announced that the rector was to leave the parish to take up community work, he said of his successor, 'he likes the important things, bingo and raffles – so he'll be alright in Staithes'.

Lay preachers voice similar criticisms. In the spring of 1976 a lay preacher from a nearby village referred in a sermon to the 'ridiculousness' and 'impracticality' of keeping two Methodist chapels open in the same village. When the service was over and the congregation were making their way out, murmured disapproval was clearly audible and some were heard to say, 'that's the last time we go to hear him'. On another occasion, during a week of prayer for Christian Unity, a lay preacher in his early twenties, and still 'on note',[9] came to conduct a service in the Wesley chapel and began his sermon thus: 'When I said to my friends that I was coming to Staithes today, they told me not to go into either of the chapels, but to stand in the middle and preach in the street.' Continuing in similar vein, he was soon stopped short when one of the stewards stood up and interrupted him saying, 'Now then, there's no need for that. We have our differences, but we speak to each other. Don't come down here talking like that when you don't know anything about it.' Criticism from the pulpit was not readily received, and while the interruption of a preacher may seem exceptional, the incident may have been typical of others in the past, when young preachers or ministers clashed with the elder statesmen of the chapels.

Naturally, the ministry tend to attribute such animosity and criticism to individual idiosyncracies or a more general stubbornness. As we have already suggested, however, this type of opposition might more profitably be viewed as an aspect of the encounter between popular and sacred cultures, which still occasionally produces friction. The opposition signifies not so much a rejection of the sacred culture, but an attempt to keep alive villagers' own version of Methodism. In so doing they prove a constant thorn in the side of the Methodist Church, at both circuit and district level, for the tension between ministry and laity is only the frontline expression of a more fundamental opposition between the people and the authorities of the institutional church. The polarisation of the two sets of interests is clearly apparent in the following case study.

Union, independence and identity: a short case study

It will by now be apparent that formal Methodist Union, which took place in 1932, gave rise to an intriguing pattern of commensality in the case of the Wesleyan and Primitive chapels in Staithes. At a local level, and barely consistent with the spirit of union, traditional rivalries persisted, but were enacted in new arenas and before a different audience. Indeed, the old hostilities seemed at times to serve as the expression of common grievances felt by both sides in the face of an increasing alienation from the broader body of Methodist fellowship and administration. The protracted debate which ensued was made worse precisely because of the rift which had opened up between Methodism in the village and Methodism as a bureaucratised, church-like, multi-national organisation.

Preparations for union began to take place within the two circuits in March 1929 and took the form of mutual cross-representation of Primitives and Wesleyans at the Quarterly Meeting.[10] The following month there was an 'interchange of pulpits'.[11] The principles of union were duly espoused in carefully worded resolutions.

We, the members of the Loftus Wesleyan Methodist Quarterly Meeting, send cordial greetings to the Staithes Primitive Methodist Quarterly Meeting. We remind ourselves that before this communication reaches you, Methodist Union will have been consummated and the two denominations become one. In view of this fact, we feel the time opportune to consider its practical bearing on the relationship between the two circuits. The amalgamation of circuits is under contemplation throughout the district and in some instances definite schemes have been proposed. The two Methodist Circuits in the Loftus and Staithes area practically cover the same ground and in the interests of the work of God and a more economical and efficient use of resources, the question of amalgamation is bound to arise. Subject to your approval, we beg respectfully to recommend that the subject be introduced for discussion at a meeting of the Union Committee of the two circuits as soon as possible. Such a discussion may result in a scheme of amalgamation; it will certainly foster the spirit of fellowship and goodwill which already exists between the two circuits.[12]

Two years later, in 1934, the Local Preachers' Meeting for the new circuit passed a motion proposing joint services at Loftus, Skinningrove and Staithes.[13]

Despite such conciliatory gestures, the practicalities of union were slow to get under way. Not until 1937 did the name 'Methodist Church' replace 'Wesleyan' and 'Primitive' on the plans, which continued to be published separately each quarter. Indeed, it was not until 1939 and the outbreak of the Second World War that the first joint plan for the circuit of Loftus and Staithes was printed. This 'Emergency Plan' listed seventeen chapels in all, including three at Loftus,[14] three at Brotton, and two each at Staithes, Hinderwell, Skinningrove and Carlin How. Local preachers were still listed separately under the old circuit names, though no reference was made to the former allegiances of the four ministers.[15]

The post-war years continued the pattern of piecemeal union, with increasing emphasis on the contingent rather than the reformist aspects of amalgamation. In 1946 two societies were merged at Loftus, followed in 1947 by similar mergers at both Skinningrove and Hinderwell. In the following year, two more chapels (Brotton West and Street Houses) were removed from the plan.[16] By 1959 discussions concerning the unification of the two chapels at Carlin How were set in motion and union was achieved there two years later.

In general, the 1950s was a difficult decade in which the circuit confronted increasing economic and organisational problems associated with dwindling membership and a decline in the number of local preachers. It was, of course, a situation which was subsequently examined more generally by the Commission on Rural Methodism (1958). By 1961 the circuit was in debt and looking for ways to place its finances, in the words of the circuit steward, 'on a business-like footing'.[17] The methods which ministers employed in tackling these issues were not always popular and in two cases ministers were not invited to remain in the circuit beyond the minimum period.[18] In 1969 the Darlington District, of which the Loftus and Staithes Circuit formed a part, set up a Replanning Commission, which in its report of July of that year recommended the closure of five chapels in the circuit. Three of these closures were to be in villages which were still struggling to maintain two Methodist chapels. These villages were Loftus, Brotton and Staithes. The motives behind the recommendation were two-fold. Firstly, and pragmatically, it was regarded as economic foolhardiness to persevere with two chapels in the same community, with all the attendant costs of heating, lighting and repairs. Rationalisation was therefore imperative on monetary grounds. In addition, there was a feeling that two chapels in the same village constituted something of an anachronism and presented a poor public image to the community; in the words of the Commissioners, it was a 'bad witness' for Methodism. The closures would therefore facilitate financial solvency and improve Methodism's reputation for reason and good sense. In Brotton and Loftus the proposals were successfully upheld, but in Staithes they gave way to lengthy debate.

Proposals concerning the amalgamation of the two Methodist societies in Staithes had first been aired, as we have seen, in 1934, yet almost thirty years later, in 1962, a meeting of local preachers could report 'no progress' towards even a tentative resolution of the issue in the form of a joint Sunday morning service during the winter months.[19] In its investigation of the situation at Staithes the Commission therefore faced acute problems and firm convictions. Perhaps sensing this, it chose to focus attention on the relative physical condition of the two chapels, comparing the favourability of each in terms of access, car-parking, safety, and so on. The state of the Wesleyan chapel was judged to be rather worse than that of the other, which was also considered to be more favourably situated in the High Street. Furthermore, the Primitive Methodist chapel, along with its adjacent Sunday School, was a 'listed' building of special architectural interest. The Commission therefore recommended that the Wesleyan chapel be closed, sold, and the resulting revenue used to improve facilities in the remaining chapel, in which all future services and meetings were to take place.

Serious doubts were quickly cast on the thoroughness of the enquiry. A leading Wesleyan told me that the Commissioners had only spent twenty minutes in each chapel and that it was felt that this was insufficient time in which to make a valid and accurate assessment, especially when the repercussions were to be so far-reaching. The Wesleyans argued that if they could maintain the building and pay their quarterly returns to the circuit (their financial position was said to be good) then they should be allowed to remain open. The main thrust of their argument stemmed from a deeply felt sense of history; two chapels had been built in Staithes and two should be kept open. Any thought of closure was an insult to the men and women who had struggled to build the chapel and who remained very much alive in Wesleyan memories following the centenary celebrations of 1966. Indeed, the issue for some had not merely been 'why close Wesley?' but 'why close either chapel?'. In November 1969, therefore, a resolution was sent from the Wesleyan trustees, rejecting the Commission's proposal.

The Primitives, on the other hand, whilst disliking outside interference as much as the Wesleyans, felt, perhaps understandably, that the decision of the Commissioners should be accepted. Meanwhile, the Wesleyans remained adamant in their opposition and in a joint meeting with the Commissioners, held at Staithes in February 1970, they once again reiterated their refusal to give up the chapel. In turn, the Commission stood by its decision. The deadlock was eventually eased through an agreement to attempt, for a trial period, to bring the two Societies together whilst at the same time keeping both chapels open. This was to be achieved by using each chapel on alternate Sundays. The two were to operate as one Society, but trust funds were to remain separate. One Sunday School was to be organised, incorporating teachers and scholars from both chapels, and all special groups (e.g. Home Missions, Women's Work, Overseas Missions) were to combine their efforts.

The new scheme began in the spring of 1970 and though intended for a trial period of one year only continued until the spring of 1975. During the trial period, the two chapels were to be considered as one Methodist Society, but whilst joint committees were formed the unity which attended them was tenuous indeed. Old rivalries lay close below the surface and since the two chapels retained separate trust funds (i.e. those which support the maintenance of the building itself) it was possible for competition to continue in money-raising events like Sunday School Anniversaries and Harvest Festivals. In short, the co-existence seems to have been both precarious and fractious.

In 1975 the matter again came to a head. On this occasion the point at issue was the choice of dates for special forthcoming events, which each chapel was required to submit to the joint Church Council Meeting. A problem had arisen over a clash of dates, though this was clearly only the tip of an iceberg of grievance and disaffection. In the meeting of 10 February 1975, discussion had turned on the submission of dates for future events when, the minutes record, Mr A., a member of the Primitive chapel, 'interrupted by saying that in his opinion if both chapels were open each Sunday there would be no reason for differences over dates'. The minutes continue:

Mr A. proposed that each chapel be open each Sunday evening but dispense with Sunday morning services. After a varied discussion Mr B. [a Wesleyan] put forward an amendment to the effect that Wesley remain open for both morning and evening services. The Minister then put this proposition to the vote . . . The result was: seven for the motion; three against; with two abstentions.[20]

The following month the proposal was taken to the Quarterly Circuit Meeting, at which it was reluctantly ratified. The Wesleyan chapel was to open once again for both morning and evening services on a Sunday and the Primitive chapel was to open on Sunday evenings only.

In addition to the issue over dates, various other more deep-seated differences had been instrumental in reinforcing the division. Both sides felt the alternate Sunday system to be unworkable, principally because members refused to attend services anywhere other than in their own chapel. Some Primitives would not attend Wesley and vice versa. As a result, attendances remained low, even though the congregations had joined forces. This had naturally taken its toll on the revenue from collections which between March and May of 1972, for example, was averaging less than £7 per week.[21] Furthermore, the proposed union of the two Sunday Schools had never been implemented and leaders from each chapel continued to organise their own children's activities and events. After a protracted and difficult period, it had therefore been decided to revert to the former system. As one man told me, 'we just couldn't go on as we were, we had to take one step backward to take two steps forward'.

Whilst these proposed changes had been discussed in the months before fieldwork began, when I arrived in the village, at the beginning of April 1975, the earlier joint system was still in operation, albeit about to be terminated. I was thus presented with the fortunate opportunity of observing the immediate effects of the changeover. During April I attended services at both chapels and made initial contact with as many chapel folk as possible. The split between Primitives and Wesleyans was immediately apparent and I soon learned which were which. This was not a difficult task, since in the services themselves Primitives and Wesleyans refused to sit with one another, preferring instead to occupy separate pews. This was no secret and the minister admitted to me, 'they are divided in two – right down the middle'. When the new quarterly plan commenced, the division was once again forcefully illustrated.

The first Sunday of the new plan saw me at Wesley, which, unlike its rival, was holding a morning service. I was somewhat surprised to see that twenty-five people were in the congregation. Previously, under the joint system, I had observed morning attendances of between fifteen and twenty. *Division*, rather than unity, seemed to have produced a renewed strength. Still more interesting was the observation that none of the regular Sunday morning attenders from the Primitive chapel were present. That is to say, those Primitives who even under the previous arrangements had always attended on Sunday mornings, irrespective of where services were being held, were now no longer going to the only Methodist service available on a Sunday morning.

After the service I talked to the stewards as they counted up the money received in the collection that morning. When it was totalled they pointed out that the sum received, over £6, was almost as much as had been averaged for a complete Sunday under the joint system. One of them said, 'We knew this would happen, they were holding back' (i.e. in their offerings). He had expected an increase in collection revenue because, he claimed, those Primitives who had attended Wesley had only given small amounts. Later I heard the Primitives accuse the Wesleyans of the same form of parsimony.

A similar pattern was repeated that evening in the Primitive chapel when over thirty people attended, giving in the region of £7. Naturally the first Sunday under the new scheme could be expected to result in an enthusiastic response and clearly members of both chapels, in the manner of political party 'whips', had made some effort to ensure good attendances. What was altogether more striking was the continuance of this trend. Subsequent months saw a sustained two-fold increase in the total number of Methodists now regularly attending chapel and a corresponding improvement in the revenue from collections.

I also became acquainted during this period with another enduring aspect of dissonance in chapel life. This concerned the structure of the quarterly plan. The burden of preaching in the eight chapels in the circuit was shared between two full-time ministers and fifteen lay preachers. A growing problem in recent years had been that of adequately deploying a diminished number of preachers throughout the circuit. Inevitably, when each quarterly plan was drawn up, gaps would occur on particular Sundays when preachers could not be found. Thus, instead of the name of a preacher appearing on the plan for a particular chapel on a given Sunday, the word 'supply' would be inserted and the onus was then placed on the chapel in question to make arrangements for a preacher to come on that day. This was usually achieved through contacts and associations with nearby Methodist circuits.

For the plan covering the period May to July 1975, Wesley had been allocated five supplies and the Primitive chapel, four. However, the former was offering a total of twenty-six services and the latter only thirteen. The discrepancy became the source of considerable adverse comment. Criticism of the planning represented two distinct modes of disaffection. Firstly, there was a dissatisfaction, common to both chapels, concerning the allegedly excessive number of supplies which they had been allocated. This was felt to be deliberate victimisation and a clear expression of the lack of favour which Staithes had with the rest of the circuit. The supposition was partially borne out by the evidence of the plan: two other chapels in the circuit had four 'supplies', but the remaining four had none or one. Secondly, and in addition to this *common* grievance, there was also a sense of injustice on the part of the Primitives, who complained of unfair treatment at being allocated four 'supplies' when they were only operating evening services; in effect they were having to find for themselves one third of their preachers for that quarter. Wesley on the other hand, had twice as many services but only one more 'supply'.

One month after the new arrangements had been introduced, I attended a coffee-morning organised by the ladies of the Primitive chapel. I chatted with several regular Sunday attenders and asked one of them, 'how are things going under the new system?'. There seemed to be a general consensus that they were 'better off', since, as one of them put it, 'they [the Wesleyans] would never come over here and the collections were poor'. Then another asked, 'have you seen t' plan? We've got four supplies to Wesley's two.' Again, this was not entirely accurate, since the plan showed five 'supplies' for Wesley – two for morning services, but also three for evenings. Nevertheless, a *sense* of injustice existed and this was capable of overriding any appeal to 'objectivity'. It was the circuit superintendent himself who was blamed for this alleged anomaly, which, I was told, constituted just one more example of his favouritism for Wesley. 'Why do you think he has a preference for them?' I asked. 'We didn't buy him a new carpet for his lounge', one of the women replied vitriolically. 'Bait a trap and you'll catch something.'

The sense of injustice provoked the Primitive Methodists into establishing themselves on the same footing as the Wesleyans. The next development in the saga, therefore, came in the middle of June, 1975, when rumours began to circulate that the Primitive chapel was to hold morning services when the new plan started in August. When a proposal to this effect was put to the Circuit Meeting, there was little choice for members but to endorse it.

In the face of combined opposition from both circuit and district the Staithes Methodists had thus achieved the remarkable result of returning to the pre-1969 arrangements. Their tenacity in this stemmed from a powerful desire to preserve both the sense and the reality of a religious tradition which they felt was under threat from uninformed and misguided influences. It would be a mistake to pass off this desire as a piece of short-sighted, parochial pig-headedness. Rather it should be seen as an attempt by a small group of men and women to maintain some influence over their chosen religious tradition.

Summary

Passages in this chapter have referred to the 'idiosyncratic Methodism' to be found in Staithes. A similar phenomenon is depicted in Moore's (1974) study of the Deerness Valley, in which he argues that village Methodism may have certain characteristics that distinguish it from Methodism in general. The distinction arises out of changes taking place in the movement over time, affecting factors of community and association at different institutional levels. He writes, 'Methodism has progressed from a sectarian to church-like structure whilst village Methodism has become more communal and possibly less associational, only formally and lightly linked to the wider association through a few officials' (1974: 123).[22] Moore shows that the village Methodists he studied have little concern with the religious issues being discussed in the wider setting. A similar situation prevails in Staithes where, for example, in the same year that the Methodist Conference voted on the important ecumenical matter of Anglican–Methodist relations, the leaders of the Wesleyan chapel unequivocally rejected the proposed union with their Primitive Methodist rivals. Parallels also emerge between Moore's description of village Methodism's weak links with the church as a whole and the overt tension between the two which was found in Staithes. The aspects of village Methodism which we have discussed and which are most relevant to a distinction of this type are nominal affiliation, chapel rivalry and the tension between ministry and laity.

Nominal affiliation exists as a vague and generalised attachment to a particular chapel building, its traditions and the people and memories associated with it. As such it may have little to do with the broad principles of the Methodist creed. Those who are attached to the chapel in this way express their religious feelings through sporadic attendances, often limited to special occasions in the calendar or communal rites of passage. All the evidence suggests that this form of nominal affiliation represents an important source of religious legitimation, albeit one which does not find expression in official terms. Nominal affiliation is closely linked to chapel rivalry, which also derives from attachment to the chapel as a building and as a symbol of communal values. Chapel rivalry, however, is more especially the domain of members and more regular supporters, whereas nominal affiliation assumes a certain passivity on the level of religious practice – although it has been seen how support from this sector can quickly be generated when necessary, viz. the attendances at services after the renewed division in 1975. Paradoxically, since its very object is the institutional church, chapel rivalry comes close to what we understood in Chapter 1 by the term folk religion. Pride in, and affection for, the chapel run counter to any concern with the contingencies, reforms and rationalisations made necessary by the difficult position of the Methodist Church and reveal the existence of a set of values which are not sanctioned by it. Likewise, the continued use of the labels 'Primitive' and 'Wesleyan' some forty years after their abandonment by the Methodist Conference points to a rejection of externally imposed change and a tenacious hold on old ways and traditional practices. Beliefs appear to lag behind or repudiate those of the wider society. As Moore states, village Methodism 'remains apart from the development in national religious organisations: the ecumenical movement and the discussions of secularisation and the "death of God" remain the activities of metropolitan Methodists' (1974: 123). Again it is the beliefs of the *community* which are cherished – beliefs held by earlier generations, deviation from which would run counter to tradition. Communally held values of this order are at the very root of chapel rivalry, which is partly motivated by a respect for the men and women who laboured and toiled to build the chapel. Thus, chapel is as significant as a monument to previous generations as it is the House of God. In a sense, then, the minister is correct in his assertion that the people are 'worshipping the bricks and mortar', since the importance of the chapel and the values associated with it seem to have supplanted its official function. The outcome of such a situation is an immanent tension between ministry and laity, which regularly expresses itself in the form of mutual criticism. At a general level the tension must be interpreted as a widespread and possibly inevitable conflict between two cultural and religious forms: the popular and the sacred, the folk and the official.

Other writers have noted the relationship between local sentiment and religious affiliation. It is one which seems to be particularly striking in nonconformity. As Rees writes of rural Wales, 'there is the emotional link between the individual and a particular chapel which is also attended by many of his kinsmen and by neighbours whom he has learnt to know better than others through meeting them there' (1950: 115). *Attachment* to the chapel may not diminish even when attendances become sporadic. Similarly, the chapel may be defended to the last against those within the church who wish to close or amalgamate it with others. Again to quote Rees, in a passage which could equally be applied to the situation in Staithes,

such allegiance as survives is an allegiance to a particular group and its chapel, and this would be largely undermined if the chapel were closed and the group merged with another. To attempt to unite two moribund Nonconformist churches would be like trying to create a new living organism by grafting together two dying ones.

(*Ibid.*: 115)

Such insights appeared to be lacking on the part of Methodist officials in the Darlington District who continued to press for amalgamation of the two chapels in Staithes. It is just possible of course that the determination of the authorities may in fact stem from the realisation that much of what is at stake in the village has little to do with Methodism. By attempting to enforce the union of Primitives and Wesleyans the Methodist Church could therefore have been attempting to squash once and for all the rich underlife of denominationally impure folk religion. R.E. Davies provides some evidence for this interpretation:

It is one thing to be generally in favour of the unity of Christian people; it is quite another thing to work from day to day with people whom you have previously regarded as 'ranters' or 'snobs', and yet another thing to consider the closing down of the place of worship which you have attended since childhood, and your father and your father's father before you. A great number of 'non-theological factors' combined to slow down the rationalisation of Methodist work and witness on the local level, and the amalgamation of circuits, obviously desirable on religious and practical grounds, has not even yet . . . been satisfactorily carried out in many 'black' areas. The hope is that the departure into eternity of those who have dominated the life of local congregations since before the time of Union will gradually complete the work which vision, enterprise, and faith began.   (Davies 1961: 74)

Methodists holding such a viewpoint would clearly find the notion of folk religion, as expressed here, completely inadmissible. Whilst the Methodist Church may prefer to ignore folk beliefs and practices, there is every reason that they should command attention from sociology which can no longer consign folk religion to decay and disappearance, as a transitory phenomenon, worthy only of a quaint, folkloristic interest. The evidence from Staithes clearly points to its persistence and vitality, and there can be little doubt that it constitutes a more important subject for study than institutionally bound and officially vouchsafed definitions of religion might suggest.

6

The annual cycle

So far, our discussion of the impact of nonconformity upon the fisherfolk has directed us towards the ways in which the sacred culture was institutionalised in the routines of chapel office and worship. Over time, traditions of affiliation served to bind individuals and families to their chapels, and deep-seated loyalties, rivalries and prejudices gradually overrode the theological and doctrinal differences which had existed hitherto. But as we have seen, religious zeal, along with accompanying enthusiasm for duty as trustee, steward or even society member, did not take a hold on all villagers. For some, it was not the regular routines of devotion and week by week attendance at Sunday worship – morning, afternoon and evening – which served as the public expression of their private religious commitment. For such people the sacred culture struck its deepest and most resonant chords at times of personal triumph or tragedy, or on occasions within the passage of the annual cycle: times which, even today, call for some collective expression of village society's concerns, aspirations and needs. If we consider the calendar of ritual events in Staithes we detect *both* sacred and popular elements, *gravitas* and *levitas* juxtaposed in an opposition which helps to give the society its texture, contrast and tension. Some of the events reveal the interplay and cross-fertilisation between Methodism and village life and demonstrate the remarkable, if at times ironic, legitimating power which resulted from those occasions when vital drops of the new wine found their way into old bottles. Beliefs of high antiquity juxtapose with medieval traditional Christianity which in turn rest uneasily alongside the sterner aspects of nonconformity. Their separate and collective observation during the course of a calendar year in the village therefore constitutes a striking illustration of the uneven qualities of social experience, in a context where, as Eliade puts it, 'For religious man, time . . . is neither homogeneous nor continuous' (1959: 68).

New Year

Let us begin with the rites which usher in the New Year. The festival, which is significant in the ecclesiastical calendar as the Feast of Circumcision, is not the object of any special services in the chapels in Staithes and passes

unmarked by any institutionalised religious celebrations. Yet whilst the
chapels themselves do not constitute the foci for religious events there is
considerable activity in the home, and to a lesser extent in the public houses
of the village. Here the New Year rites express the sense of guarded
optimism with which the villagers anticipate the coming year and are above
all concerned with the protection and well-being of the home and household.
Celebration commences on the night of 31 December and continues into the
early hours of 1 January. Large numbers of people are found crowded into
the three public houses in the old village, where considerable quantities of
alcohol are consumed amidst boisterous and animated scenes. At around
eleven p.m., most people begin to make their way back to their homes or to
those of friends and relations. Once there, attention is turned towards the
clock and the ticking away of the final minutes before midnight. At this point
it is usual for the woman of the house to sweep and tidy the fire-hearth of any
fallen coals, cinders or soot. Those women who are particularly fastidious
will also wash any dirty crockery which may be about. The meaning of these
acts comes across strongly as an attempt to avoid the carrying-over of 'dirt',
defined by Douglas (1970) as 'matter out of place', from one year to the
next. Specifically, dirt must not be allowed to contaminate the liminal
period of transition at midnight. At that time on 31 December the untidy
hearth or the dirty cup is, again in Douglas's terms, an anomaly. To
understand the full significance of this act it is necessary to refer to the strict
cleanliness and houseproud nature of many Staithes women. In keeping
with Methodist standards, most women would disapprove of dirtiness or
untidiness at any time, but for these to be carried over into the beginning of a
new year would be anathema. As one woman put it, 'I always go round just
before midnight and tidy everywhere up, then I sweep the hearth. It would
be terrible if you let the New Year in with the place a mess.' Eliade has
argued that the significance of the New Year in primitive and archaic
societies is:

a reactualization of the cosmogony, it implies *starting time over again at its
beginning*, that is, restoration of the 'pure' time, that existed at the moment of
Creation. This is why the New Year is the occasion for 'purifications' . . . for it is not
a matter merely of a certain temporal interval coming to its end and the beginning of
another . . . it is also a matter of abolishing the past year and past time. Indeed, this is
the meaning of ritual purifications; there is more than a mere 'purification'; the sins
and faults of the individual and of the community as a whole are annulled, *consumed
as by fire*.   (Eliade 1959: 77–8, emphasis in original)

Seen in this way, the sweeping of the hearth, the washing of crockery, and
the tidying-up represent the scourging of the passing year's accumulated
'dirt'. This might be viewed in both a physical and a moral sense, whereby
past actions, misdemeanours, failings or whatever are ritually expelled: the

slate thus wiped clean is prepared once more for the imprint of 'New Year's resolutions'.

A few minutes before midnight all the men present in the family home step outside. One man in particular will have been chosen to 'let in the New Year' – perhaps because having done it in a previous year the household concerned enjoyed good fortune, or because he meets the favoured physical requirements by being of dark complexion and hair. This man, who is known as the 'first footer', performs his ritual duty by being the first person to enter the house after midnight; his is literally the 'first foot' to cross the threshold after the stroke of midnight. He carries with him a piece of coal and a silver coin and upon entering is greeted by the women, who have remained indoors. He then gives one of them the coin and places the piece of coal on the fire saying, 'May your hearth never grow cold.' Greetings are then exchanged all round before the 'first footer' is asked to cut a special 'New Year's Cake' and to make a short speech. The speech usually invokes good fortune for the household, typically by wishing them 'health, wealth and happiness'. For many villagers the revelries of eating and drinking may carry on into the early hours and it is common for groups of men and women to go around the village visiting the homes of relations and friends where they are immediately offered alcoholic refreshment and a piece of the New Year Cake, which is traditionally eaten with Wensleydale cheese.

The following morning sees the turn of the younger boys in the village to take part in the celebrations. The boys, known locally as 'lucky birds', are seen as the carriers of good fortune. Up and about very early they take great pleasure in stirring late sleepers by knocking on doors to the accompaniment of the chant,

> Lucky bird, lucky bird, Chuck, Chuck, Chuck.
> All the year you'll have good luck.
> If you haven't got a penny a ha'penny will do,
> If you haven't got a ha'penny, God bless you.

Even in those houses where the New Year has already been introduced by an earlier 'first footer' children are invited in and given food and money before passing on elsewhere. Many of the children carry small individual gifts of bread, coal, holly and salt. When I asked one of them about the significance of these gifts, he replied confidently, 'Bread means you'll never go hungry; coal's so you'll always have a fire; holly's so that our friendship'll always be green and salt's for the salt of the earth.'[1] New Year celebrations finally draw to a close in the evening of 1 January, after families have gathered together for a large celebratory meal.

Three features of the New Year rites merit further attention: firstly, those aspects which relate to the home – indicated in the attention given to the hearth and in the threshold rites and developed in the concern shown for the well-being of members of the household; secondly, the sexual role differences which the rites display; and thirdly, the content of folk religious symbolism.

The hearth clearly retains its effect as a powerful symbol of home life. The continuance of this in Staithes is related to the predominance of homes which are still heated by open fires, many of which are also used for cooking purposes, heating kettles, and so on. Collecting firewood from the beach and scaurs is also an activity in which many men are involved in their spare time, particularly in the winter months when rough seas deposit large quantities of driftwood along the shores around the village. The invocation, 'may your hearth never grow cold', is no mere token therefore, but has a very real significance. In most homes in Staithes it is the hearth and fire which form the focal point of the kitchen or living room, around which the family groups itself and to which the visitor is drawn. That it should be unsullied by dirt as the New Year dawns is a reflection of its potency as a symbol of family and home life.[2] Further attention is drawn to the importance of the home in the threshold rites wherein the borderline between home and wider society, or as van Gennep sees it, 'the boundary between the foreign and domestic worlds' (1960: 20), is ritually crossed. The rites therefore represent the ritual and symbolic introduction of the New Year into the household.

It is interesting that the principal actors in the New Year rites are male, always adults in the case of the midnight ceremony and boys the following morning. Importantly, it is these 'first footers' or 'lucky birds' who are regarded as the bearers of good luck and who by carefully following the ritual procedures may introduce good fortune into the home for the coming year. It would be considered quite improper and most impropitious for a woman to be asked to let in the New Year; indeed it would not be considered at all. That women tidy the house before midnight but do not take on the task of 'first footer' is a reflection both of their domestic role and an anomalous ritual potency. Women's roles are further enforced in this manner through other superstitious practices relating to fishing and mining, wherein they are typically seen as portents of ill fortune (see below, Chapter 8). Why should men and not women be considered as carriers of luck? The answer may be related to the role which women play in other rituals. We shall see in the next chapter that in the context of certain life cycle rituals it is women rather than men who are the object of taboos and who are most subject to the constraints of structural liminality. Women bear the children; women must be churched; women lay out the dead and women to a much greater extent than men are constrained by mourning rules. It seems likely, therefore, that these injunctions effectively prohibit them from any rites which rely for their success upon the fickleness of luck and fate.

The rites of the New Year suggest that symbols of high antiquity continue to be operative in some of the rituals taking place outside the institutional church. This can be seen, for example, in the use made of salt and evergreens. More recent symbolic accretions are found in the deployment of coal and silver. All of these clearly belong to a tradition originating outside of any official religion. An interesting feature of their use is the considerable knowledge of symbolic content which villagers display. I discovered few cases, for example, such as those described by Barker (1972: 614) in her study of wedding rituals, where individuals carried out a rite involving a particular symbol *without* having any conception of its meaning.

What then is the significance of such an elaborate set of New Year rites? One interpretation might be that they constitute ritual procedures emanating from the popular culture in a situation for which the official religion has no related beliefs or practices. The activities just described are clearly not the product of the institutional church but derive from the folk context and are sustained in the communal setting. The folk items take as their focus the home and family – a setting into which the official religion rarely penetrates. It is true that in certain churches in other parts of the country it used to be the custom, initiated during the nineteenth century, to hold midnight services on 31 December; the practice, it seems, is now dying out. In the local situation, where neither chapel nor church officially recognise what is perceived as an important period of transition, the religious vacuum has been filled by elements from the folk milieu. The outcome is a set of clearly defined and symbolically charged rituals.

Sunday School Anniversaries

The next important occasion in the annual cycle is the sequence of Sunday School Anniversaries which take place in the chapels in February and March each year. Custom in Staithes seems to differ from Methodist practice elsewhere, where such events are usually held in the spring or summer months. But despite the threat of inclement weather and the not unusual occurrence of cuts in the electricity supply, the chapels continue to hold their most important annual festival in the winter. My first enquiries concerning the reason for this were directed towards the Wesleyans who maintain that their appointed date, always the first Sunday in February, is the *actual* anniversary of the opening of the Sunday School – unlike the other two chapels. However, further enquiries produced similar statements from both Primitive Methodists and from members of Bethel. In fact a more likely explanation is the one which relates the timing of the Sunday School Anniversaries to a particular changeover in the annual fishing cycle. During the nineteenth century, February and March saw the transfer from distant water fishing by the yawls back to inshore fishing in the cobles. Consequently

many men were back in the village after a considerable absence and were
therefore able to participate in community events once more. Thus, it was
natural that the anniversaries should be held at the same time.

Anniversary celebrations, preparations for which will have been under
way for several weeks, commence on the Sunday afternoon of the
anniversary weekend, when special services are held involving the children.
The service at the Wesleyan chapel includes one notable feature which is
absent from the others: 'scholars' are examined by the Sunday School
superintendent in the Conference Catechism. Presided over by the preacher
for that evening, each child is required to answer a number of questions, the
length and theoretical complexity of which are dependent upon age and
ability. It is a ruling that only those who successfully pass this test may later
take a place on the platform in the chapel for the singing and recitations. In
practice, however, there are no failures, and stumbling and – in the case of
the youngest children – faulty memories are generously helped by judicious
prompting.[3] Staithes Wesleyans claim that examination in the catechism is
practically extinct elsewhere in the country, and its persistence in the village
is a matter of some pride; certainly none of the Methodists suggest that its
abolition almost everywhere else could be seen as a change for the better. In
such matters Staithes people show considerable deference to the legitimacy
of tradition, irrespective of its content. Accordingly this 'custom' is grouped
along with other activities found in the village, both religious and secular,
such as the wearing of bonnets by women in the summer or eating special
foods at a funeral, which are also felt to be worthy of preservation. As one
man said of the catechism examination, 'folks in towns don't bother with
this sort of thing, but we like to keep the old customs up'. Traditional
practices of this sort therefore have the effect of maintaining communal
identity and of marking off the traditional mores from those of the wider
society and the undesirable changes which it has undergone.

Large congregations in the chapel on the Sunday evening mark the high-
point of the Sunday School Anniversary weekend. At each of the chapels I
observed attendances in the region of 120 to 150 people. These included
members, who in some cases were often poor attenders Sunday by Sunday,
as well as those who were nominally affiliated, such as former scholars and
the parents of children taking part. A notable feature of this latter group was
the high proportion of fathers present to watch their children perform; these
men in particular were normally distinguished by their non-participation in
chapel matters, but for the Sunday School Anniversary were very much in
evidence, albeit frequently looking ill at ease. Older people are also well
represented at the service, often in the capacity of grandparents as well as of
long-standing supporters of the chapel.

A special platform is erected for the evening service in front of the pulpit,
which extends out over the front pews. Children taking part are seated on

this platform, dressed in their best clothes. At Wesley there is a strict rule that girls must wear white, though at the other two chapels this tradition has fallen foul of the dictates of fashion, so that many girls now appear in long party dresses. Most parents seat themselves in the gallery of the chapel, from where they can obtain a better view of their children on the platform. Sunday School Anniversaries and funerals were the only occasions upon which I saw the gallery contain more than a handful of people.

The service commences with a hymn sung by the entire congregation (the Wesleyans print a special sheet of anniversary hymns which are sung during the course of the weekend). Thereafter the children dominate the proceedings with a series of recitations and songs. In solos and group items the children work their way through a variety of poems and musical interludes. The poems, both from the smallest children and the teenagers, frequently have no religious content whatsoever, but are usually anecdotes about animals ('Old Rover', 'Little Mouse'), the seasons or, in the case of older boys, the sea – the lengthy saga of disaster and shipwreck being a particular favourite. Most of the children clearly find performing a matter of some discomfort, something to be rushed through at a rapid rate, and in which an iron-like metre leaves little room for personal expression. This, coupled with the size of the congregation, the formality of the occasion and the wearing of one's best clothes, combine to make the experience somewhat traumatic. Most of the children on the platform have a manifest air of bewilderment mixed with excitement and fear. Despite all this the congregation delights in the performances and is totally indulgent of unintelligibility, errors and inaudibility. In fact the songs, poems and general spectacle seem to please the adults far more than they do the children.[4] After the service, for example, typical overheard comments might refer to a particular child's performance or the attractiveness of the girls' dresses. Whatever the balance of enjoyment between adults and children, there is no doubt about the lasting impression which 'standing on the platform' makes on the child. Many adults made reference to their memories of the occasion, some recounting, not without a degree of pride, how after appearing in the anniversary for the seventh time, they received their own bible, a practice which still persists today.

Celebrations continue on the following day, Monday, when in the afternoon members of the Methodist chapels parade around the village, carrying the chapel banner and singing their anniversary hymns. Paying particular attention to singing outside the homes of their own brethren, especially the sick and infirm, the group tours the yards and streets of the village before making their way back to the chapel Sunday Schoolroom for tea. The 'faith tea', so called because its success is dependent upon the voluntary donation of food, is an essential ingredient of the weekend. Large numbers are attracted, usually in the region of 100 people, and a general celebratory atmosphere prevails, accompanied by much banter and joking. The tea is again a manifestation of communality; individuals lapse into broad Staithes dialect and many in-group jokes and references pass to and fro, intelligible, in the main, only to villagers.

The final event in the Sunday School Anniversary celebrations takes place on Monday night, when the children repeat their performance of the previous evening. Once again they run through the poems and songs, though this time in a rather more relaxed manner and in an atmosphere of greater levity. Unlike at the previous service, which takes place upon the Sabbath, applause is permitted and encouraged. The Monday night service provides yet another opportunity for money raising. Collections are held throughout the weekend and a charge is made for the anniversary tea which, since it relies entirely upon donated foodstuffs, incurs no drain on chapel funds. As a result, the Sunday School Anniversary constitutes one of the largest single contributors to a chapel's trust funds.[5]

The Sunday School Anniversary stands out as perhaps the most important annual event in the religious life of the village. There are a number of reasons for this. Many people who do not attend a chapel at all during the course of the year, including the young married men, will be present for the Sunday evening service. The anniversary draws in even those with extremely weak nominal ties as well as the more sporadic Sunday attenders. All come together for a service which reaffirms the strength of the chapel. In so doing each chapel is able to present a picture of success and continuity through large congregations, the presence of 'old scholars' and a platform filled with Sunday School members. Problems of finance and attendance are temporarily masked by a collective statement of institutional vigour. The choice each year of the same preacher, ironically the same person for both Wesleyan and Primitive chapels, further affirms the desired image. The preacher can be relied upon to idealise the role of the chapel in village life and point to its continuing relevance. The sense of continuity between past and present is no mere illusion, however. As the following quotation illustrates, the sentiments and activities of the Sunday School Anniversary weekend have changed little in over a century.

Staithes – At the anniversary recently held here . . . two short sermons [were preached] on the importance and utility of religious training, to large and respectable audiences; and after each session several scholars gave good evidence of the efficiency of their teachers, by their excellent recitations and singing.

They processioned the streets with a large banner on the Monday; and as the day was fine, a large train accompanied them, while their beautiful hymns vocalized the surrounding air. Having arrived at the chapel at about two o'clock, p.m., they were plentifully supplied with spiced bread and tea; and a public tea-meeting of adults afterwards took place. All present seemed happy; and at the evening's meeting, the addresses, recitations, and devotional services were highly exciting and profitable.

A greater collection than usual was obtained, and the teachers, pupils, parents, and friends separated, blessing God for the golden days of the nineteenth century.

(Primitive Methodist Magazine 1849: 182)

Robert Moore reports a similar situation in Sunday School Anniversaries in Esh Winning, which he describes as 'a celebration of the traditional values of the Methodist family and community' (1974: 218). Moore demonstrates this in the case of parents and Society members who insisted upon the retention of a traditional Sunday School Anniversary, even in the face of opposition from the Sunday School teachers themselves, who wished to up-date the proceedings. He refers to a situation having numerous echoes in Staithes, and which in terms of the present analysis might well be seen as an aspect of folk religion: 'whatever the goals of the chapel officials may be they are constrained by the orientations of the parents and congregation towards seeing that the children do their pieces in a traditional anniversary, not towards the formal goals of Methodism or Christian education' (1974: 218). One important consequence of this form of Sunday School Anniversary in Staithes may be that it refurbishes collective sentiments which are at variance with those of the local Methodist circuit and district, and, indeed, with the wider society in general. Whilst, within the chapel, there is no conflict of the type described by Moore (since all are in favour of the type of anniversary which exists), in holding successful Sunday School Anniversaries independently of each other the two chapels demonstrate their ability to prosper and flourish and, in turn, provide themselves with a justification for continuing the conflict with the circuit. Viewed in this way rivalry between the chapels, for example over the amount of money raised, is essentially secondary to their joint defiance of the Methodist hierarchy.

Lent

The final Sunday School Anniversary, that of the Primitive Methodists, coincides roughly with the beginning of Lent. The Lenten period provides another opportunity to compare certain aspects of official religion with their folk counterparts. Whilst some elements of folk religion, as conceptualised in Chapter 1, are thought to be pre-Christian in origin, the examples associated with Lent seem to have grafted themselves onto the Christian tradition at a later date. Shrove Tuesday activities are a case in point. In the middle ages the day was one of confession, or 'shriving' in preparation for Lent. The custom of eating pancakes is thought to owe its origin to the practical expediency of using up remaining eggs and fat which were forbidden during the Lenten fast. However, the shift which took place, probably in the fifteenth century, from 'shriving' to 'shroving', confession to carnival, signalled a remarkable transformation in the accepted activities of the day. From austerity and spiritual preparation the emphasis changed to one of merry-making and boisterousness in the form of a letting-off of steam before the gravity and solemnity of Lent. It is this aspect of the day which has survived,[6] not an occasion for shriving, but 'pancake Tuesday', a day for both eating and running races with pancakes.

The consumption of pancakes on Shrove Tuesday is still common in Staithes, although all reference to the original Catholic meaning and practice has gone and in recent years an element of levity has been introduced in the form of a children's pancake race, which takes place on the sea-front. Children of all ages may enter for the competition, and like other village events it has the dual function of being at once entertaining as well as a useful means of raising money, in this case for the funds of the local branch of the Royal National Lifeboat Institution. In the days which follow Shrove Tuesday, Lent receives little formal recognition within the chapels, and it is doubtful if it has any impact upon the lives of most villagers.

Easter

Although the Easter period is arguably the most important in the Christian calendar, it does not stimulate the people of Staithes into an exceptional amount of religious activity. Once again, the events to which villagers attach greatest importance seem to be external to, if not at times in conflict with, the officially prescribed religious themes of the festival. Important Easter events in the village therefore include the presentation of prizes to Sunday School scholars, the wearing of new clothes on Easter day and certain customs relating to the decoration and eating of Easter eggs.

On the afternoon of Good Friday it is usual for the Methodist chapels to hold a service; one of the few examples of intra-Methodist ecumenicity to take place, it is held jointly, using alternate chapels each year. A visiting preacher is invited and attendances are in the region of fifty persons. Afterwards a tea is held in the Sunday Schoolroom at which a general atmosphere of merriment prevails. The irony of the situation prompted one local preacher to remark: 'For everyone else in the church Good Friday is a day of prayer and great sadness, but in Staithes they use it as an excuse for the biggest bun-fight you've ever seen.' Once again local variations on particular religious themes seem to be incongruent with the official version.

The most interesting aspect of Easter Sunday services in Staithes is their relatively poor attendances. Easter day attendances in 1976 were estimated at between thirty and forty persons for each chapel in the morning and on or about the average normal Sunday attendance of twenty-five in the evening. Therefore, while there is no significant increase in attendance at Easter, there is a reversal of the normal Sunday pattern in the village whereby the largest congregations are usually to be found at evening services. What is interesting about the attendances is how low they appear when compared with those for Sunday School Anniversary weekends or Harvest Festivals. On the afternoon of Easter Sunday, however, more people are to be found in the chapels since this is the time chosen for the presentation of prizes to Sunday School scholars. Thus, as the emphasis shifts away from the broader concerns of the official religion to more specifically communal sympathies and concerns, there is a proportionate increase in interest and activity on the part of villagers. At 2.30 p.m. scholars, with their parents and families, assemble for the prize-giving. Unlike the anniversary services, this is quite simple in form. An 'old scholar', usually someone who has subsequently been distinguished by worldly success, such as a teacher or professional person, is asked to award the prizes and as each name is called, children walk to the front to recite their 'piece' for the final time, before receiving a prize.

Receipt of a prize is theoretically dependent upon the achievement of a specified minimum number of attendances for the year, but in practice all children who are on the Sunday School register usually receive their reward. The practice of giving a prize to everyone thus guarantees a numerically strong display of scholars at a time when public attention is considerable, and whether intended or not, contrives to present an image of institutional vigour. Certainly, similar ideas were not far from the minds of some villagers and were known to result in criticism of one chapel by another. I remarked, for example, to a Wesleyan about the substantial number of children at the Primitive Methodist prize-giving who had not come forward to claim a prize when their name had been called out: 'That's because half of 'em aren't from Steeas . . . they're from Saltburn, Marske, Carlin How and all over . . . they might have belonged here once over, but not any more', he said. Another remarked, 'They make up half the names.' Allegations of this sort probably tell us as much about chapel rivalry as falsification of the number of scholars; nevertheless, there was evidence to show that the Primitive Methodist chapel successfully marshalled the support of 'former scholars' at Anniversaries and other important events in the chapel year. For example, I observed several teenage boys and girls taking part in the Sunday School Anniversary whom I knew to be no longer in attendance at the Sunday School. Practices of this sort at the anniversary and the prize-giving seem to be connected with the variety of unofficial aspects of chapel affiliation which were discussed in Chapter 5 and illustrate an overriding concern that the image, if not the reality, of the chapel's vitality must be preserved at all costs.

Easter day observance presents us with something of a paradox, low or average attendance at the chapel and high attendance at the Sunday Schools. This might be viewed as an implicit repudiation of central

Christian themes, where the effect of the different emphasis is to undermine official religion in favour of the folk or community. Obelkevich notes a similar example of the popular culture's persistence in nineteenth-century rural Lincolnshire where it was a common practice among Methodists to hold Sunday School Anniversaries on Good Friday, thereby providing a local celebration which was counterposed to the general tenor of that day for the rest of the church (1976: 267).

But whilst in terms of official religion collective responses to the Easter period may be weak, when we turn our attention to the folk or popular realm, a rather different picture begins to emerge. In fact, Easter is important for a variety of folk traditions. For example, Easter day is associated with the wearing of new clothes, a custom which is rigidly adhered to by most families in the village, especially where children are concerned. Those who fail to put on new clothes are said to run the risk of being excreted upon by birds[7] (though it must be acknowledged that seagulls represent an ever-present danger in this respect, throughout the year). The decoration of Easter eggs, whose significance as a symbol of fertility is probably pre-Christian in origin, is also popular in the village and during the week before Easter the eggs are to be seen on display on many window ledges. On Easter Sunday they are cracked in 'Jarping' competitions, where opponents strike their eggs together, the winner being the person whose egg withstands the blow intact. Above all, for children, Easter is synonymous with the receiving of large, and often expensive, chocolate eggs. The folk customs of Easter are therefore capable of eliciting considerable involvement, particularly in the familial setting, whilst in the chapels Easter day attendances can barely be distinguished from other Sundays. Once again, the official themes appear to assume a secondary importance in comparison with the always vital concerns of communal religiosity and chapel tradition.

Chapel Anniversaries

Chapel Anniversary celebrations are held in the summer months, between June and August, and while they constitute important events in the chapel year, activities are not on the same scale as the Sunday School Anniversaries. Again, the celebrations take the form of a mixture of religious and more secular pursuits. It is customary for each chapel to invite its regular 'anniversary preacher', who comes along each year to take the Sunday evening service. The preacher usually has some connection with the village; the Wesleyan anniversary preacher, for example, is a middle-aged man, born in Staithes, who is now the head teacher at a large comprehensive school. Much respected by Wesleyans, a historian by training, and a keen researcher into the local history of the area, he is extremely popular for his wealth of knowledge concerning Staithes in former times. At the anniversary service in June 1975 his sermon consisted largely of a history of the Wesleyan chapel, liberally spiced with popular anecdotes and references to well known characters from the past. Emotional in tone and delivered with a measured dignity, the sermon left a lasting impression on all who attended and was often referred to during the following year. Preachers of this kind are popular in so far as they put forward a view of the past couched in terms of traditionally cherished values such as honesty, cleanliness and Godliness. They are also required to transcend, albeit temporarily, the immediate pressures and contingencies experienced by the chapels. Whereas regular week by week preachers tend to contrast the historical and idealised picture of chapel life and piety with the contemporary one, at the anniversary, contemporary apathy and difficulties within the chapel are overlooked or temporarily ignored. Preachers therefore point to the continuing success and vitality of the Sunday School, the traditions and memories which are associated with the chapel, and, above all, the great achievement of Staithes people in keeping open their places of worship in the face of varied opposition. The important function of the Chapel Anniversary is, like that of the Sunday School Anniversary, the consolidation of shared and traditional mores. That large numbers of people feel the importance of this is proved by the attendances, which though not as great as for Sunday School Anniversaries are nevertheless two or three times that of a normal Sunday evening congregation.

The following day, celebrations continue, now taking on a more secular tone. Each chapel usually holds a coffee-morning and sale in support of trust funds. These coffee-mornings provide a good opportunity to observe the significance of nominal affiliation. They depend heavily upon those who almost never attend services, but who nevertheless consider themselves 'Primitives' or 'Wesleyans' and who can be relied upon for support in money-raising events. Later on in the week one of the several religious choirs from the surrounding area may be invited to give a 'sacred concert', and film shows or illustrated lectures are also popular anniversary activities. On one occasion during fieldwork, the Wesleyans had the novel idea of giving their anniversary coffee-morning a special theme. Through their considerable network of members and sympathisers they were able to gather up a vast collection of village memorabilia, including old photographs, paintings and, in particular, models of Staithes fishing craft made by various local men. In this manner the schoolroom was successfully transformed into a folk museum of village life which attracted several hundred people, including both villagers and visitors. An enormous sense of pride emanated from those whose idea it had been and who had organised the event, and one sensed that this pride went far beyond the satisfaction of a successfully executed money-raising scheme. They had shown the outside world and other villagers something of the rich heritage of 'Steeas' and the place of the

Wesleyan chapel within it, and this was the real source of gratification. Dwelling on the past seemed once again to be a means of mitigating contemporary difficulties.

Harvest Festivals

The celebration of the harvest within the church was unknown prior to the 1800s, though for centuries before its secular counterpart, the harvest supper or harvest home, had been a regular feature of village and rural life (Obelkevich 1976: 57–9; Baker 1975: 30–5). Harvest Festivals in the modern sense were not practised in the Church of England before the 1840s (Cuming 1969: 196) and although a prayer of thanksgiving for the harvest had appeared in 1796 (*ibid.*: 169) it was not until 1862 that an official form of service for the Harvest Festival was introduced. The consolidation of the Harvest Festival and its appearance in the Book of Common Prayer is generally attributed to the innovative energies of the Rev. Hawker in Cornwall during the 1870s, but was also part of a broader, ritualistically motivated movement within the Anglican Church. In Staithes, Harvest Festivals seem to have been a popular part of *chapel* life from the 1870s onwards, though they were of course popular elsewhere among nonconformists. There is a certain touch of irony in the fact that a product of Anglican ritualism should have taken root and thrived in such a setting.

Preparations for the Harvest Festival begin about one week before the event, when the active members of each chapel visit the homes of all those who have some affiliation. Their main purpose is to importune gifts in kind such as tins of food, bags of flour, sugar, vegetables and flowers; they will also accept any monetary gifts which may be offered. Members of the Sunday School, or more often their parents, also contribute substantial gifts. On the morning of the Harvest Festival each child usually brings to the schoolroom a decorated hamper containing fruit and vegetables as well as tinned and packed produce. In the afternoon, a special platform is erected in front of the pulpit, upon which the various donations are displayed. The village's connections with the sea are strongly emphasised. The display always includes a selection of lobsters and crabs, the balconies are draped with fishing nets and small model replicas of Staithes's cobles past and present are set out around the pulpit. These maritime symbols are all expressions, say villagers, of 'the harvest of the sea'. At a more fundamental level, this transmutation of the harvest theme represents both an expression of the sea's bountifulness and also a general antagonism towards matters concerning the land and farming (see Chapter 8).

The popularity of the Harvest Festivals, like that of the Sunday School Anniversaries, seems to represent a level of chapel activity which is rarely achieved at other times of the yearly cycle. They are attended by dilatory members as well as the broad span of sympathisers, many of whom would never dream of missing the Harvest Festival or the Sunday School Anniversary. The service undoubtedly has many attractions: it is colourful, the Harvest hymns are rousing and, above all, there is the sense of occasion. Preachers are especially invited each year because of their ability to preach a good 'Harvest sermon'. That chapel members have clear expectations about what is and what is not appropriate is well attested by the following incident, observed at the Bethel chapel. During the collection the organist played the hymn 'I Will Follow Jesus' and in accordance with a tradition found in all the Staithes chapels, the congregation immediately joined in singing as the collection plate circulated. When the stewards completed their duties, the assembly concluded with a rousing chorus of,

> Follow, follow, I will follow Jesus,
> Everywhere, anywhere, I will follow on.
> Follow, follow, I will follow Jesus,
> Everywhere he leads me I will follow on.

The chorus faded away, whereupon the preacher, instead of giving a prayer of thanks for the offertory, paused and, pointing an accusing finger at the congregation, cried out, 'I wonder? Would you? Would you follow Jesus? Would you give up your job to go after him? Would you follow him into a Russian prison? I wonder my friends!' The congregation were clearly taken aback by this unprecedented outburst and outside afterwards several people were heard to remark indignantly, 'that's not what we come to the Harvest for!'. The 'serious' concerns of religion, it was felt, should not be allowed to interfere with one's enjoyment of the Harvest Festival. Prickly moral issues clearly have little place in popular religion.

The symbolism of the Harvest motifs also reflects the strength of the folk religious influence. Chapels are decked out with all the symbols of largesse – corn sheaves, newly cut vegetables and fresh sea produce, in what in many ways can be seen as a celebration of the potency of nature rather than a thanksgiving to God. Indeed, to see the chapel decorated in this way evokes nothing so much as the aura of a fertility rite or symbolic reiteration of the bountifulness of earth and sea.

Finally, mention must be made of a most unusual feature common to all three chapel Harvest Festivals in the village, though not to that of the Anglican Mission Church. While in many churches it is usual to distribute the donations of produce to the needy, the sick and the aged, in Staithes, precisely the reverse takes place. Instead of being shared out among the deserving, the goods are instead auctioned off to provide money for chapel funds. At 6.00 p.m. on the three successive Monday evenings following the Harvest service, each chapel holds an auction at which every donated item is sold off to the highest bidder. The sales are extremely popular amongst housewives and provide a real opportunity to purchase good quality home-grown produce at low prices. Revenue from the sales is usually in the region of £100, an important contribution to trust funds. The services thus have a strong popular appeal to villagers, who see in them an enjoyable and impressive spectacle and capitalising on this appeal, chapel members in turn exploit the Festivals as occasions for displaying institutional strength and for gaining revenue.

Hallowe'en

A little later in the year, on the night of 31 October/1 November, Hallowe'en is celebrated. Situated at the transitional point between autumn and winter, the period has had religious significance far back into antiquity. For the Celts the present 1 November was the festival of *Samhain* when evil forces were expelled and the powers of fertility renewed. Since that time the festival has taken on other meanings. Victor Turner writes, 'In European folk beliefs, the midnight of 31 October has become associated with gatherings of the hellish powers of witchcraft and the devil . . . Subsequently a strange alliance has been formed between the innocent and the wicked, children and witches who purge the community by the mock pity and terror of trick and treat' (Turner 1974: 172). In Staithes, Hallowe'en sees the streets and alleyways of the village filled with young children who delight in leaping out from behind corners and rushing at unsuspecting adults. Most of these children wear strikingly elaborate masks of multi-coloured papier-mâché and cardboard and carry lanterns made from hollowed-out turnips with holes for eyes, nose and mouth and with a lighted candle inside.[8] For this one night of the year they are permitted to terrorise the adults of the village with their exaggerated howling and terrible movements, and may accost their elders crying,

> The sky is blue, the grass is green
> Can you spare a penny for Hallowe'en?

A monetary contribution is expected and rarely refused. When asked about the meaning of Hallowe'en, children combine a knowledge of the supernatural with a down-to-earth pragmatism; as one boy put it, 'Hallowe'en's the night when witches and toads come out – but we just do it for money.'

Children's activities on Hallowe'en clearly fall into the category of what Gluckman (1956) has called 'reversals', or rituals in which customary hierarchies are inverted. The rites symbolise protest against the established order of adult–child relationships so that for a short time children are licensed to wreak revenge for their structural inferiority vis-à-vis the world of adults. The fact that the rites are restricted to one night in the year results in the reaffirmation of existing roles and may indeed serve to strengthen the existing hierarchy. Hallowe'en is also known as 'mischief night' in Staithes,[9] and children get up to all kinds of general mischievousness, such as tapping on the windows of houses to frighten those inside or writing slogans in 'crazy foam'.[10] Most adults indulge this sort of behaviour. For example, on Hallowe'en in 1975 some children tampered with and rearranged a 'fleet' of stacked lobster pots near the harbour. Next morning I saw the owner of the pots rearranging them. He informed me with a grin: 'you expect this sort o' thing on mischief night'. Such an act occurring at another time would have resulted in serious repercussions, leading to some form of punishment for the children concerned.

Christmas

The religious significance of Christmas in Staithes, as elsewhere, competes in pluralistic fashion with alternative meanings – gift-giving, card-exchange, spending, consumption, holiday-time, and so on. The meaning which Christmas has for the individual may therefore vary from a purely secular holiday to an important religious occasion which is felt to have been adulterated and perhaps devalued in the wider society. In Staithes the representative picture lies somewhere in between and once more a fusion of folk and official items can be shown to coexist. Beliefs and actions relating to Christmas are dispersed into three major institutional settings; the chapels and church, the family and, taken together, the pubs and the club. Christmas is surrounded by a different set of meanings in each, and while these may seem to be in conflict or to be mutually exclusive, research suggests that for most villagers the distinctions are blurred and 'Christmas' manifests itself in the activities of all three institutions.

Within the chapels, preparations for Christmas begin early. Both Primitives and Wesleyans hold their own Christmas fairs, where gifts and home-made products of various kinds are sold. These provide a useful boost to chapel funds and, as many people put it, 'make you feel that Christmas is on its way'. On Christmas Eve, in keeping with long-standing local practice, carol singers from both Methodist chapels tour the village in separate groups. This always brings out a large number of singers and is much appreciated by villagers. As one man put it, 'when I hear those singers coming round on Christmas Eve, then I know Christmas really is here'. Both groups make considerable effort to reproduce the imagery of a traditional English Christmas, eschewing the more recent carols in favour of old Methodist tunes and traditional folk carols. The Wesleyan singers dress in Victorian costume for the occasion, whilst the Primitives accompany their singing with an old portable organ. Both groups make a special point of singing at the houses of other chapel folk.

In recent years it has been the practice to hold a midnight service in one or other of the Methodist chapels, but this has only been poorly supported. The practice was initiated by the present minister but does not, so far, seem to have captured the imagination of local Methodists. Midnight Mass and Communion are held in the Roman Catholic and parish churches and both are well attended. Services are also held on Christmas Day in these churches, though not in the chapels.

Within the private sphere of family life, traditions and customs relating to Christmas are similar to those found elsewhere in our society. Great emphasis is placed upon card- and gift-exchange between friends and relations and considerable expense is incurred thereby. It is interesting to note the extremely large numbers of presents received by many children, since for those who come from long-standing 'Steeas' families, in particular, and who in consequence form part of an extensive kinship network, a large body of kin are represented as potential gift-givers. This became quite apparent during fieldwork whilst visiting various local families on Christmas Day, when the rituals of gift-exchange emerged as powerful agents of community maintenance. Several anthropologists have, of course, pointed to some of the functions and meanings which underlie gift-giving systems (Malinowski 1922; Mauss 1970). Lévi-Strauss, writing of the contemporary American Christmas, emphasises the status gain which comes from the giving of gifts and the ostentatious destruction of wealth: 'the exchange of gifts at Christmas, for a month each year, practised by all social classes with a sort of sacred ardour, is nothing more than a gigantic *potlatch*, implicating millions of individuals and at the end of which family budgets are faced with lasting disequilibrium' (1969: 56).

The Christmas activities in the public houses and social club in the village are essentially charitable. Each organises its own Christmas draw, or lottery, and the profits go towards buying hampers and Christmas gifts for the elderly. The pubs are frequently crowded on Christmas Eve and it is also the habit of many men in the village to visit their 'local' at lunchtime on Christmas Day. On both occasions the singing of carols is popular. As in the domestic sphere this is once again a time of intensive conviviality, with much buying of drinks and displays of generous sociability.

Summary

The beliefs, practices and symbols associated with the annual cycle in Staithes indicate the interplay of communal factors with those of both official and folk religion. Emerging from this interplay is a complex pattern of sociability and religiosity in which important religious times are often those when villagers gather to celebrate not, for example, the birth or resurrection of Jesus Christ but rather the founding of the Sunday School or the building of the chapel. Such occasions are typically marked by concerts or special teas and not solely by a religious service; they have, in consequence, the overriding quality of being enjoyable for those taking part. Their importance, therefore, lies in the fact that they are underscored by communal rather than, say, specifically Methodist values; they are occasions for recalling past times and for reconstituting shared sentiments, often expressed in terms of an idealised view of village and chapel life in earlier periods. Moreover, the traditional content of some of the celebrations serves to differentiate the community from the wider society and emphasise the *gemeinschaftlich* quality of folk religion.

The pleasurable aspect of many activities associated with religious life in the Free Churches has been noted by various writers. Horner (1971) and Obelkevich (1976), commenting on the situation in the rural areas in the nineteenth century (Northumberland and Lincolnshire respectively), have drawn attention to the warmth, both literal and emotional, which drew many members of the working classes into the chapels. More recently, research carried out in the north of England by Pickering (1968) has suggested that for chapel-goers the pleasure derived from the hymn-singing and sermons is the main reason for attendance. As Pickering puts it, 'the pursuits are recreational. If they do not fulfil this function, they are dropped and membership ceases' (*ibid.*: 86). Such a position is akin to that in Staithes where, as we have seen, the events of the chapel year draw large support even amongst irregular Sunday worshippers, who in attending Harvest Festivals, Anniversaries and so forth, keep alive their affiliation to a particular chapel. It is also possible to pick out within the annual cycle both institutional and non-institutional religious elements. Bock, for example, sees two coexistent symbolic systems associated with various types of holiday behaviour in the United States, one set of symbols being directly connected with Christian theology and the other deriving from 'ancient folk religions' (1966: 207). The essential point is that whilst, as we have already attempted to demonstrate, the origins of these symbols may go back to before the time of the Early Church, many of them continue to validate changes and annual events today. They do this by fusing, often in a striking manner, with official and institutionally sanctioned beliefs and practices into what can be seen as a persistent and resilient communal folk religion.

7

Birth and death

Birth, death and rites of passage

Birth and death constitute the most perplexing aspects of the human condition. None ask to be born, few wish to die. These simple realities spell out the existential dilemma which has taxed philosophers and theologians over the centuries. For some sociologists, religion is entirely a response to these aspects of human existence. Yinger, for example, defines it as 'a system of beliefs and practices by means of which a group of people struggle with ultimate problems of human life' (1970: 7), whilst for Daniel Bell 'The ground of religion is existential' (1977: 447). How and why do these enigmatic aspects of the human situation, especially birth and death, result in religious responses?

The human biography proceeds through a number of biological stages: conception, gestation, birth, infancy, puberty, maturity, old age, death. In all societies, but to varying degrees, these stages are attended by culturally prescribed expectations relating to role, status, and so on. In this manner, being a teenager or an old man signifies far more than simply having reached a certain age of biological maturity and summons up a whole set of norms, values and behaviour. In terms of religion, it is the points of transition between the phases or cycle stages which are important, since they demand some system of socially recognised legitimation; these are the transitions which, as Lloyd Warner puts it, 'all societies ritualize and publicly mark with suitable observances to impress the significance of the individual and the group on living members of the community. These are the important times of birth, puberty, marriage and death' (quoted in Turner 1974: 157). Their importance is such that the term 'life crises' is frequently used to describe them. They imply significant changes for both individual and society alike. Birth and death probably constitute the greatest crises of the life cycle, since within them cultural and structural transfigurations are underpinned by fundamental physiological changes in the individual. At birth the transition of the infant from an undifferentiated, thing-like existence in its mother's womb to that of unique individuality is one of enormous magnitude. Frequently it is accompanied by doubts and fears concerning the successful outcome of the process, which when duly accomplished may then give rise to speculation concerning the child's future prosperity, good health, intelligence, worldly success, and so on. Death raises similar questions and constitutes a crisis not only (and self-evidently) for the individual concerned but also for his or her significant others. The death of any individual therefore involves a momentous relocation into another social category – from the world of the living into the world of the dead. Indeed, the example represents one of the few aspects of human experience which appears to have remained relatively immune from secularising forces, so that the disposal of the dead in Britain still almost invariably takes place with some accompanying religious ritual (Pickering 1974).

It is important not to overlook the rich variety of 'folk' responses to these life crises, which emanate from outside the churches. These may take the form, for instance, of superstitions which regulate the behaviour of those coming into contact with birth or death; or of explanatory beliefs of one sort or another, such as *why* a woman gives birth to a girl and not a boy or *why* an individual should die at a particular time. As we saw in Chapter 1, these are essentially questions on the level of theodicy and represent a set of dilemmas which institutional religion in its various guises frequently finds it difficult, or is reluctant, to comment upon. Thus in the cases of birth and death, resolutions to these problems are often sought through a combination of official and unofficial elements within the rites of passage and bolstered by a variety of legitimating beliefs. We should note that the rites can only be interpreted along with and in terms of these beliefs. To examine the rites merely in terms of their function at the level of structure would be to fall into the major error of those functionalists who have so often overlooked the meaning which ritual has for the participants. Explanations which centre on the rites' contribution to an overall state of social equilibrium therefore fail to acknowledge that they have meaning for the actors, either by ignoring them completely, or by bracketing the meanings as 'false' explanations of what is 'really' taking place.

Berger and Luckmann's (1971) comments on the rites of passage are instructive at this point. They point out, using the example of primitive society, that the rites function at both the macro and the micro level, in so far as they constitute a nomic or ordering process which is effective on a structural plane as well as being meaningful within individual consciousness. Accordingly, 'the periodization of biography is symbolized at each stage with reference to the totality of human meanings' (*ibid.*: 116). The rite of passage *does* therefore achieve a measure of social solidarity through a sense of personal belonging and security, which in turn operates psycho-logically in demonstrating to the individual concerned that he or she is living 'correctly' (*ibid.*: 117). It is worthwhile quoting Berger's *Social Reality of Religion* at some length here.

The nomos locates the individual's life in all embracing fabric of meanings that, by its very nature, transcends that life. The individual who adequately internalizes these meanings at the same time transcends himself. His birth, the various stages of his biography and, finally, his future death may now be interpreted by him in a manner that transcends the unique place of these phenomena in his experience. The point is made dramatically clear in the case of rites of passage, in primitive societies as well as more complex societies . . . The social ritual transforms individual biography into an episode in the history of the society. The individual is seen as being born, living and suffering, and eventually dying, as his ancestors have done before him and his children will do after him.   (1973: 62)

Van Gennep (1960) defined rites of passage as those which 'accompany every change of place, state, social position and age' (quoted in Turner 1974: 80), and saw all the rites in terms of a now famous tripartite process wherein each reveals a stage of separation (*separation*), transition (*marge*) and incorporation (*agrégation*). The first stage of this sequence places the participant in a state of symbolic separation from the rest of the group. From here the individual passes into a transitory or liminal stage which is 'betwixt and between' (Turner 1974) two social states. From which position the process reaches its resolution by the final rite of incorporation of the individual into a new social location. For van Gennep, all rites of passage illustrate this sequence, and his schema has been used by anthropologists to explain a variety of customs and practices (Goody 1962; Malinowski 1954). But whilst the anthropologists have employed the van Gennep triad in order to illustrate the processual structure of the rites, in sociology the term 'rite of passage' has signified little more than that which takes place inside a church building at a baptismal, marriage or funeral service. With the exception of recent work by Bocock (1974) and Leonard (1980) few attempts have been made at systematic sociological analysis of the content and meaning of ritual in contemporary society. As Kimball wrote in the introduction to the English version of van Gennep's work, 'by and large, rites of passage have not been incorporated in sociological theory or thought' (1960: xiv). Discussions of rites of passage, even in the sociology of religion, have usually been concerned with their quantitative rather than qualitative aspects. For example, measures of persistence have been used to question certain assumptions in the secularisation thesis and in order to demonstrate the continued propensity among large sections of the population to mark important life-critical changes with the offices of the church (Martin 1967: Chapter 2; Pickering 1974). Such an approach, however, has so far told us little about the meanings which the rites have for their participants. Elsewhere, the community studies have significantly failed to grasp the opportunity they so clearly afford for furthering our knowledge of the organisation and make-up of the rites. The present chapter therefore represents a small attempt at rectifying this deficiency by way of a detailed description of the rites of birth and death in Staithes, taking a processual approach as its organising principle. Our analysis is thus not merely confined to the ritual which takes place in church but extends to a consideration of the entire *process* of birth and of death. Through it we seek to understand how two significant life crises are communally managed within the context of folk belief and practice.

Birth

It would be a mistake to identify the *rite de passage* of childbirth exclusively with the church's baptismal ritual; this, of course, has often been the case among sociologists, who, for practical purposes such as the measurement and comparison of baptismal rates, have tended to neglect the content and structure of the rite as well as the subjective meanings which it has for the participants. In order to grasp the importance of rites of passage within folk religion, then, each life cycle rite should be seen as a *process* which might last for several days, weeks or even longer. Thus in the case of childbirth, the rite begins prior to the woman's delivery and is not resolved until some time after it. The official rite of baptism, seen in this light, forms only a part of the total ritual process, which also includes diverse folk elements. It is the nature of these elements and their relationship to official counterparts which concern us here.

In fact the rite of passage involved at childbirth implies not one, but two ritual processes; one of these centring around the mother and the other around the child. This is acknowledged, for example, in van Gennep's (1960) account which considers 'pregnancy and childbirth' separately from 'birth and infancy'. In many ways, however, van Gennep's is an unnatural division, especially in the context of a specific empirical study, since the ritual states governing both mother and child are intimately bound up with one another and should be considered as a whole. Both aspects, which are in effect two sides of the same coin, are therefore considered here within the general context of the ritual process relating to birth. This reveals that both mother and child pass through respective states of ritual separation, transition and incorporation. We begin by describing the process as it took place in the early years of the century, before moving on to a discussion of the contemporary situation.

Childbirth in Staithes in the early twentieth century

In considering the religious beliefs and practices associated with birth, a primary factor which must be taken into account is that of the material and ecological conditions in which gestation and childbirth take place. At Staithes these conditions have changed enormously during the present century. As we saw in Chapter 2, piped water in the home and the provision of electricity were innovations which significantly improved the conditions of family and home life. This is important in that, at the beginning of the century, birth was still an event to be handled in the home, by the family and with the assistance of other members of the community. Later, the effect not only of better living conditions but also of the emergence of welfare services and medical facilities greatly affected the content of religious beliefs and practices relating to childbirth.

In the early part of the century, however, the situation in the village was still characterised by poor and inadequate housing and overcrowding, made worse by the rigours of a fishing economy which had traditionally involved the utilisation of the home in various aspects of the work process. Set in these conditions, birth, in Radin's term, was an important 'social precipitate of fear' (1957: 5); a reason for trepidation, anxiety and apprehension, made worse by economic pressures and difficult conditions.

For the expectant mother, the ritual process began some time before childbirth. Women who became pregnant were referred to as having 'fallen', a notion of pregnancy, which has been noted elsewhere (Chamberlain 1976a: 11). To become pregnant was to 'fall' and having done so various observances contrived to set the woman apart from the rest of the group. These usually involved events or situations which the woman should avoid, both for physiological and magical reasons. Accidents, falls, and so on were often said to produce permanent and unfavourable effects in the unborn child. For example, one old woman told me how, during a pregnancy, she had been struck in the face by a ball and was told by her friends that her baby would have a birth-mark on its face. Another woman told how years before she had slipped on the ice whilst pregnant and upon consulting her doctor was told to 'forget about old wives' tales' which predicted unfortunate consequences. Above all, pregnancy was a time of vulnerability when a woman sought to avoid dangers which might be harmful to her unborn child; such avoidances served in turn to keep her in a state of symbolic separation.

The act of childbirth marked the commencement of that aspect of the ritual process with the *child* as subject. The process was initiated by a physical act of separation in the cutting of the umbilical cord. Carried out by the woman in attendance at the birth, either a midwife or a neighbour, cutting the cord was not only essential to the successful accomplishment of the birth but also had a ritual and non-utilitarian act associated with it. It was customary for the newly born child to be taken immediately by the midwife into the attic room of the house and there held aloft. Should no such room exist, the midwife would stand on a chair in the bedroom and hold the child above her head. The purpose of this ritual, I was told, was that 'the baby had to go up in the world before it went down', i.e. it was directed towards ensuring material success for the child in its future life. Acts of this type are what van Gennep, following Tylor (1871), calls 'sympathetic' rites, i.e. 'based on belief in the reciprocal action of like on like' (van Gennep 1960: 4). Naturally such a rite might be invested with various other levels of meaning, and while the explanation which we cite here is the only one offered by villagers, it should be remembered that it is based upon individual memories of an act which is now hardly ever practised. The folk memory may be both selective and defective and some alternative interpretations could have been lost. For example, one immediate interpretation which springs to mind is that the uplifting of the child might have constituted a symbolic offering to God. On the other hand van Gennep draws our attention to a pressing social function of such rites: 'the child must first be separated from his previous environment, which may simply be his mother. I think this necessity accounts for putting a child in the care of another woman for the first few days, a practice which has no relation to the time required for the appearance of milk' (*ibid.*: 50). Seen in this light, the lifting-up of the infant or its removal to the attic room of the house by the midwife would constitute the first physical separation from the mother and, by implication, the onset of individual identity following the socially undifferentiated state of the womb.

One cannot take this interpretation too far, however, since the period after childbirth was characterised by a liminality in which both mother and child continued to be the objects of ritual taboos and observances. During this period they existed in a transitory state; the mother not yet able to return to her normal pattern of social relationships and the child still awaiting ritual acknowledgement and acceptance as a member of the group. Let us look at the position of each in turn.

The social liminality of the mother after childbirth was expressed through restrictions on her behaviour and movements. Principally, these prevented her from engaging in day to day social activities outside the home. Restrictions on her movements were lifted only after she had been 'churched', until which time it was considered improper for her to leave the house. Were she to venture outside, it was made clear that she would be forbidden to enter other people's houses. As one old woman put it, 'They didn't have 'em in until they'd been churched, they were scared something might happen.' To allow an unchurched woman to enter one's home would therefore be 'asking for trouble, they'd say it was bad luck'. Comments of this kind suggest that the post-natal woman was seen as a ritually impure and dangerous object. Until this impurity was removed, through churching, a woman could not resume her normal activities. Van Gennep, in a highly apt phrase, sees the churching rite as embodying the 'social return from childbirth' (1960: 46).[1]

The social liminality of the *child* at this point was expressed in a number of ways. In the first place it was 'betwixt and between' (Turner 1974) two social states, as Lévi-Strauss would have it, of culture and nature. Born into the world as an individual, it had transcended the state of nature in which it existed in its mother's womb, but had not yet gained entry into the cultural realm where it could exist as a social being. This entry was facilitated by baptism, which recognised the child's existence, gave it a name and drew it into the life of the community. The liminality of the unbaptised child in Staithes was reinforced by particular taboos, the most important of which was the custom which prevented a new-born and as yet unbaptised infant from being taken into other houses in the village. To allow an unbaptised child into the house, like the entry of an unchurched woman, was unthinkable. As one woman told me, 'They would stand and look at the baby at the door, but they wouldn't have it in.' This particular custom tells us two things. Firstly it is indicative of the sense of impurity surrounding the infant, and secondly it illustrates that this impurity was thought to have unfavourable consequences on the home. Under no circumstances, therefore, could the child be allowed to cross the threshold and endanger the domestic world.

The liminal qualities of the unbaptised infant are of course by no means a product exclusively of the folk realm. Parallels can be found in official doctrine, for example, in the church's teaching on the eternal fate of the unbaptised. Thomas's *Religion and the Decline of Magic* contains a discussion of the development of the church's attitude to baptism in the medieval period. He writes, 'The church taught that the ceremony was *absolutely necessary for salvation* and that *children who died unbaptised were consigned to limbo*, where they would be perpetually denied sight of the vision of God, and even, according to some theologians, subjected to the torments of the damned' (1973: 40, my emphasis). Within the church, opinions over baptism were seriously divided, however, and after the Reformation many Puritans regarded the rite as yet another popish abomination. The Anglican Church, for its part, has never officially given great place to the concept of limbo, which was derived from St Augustine of Hippo. Nevertheless for many within the Roman Catholic Church, the idea remained a valid one. It is not our concern here to document the evolution of theological thinking on baptism; what is important is to note that baptism has traditionally been seen as a bridging point between two states. Emphases vary with church and denomination, from the notion of cleansing from original sin to merely welcoming the child into the fellowship of the assembly. Whatever the interpretation may be, underlying it there is the idea of movement from one social realm to another; sin to forgiveness; outsider to member. It is here that the significance of baptism can be located since it brings to an end the liminal state wherein the child hovers between two worlds. Baptism implies resolution and aggregation, not only in terms of official theology but also on the level of folk religion and community.

Folk beliefs relating to baptism appear to be even more diverse than theologically informed opinions within the church. A variety of them are described by Thomas; typically, they represent a re-channelling of theological thinking along more pragmatic lines. For example, the concern with the child's spiritual future, which is central to the baptismal rite, became transmuted in the medieval period into a belief which held that baptism was 'an essential rite if the child was to survive at all' (Thomas 1973: 4). The question of spiritual destiny was thus reduced to a pragmatic, instrumental level. Such a belief is congruent with the liminality of the unbaptised infant who is depicted as hovering between the unborn state and the prospect of a full human life. The child who dies before its liminality has been resolved is considered vulnerable in the extreme, viz. the concept of limbo. A limited amount of more recent material exists relating to this subject. For example, Williams found in Gosforth that whilst people were usually muddled, vague and unclear about their reasons for having their children baptised, they had strong feelings about the burial of unbaptised children.

Everyone . . . agreed that to bury a child without baptism was a terrible and shocking thing, to be avoided at all costs, and in commenting on this many people who had found it impossible to say why they had had their own children baptized were stimulated into expressing opinions. A village craftsman, for example, said 'If tha didn't get kiddy baptised by t'parson, it would have to be put in a box and stuck in t'ground like some sort o' animal.' Other characteristic remarks in this context were 'It wouldn't be right like a proper babby, it would be just like burying a dog or a sheep . . .'   (Williams 1958: 59–60)

What emerges from Williams's account is that the death of the unbaptised is not followed by the normal funerary ritual but by a procedure more appropriate to the disposal of a dead animal.[2] This suggests once again that unbaptised children are seen in a separate category from other social beings in which their identification with animals places them in closer proximity to the natural than the cultural realm.

There were few deaths of unbaptised children in Staithes in the early part of the century, for whenever a child seemed unlikely to survive for very long after its birth the midwife or doctor would immediately perform the baptismal ceremony. As one middle-aged woman told me, 'They always "did" them straight away if they thought there was anything wrong. They gave the baby a name but you could change it afterwards if you wanted to.' The practice ensured that a child did not die unbaptised: the liminal infant should not pass out of the world before having adequately been made part of it.

The case of still-born infants presents a similar and interesting situation. Still-born babies were and are buried at the back of the cemetery, almost under the boundary hedge and without a headstone. A woman who had had a still-born baby in the 1930s described the following events.

The undertaker made a box [i.e. a coffin] and then took it away. They buried it up at the back of the cemetery.
Q. Did you mark the grave with a headstone?
I wouldn't know, we weren't there, the undertaker did it all, we didn't go.
Q. Was a minister present at the burial?
No, just the undertaker and gravedigger.

This rather perfunctory disposal of still-born children clearly illustrates their structural location: they represent the liminal *par excellence*. Their very name is itself paradoxical and contradictory; they are both born and not born, they enter the world but never become a part of it. Still-born children fail to resolve their liminality and must remain forever 'betwixt and between' social states. Consequently, the disposal of such a child does not elicit the customary elaborate ritual response (see below) but is carried out unceremoniously by the gravedigger and undertaker. No official religious sanction is given to the proceedings and family members do not attend. The burial therefore has none of the usual attributes of hymn-singing and funereal symbolism; the attenuated funerary ritual and marginal position of the grave – just inside consecrated ground – all combine to emphasise the extreme liminality of the still-born infant.

In Staithes, as in Gosforth, only a short period of time was allowed to elapse between the birth of a child and its baptism. For example, in 1913, just before the outbreak of the First World War, the parish register shows that five Staithes children were baptised at the parish church; every child was less than one month old.[3] The brief period between birth and baptism[4] suggests two things: firstly, anxiety that the child might fall ill and die unbaptised and secondly, an underlying feeling about the practical efficacy of baptism. Both reflect a desire to confine the dangerous liminality of the child as much as possible by limiting it within a short space of time.

Parish records indicate large numbers of baptisms taking place in the parish church during the nineteenth century and even many chapel folk appear to have had their children baptised there. The attitude seems to have been that rites of passage were more effectively validated by the Established Church, even though Anglicanism had always remained remote from village life. While the early decades of the twentieth century see the beginning of a decline in this attitude, as revealed in the falling number of baptisms, there was no immediate and corresponding increase in chapel baptisms. Indeed, up to the 1930s, baptisms in the chapel were rare. Those who did have their children baptised there were described to me by one woman as 'the better sort of folk, everyone else always had 'em done at home'. In most cases the minister appears to have visited the home, usually about one week after the birth of the child. Again, baptism was often seen in a pragmatic and instrumental light. As in other areas, Staithes people, even today, habitually refer to having the baby 'done'. Home baptisms were therefore carried out in a simple manner with little ritual elaboration and without many of the accoutrements of baptisms in the chapel, which, when they first appeared, were associated with ostentation and 'respectability'. Baptism was nevertheless important in that it freed the child from restrictions placed on it at birth and was also seen as a rite which was necessary to protect the child in after-life, should it die in infancy.

The liminality of the mother was resolved through the ritual of churching. Official teaching on this rite has changed over time, largely from an emphasis on the *purification* of the woman, based on injunctions from Leviticus xii, 1–6, to one of *thanksgiving* for the successful delivery and birth of the child. In the Anglican Church, for example, the Old Testament emphasis on purification was removed when 'The Order of the Purification of Women' from the 1549 Book of Common Prayer (which had earlier appeared in the Sarum Missal) was replaced by 'The Thanksgiving of Women after Childbirth, commonly called The Churching of Women', in the prayer book of 1552 (Cuming 1969: 90–1, 113–14). This did not prevent fierce criticism from some Puritans who condemned the rite as supersititious and irrational. Today, the Church of England is the only major church which continues to have an official rite of churching. The rite was discontinued by the Roman Catholic Church in 1970, although vestiges of it remain in a new rite of baptism. The Methodist Church did have a 'Service of Thanksgiving of Mothers' based largely upon the 1662 Prayer Book rite, but since 1975 and the publication of the New Book of Offices has likewise abandoned the rite.[5]

In Staithes a woman was churched on the first occasion that she attended chapel after the birth of her child. Churching normally consisted of the minister offering prayers of thanks for the successful outcome of her confinement. Despite this official emphasis on thanksgiving, it is likely that the women themselves were more concerned with the element of *purification*, since it was only when they had been churched that they could resume their normal lives. As one woman put it, 'you *had* to be churched before you could go into other houses'. Churching was therefore the important rite which ended the woman's period of liminality and permitted her to re-enter the life of the community free from restrictions.

The liminality of both mother and child was therefore resolved by a rite of passage: through churching for the mother and baptism for the child. Both of these rituals were encountered during fieldwork and the evidence suggests that they have undergone major changes during the course of the century. In the case of baptism, an important shift in location, from the home to the chapel, has brought an *increase* in the level of ritual activity; whereas the provision of a formal rite of churching, on the other hand, has largely been abandoned by the Methodist Church. Where the church has denied a formal outlet for churching, however, a folk rite seems to have emerged as a surrogate.

Childbirth in Staithes today

It is now possible to go on to a description of the relevant beliefs and practices which were encountered and observed during the period of fieldwork. For the woman in Staithes, as for most women in our society, confirmation of the state of pregnancy brings about numerous new obligations and changes in behaviour. It is the family doctor who normally confirms that a woman is pregnant, after which the news that she is 'expecting' quickly travels around the village. Direct conversational references to the woman's new state may be tacit at first, for example, through enquiries about her health, but at some unspecified time, when knowledge about her condition has reached an adequate degree of generality, specific questions might be asked by friends and neighbours, such as 'when's it due then?' or 'what's it going to be, a boy or a girl?'. This latter question concerning the sex of the unborn child leads some women to carry out various experiments designed to indicate the outcome of their pregnancy. One woman, who had had a baby boy shortly before I arrived in the village, told me of the following experiment which she had tried. 'You dangle a needle and thread over your [i.e. the pregnant woman's] knee. If it sways from side to side across the knee it'll be a boy. If it swings lengthways with your leg, it'll be a girl.' To indicate the accuracy of the method, the woman added, 'and every time we did it, it came out for a boy'. Both she and her husband had carried out the experiment on several occasions during her pregnancy. Another woman told me that the location of the first labour pains was a sure sign of the sex of the baby; 'if they start in the back it will be a girl, if they're in the stomach, it'll be a boy'. For verification, she referred to a woman whose labour pains had begun in her back and who had subsequently given birth to a baby girl.

Uncertainty about the child's sex is also revealed in the precautions taken by the pregnant woman and her relatives and friends in making articles of baby clothing. Knitted garments made before the birth are invariably white in colour, whereas once the child is born, and its sex known, clothing will be produced in the traditional colour schemes of blue for a boy and pink for a girl. The choice of the neutral white before the birth indicates the sense of uncertainty felt by the mother and those around her. This is even more graphically revealed in relation to the act of purchasing a pram for the child. I was told that a couple would never buy a pram until after their child was born. As one woman told me, 'it wouldn't be right, you'd be tempting fate'. In one case which came to my attention, an expectant couple had discovered a bargain-priced secondhand pram which they wished to buy. To have made the purchase there and then would have been to break with accepted custom and, perhaps, to have tempted fate. In the end they opted for a pragmatic solution. They bought the pram, but for the remaining six months of the pregnancy kept it in the boot of their car, refusing to take it into their house. The incident illustrates both the restraining effect of folk religion and also the *ad hoc* measures by which constraint can be mitigated when it conflicts with personal interest.

Communal recognition of a pregnant woman's condition plays an important part in the ritual process and serves to separate symbolically the woman from the community at large. As the fact of her pregnancy becomes more conspicuous through the wearing of maternity clothes, this symbolic set-apartness is then signalled back to the rest of the group. Symbolic separation may also occur in the private sphere of the home, where husbands temporarily take on new and more domestic roles, ordering their wives to relax, rest, and so on. Indulgence in semi-magical acts of prophecy concerning the sex of the child also fall into this category since they serve to reinforce and emphasise the special condition of the woman.

However, by far the most important source of separation comes from the fact that women now almost invariably give birth to their children in a maternity hospital, in Whitby, or Scarborough or Middlesbrough. *Symbolic separation is thereby underscored by physical remoteness from home, family and community. The act of childbirth has been removed from the familial and communal setting and now takes place, for the most part, in unfamiliar surroundings. It has become the responsibility of doctors and nurses, who supervise the event in accordance with prescribed technical procedures and standards. The parturient mother can now be visited by friends and relatives only after they have made a long and often inconvenient journey, and even then only at times appointed by the hospital. The traditional meaning of childbirth, an event in the life of the community and managed by its members, is thus usurped by the dictates of a bureaucratically administered health service. Communal responsibility has been superseded by the services of a professional agency – a situation which we shall meet again in our analysis of death.

The context of its birth also provides a period of separation for the child, who has yet to become a part of village life. Since the birth takes place away from the community, the child is in the ambivalent situation of 'returning' to a village in which he/she has never 'been'. Upon its birth, the child emerges as another member of the social world and can become the object of direct, rather than indirect, social relations. The transition is marked both by folk customs and church rites, which conclude the liminal period.

Both mother and child occupy a position of liminality when they return to the village from the maternity hospital. The woman, especially in the case of her first child, returns to the village endowed with a new social status and has to undergo social recognition as 'mother'. As for the child, membership of village society can only be achieved through communal recognition. Shortly after their return home, mother and child therefore receive visits from friends and relatives who frequently bring gifts, such as an article of clothing, or a toy. These gifts are invariably accompanied by a silver coin, often a ten pence piece. The gifts suggest two different sorts of help or assistance; to give a garment is clearly to offer practical aid, whereas the giving of the coin is, in monetary terms, purely a token gesture, whose significance is more important on a symbolic level. The gift of the coin is interpreted in a general sense as being 'for good luck' or, more specifically, as one man told me, 'so t'bairn will never be short of money'. In some cases the gift of a silver coin is accompanied by other gifts which are also endowed with some representational meaning. A couple told me how their son, now fourteen years old, had on the occasion of his birth been given a small basket containing an egg ('for fertility'), a packet of salt ('for the salt of the earth') and a silver coin ('so he'd always have money'). The gifts in the basket were therefore seen as symbolising particular properties which the child might enjoy in later life. The egg and salt, symbolising fertility and, more usually, preservation, are probably pre-Christian in origin. Their persistence today suggests a remarkable tenacity.

The gift-giving visits are often the occasion for an alcoholic drink of some kind, even amongst Methodists. Known as 'wetting the baby's head', the practice is a good example of the transmutation of a church concept into a popular or folk idiom. The term clearly refers to the baptismal rite where the child's head is wetted with water in the sign of the cross. Of course, it is the palate and not the head which receives a wetting, and this is frequently accompanied by a toast 'to the little 'un'. Since the visits tend to contain formal elements, such as the giving of gifts and 'toasting', they serve to confirm the liminality of mother and child, who for a short period are the objects of particular observances. Yet they also begin to confirm the first time mother in her new role and provide communal recognition of the infant.

Nevertheless, in a small number of traditionalist 'Steeas' families, certain taboos relating to both mother and child in this early period after birth may still be found. In the past, as we have seen, women would not leave the house until they went to church or chapel for the churching ritual; during fieldwork only one case of churching occurred. Perhaps significantly, it was in a family who were actively involved in one of the Methodist chapels. Shortly after mother and child had returned from the maternity hospital I made a visit to the family and after a while the topic of baptism came up in our conversation. It transpired that the service was being delayed due to the fact that no minister was booked to preach at the chapel for some weeks. This delay, I discovered, was becoming a source of tension in the family, the child's grandparents being particularly anxious about a long period between his birth and christening. At this point the mother said of her husband's father, 'he wouldn't even have me in the house until I'd been into chapel . . . just to go in and out, that's enough'. 'So did you do that?' I asked. 'Oh yes', she replied; 'the day after we got back [i.e. from hospital] – his dad made me.' Despite her active involvement in chapel life, she appeared to put up no resistance to a request which could find no official warrant. When I enquired as to her motives, the husband, replying on her behalf, said, 'superstition again' – though not in derisory tones. He also seemed to see nothing incompatible in the use of the chapel for such a perfunctory folk rite. Parental pressure in these matters is reported elsewhere by Pickering (1958), Staton (1980) and by Young and Willmott, who found similar evidence in Bethnal Green where married daughters were encouraged by their mothers to be churched after the birth of a child and complied, often at the expense of sarcasm from their husbands, who appeared less concerned with the maintenance of tradition (1962: 59). Staton's (1980) recent work, in particular, suggests that the custom may be far more widespread than is commonly realised.

Attitudes to churching among ministry and clergy on the other hand seem to vary from ignorance to open hostility. The Methodist minister in Staithes during fieldwork was unaware of the persistence of the rite and told me, 'all that sort of thing is a thing of the past, it doesn't happen any more, no one asks for it'. The Anglican rector, however, had encountered the phenomenon and reported that it had been requested 'three or four times' in his three years there. The Roman Catholic priest was aware that the rite had been dropped by the Church and expressed some surprise when I informed him that his own church notice board still referred to 'churching by appointment'. Those occasions when members of the clergy have been moved to written comment on churching give us some further idea of its extent. For example, in 1941 a Lincolnshire vicar in a letter to the journal *Folklore* reported from his parish the 'widely diffused idea that a mother must not enter anyone's house until she had been churched. I am frequently asked if I will "set Mrs so-and-so at liberty" ' (Binnall 1941: 75). His tolerance of the practice is not echoed by the incumbent of an industrial parish in Middlesbrough, some twenty miles from Staithes, who almost thirty-five years later wrote in his parish magazine, 'Sometimes . . . ideas, passed from older members of the family, are loaded with superstition. Some mothers asking to be "churched" soon after their baby has been born do so because relatives won't allow them into their houses until they have been to church – as though there was something wrong or unclean in having a baby!' (Cameron: 1974).

The nature of the rite in Staithes seems to have effectively concealed it from the notice of the Methodist minister living in the village. This may be explained by two factors: firstly, a certain amount of embarrassment surrounded the act and it is therefore unlikely that it would have been a topic of conversation with the minister (attitudes to whom we have already discussed), especially for regular chapel goers. Secondly, the attenuated nature of the rite itself made it a simple matter to carry out and, at the same time, conceal from the ministry. The straightforward and spontaneous procedure of going into the chapel building contained no ritual elaboration and could easily be accomplished without exciting undue attention. What is striking about the local churching rite is that it has no connection with any official churching or thanksgiving ritual in either Anglicanism or nonconformity. No liturgy or minister is involved; the subject must simply, and in almost instrumental fashion, go into a church or chapel. The act therefore seems to lean more heavily towards a notion of purification of the mother than one of thanksgiving for the birth of the child and may be viewed more appropriately as a *folk* ritual than as an element of the official religion.

Like the practice of churching, observances of taboos relating to the unbaptised child are now less common. In certain cases, though, a baby who has not been christened will not be allowed into a person's house. This is a tradition usually observed by older women. As one woman told me, 'Some of the old folks won't have them [unbaptised children] in the house. They'll come to the door and have a look but they won't let you in.' Another much more common practice exists in relation to unbaptised children. Upon returning from the maternity hospital mother and child usually remain indoors for two or three days. The day she takes her baby out for the first time is an important rite of passage in itself, involving the start of reincorporation into the community. Once again the significance of the rite is two-fold. For the mother, it induces public recognition of her status *qua* mother, which is particularly important for the woman who has just given birth to her first child. Members of the village now see her in a new capacity, in most cases aptly attested by the sight of her proudly pushing her pram. People she meets in the street offer congratulations and ask about the state of her health. For the child, the day represents a first involvement in the social life of the community, which is marked by an interesting folk ritual. Upon meeting the child for the first time, usually in a shop or in the street, both men and women will make a point of giving it a silver coin. This is usually done in a specified ritual manner, for example, as one man in his late thirties told me, 'I always touch the baby's palm with it' (the coin); whilst a woman of the same age, also present at the time of the conversation, said, 'I always touch the forehead.' When asked why they did this, the man replied, 'it's for good luck, it's so they'll never go short' (i.e. of money). In another case a woman out with her baby for the first time was stopped by several women who wished to give her a silver coin, all of whom insisted on putting it in her baby's hand, saying, 'I've got to give it to her first before I give it to you.' These statements suggest that there are clearly defined rules which must be adhered to if the gift of the coin is to have any efficacy. The custom is extremely widespread in the village and shows no sign of disappearance. One woman told me that in the days after her child was born she was given coins amounting to 'three or four pounds' in value; even allowing for exaggeration, this points to the ubiquity of the practice. The gift of the coin is usually seen as a means of ensuring luck for the child, particularly in the financial sphere. A further interpretation might be that the ritual incorporates the child into the web of communal relations through the most efficacious method of gift-giving. As Mauss (1970) has indicated, to receive a gift is to place oneself in a position of obligation to the donor. Conversely, to give a gift is to affirm one's status position above that of the recipient. Thus, through receiving gifts of silver coins the young child makes an entry into community life and is immediately placed in a position of obligation, not just to one individual, but to many; to wit, the entire community. The custom suggests both amity and enmity, friendship and hostility. On the one hand it emphasises goodwill towards the child, and the hope that it will enjoy material prosperity and be endowed with the metaphysical property of 'luck'.[6] It also suggests a welcoming of the individual into the group. Conversely, the rite may have a darker aspect in which the child is quickly placed in a position of structural weakness and obligation.

The rituals of churching and gift-giving, then, mark the movement of both mother and child, away from their liminal states. The final rite of incorporation for both is marked by baptism, providing formalised and public recognition of a new status for the mother and a name and assimilation into the group for the child. An important feature of the baptismal rite in Staithes is the transformation which it has undergone during the course of the century. Up to the time of the outbreak of the Second World War, the children of those with chapel affiliations were, as we have seen, almost invariably baptised in the home. After the war it became increasingly common for baptisms to take place in the chapel. For the small group of Staithes Anglicans, baptisms only rarely take place in the Mission Church and are usually held at Hinderwell. On a number of occasions I was able to observe the *complete* rite of baptism, from the assembly of the participants at the house through the departure to the chapel, the service itself and the final return home. The following is therefore an account of a typical rite, taken from fieldnotes.

About an hour before the service is due to begin, the maternal grandparents, accompanied by the two godparents, arrive at the house. The parents of the baby and their two daughters are all dressed in their 'Sunday best'. The baby is clothed completely in white and is wrapped in a large crocheted shawl. This is referred to as the 'christening shawl' and in this case, as in many others, it is one which has traditionally been worn by other members of the family on the occasions of their baptism. The godparents vary, but are often siblings of the parents. They have brought a gift for the child, a small-scale silver-plated knife, fork and spoon set. General conversation follows the arrival of the guests, who each hold the baby for a short time, talking and playing with it until, at the appropriate time, the group leaves for the chapel. At this point the baby's mother hands the child to the godmother. As we walked I asked why the godmother must carry the baby out of the house and to the chapel. 'This is just the way we do it', the mother said, 'Mr M. [the Methodist minister] said I could carry him to the chapel, and J. [her husband] could carry him back, but I said we'd done it this way for the other two, so we'd keep it the same.' Her statement includes the classic elements of folk religion: an acceptance of and confidence in established rules and procedures, often in the absence of any understanding of their meaning, along with an emphasis on the continuance of family tradition and an implicit repudiation of the official religion through a rejection of the minister's proposal.

On arriving at the chapel the group enter through the large main door, which is reserved exclusively for use at the rites of passage, and sit down in the front pew which has been kept vacant for them. Throughout this time the godmother continues to hold the baby, finally giving it to the mother just prior to the baptismal rite itself.

When the service is over, the group leave the chapel and are frequently congratulated outside by other members of the congregation, who also make complimentary remarks about the baby. Then, joined by others, they set off back to the house, with the mother now carrying the child.

Upon their return, food and drink are produced and whilst these are being consumed, the godparents are asked to cut the child's 'christening cake' – a large fruit cake decorated with icing. This is done jointly by the couple, holding the knife and cutting together and being instructed as they do so to 'make a wish'. Portions of the cake are then given to all of the guests and a brief toast of 'health, happiness and prosperity' is proposed for the child. Everyone drinks to this toast and the cake is eaten. The 'christening cake' is regarded with particular significance by the participants and is often specially baked and decorated by a friend of the family or member of the chapel. Opinions are passed and comments solicited on its quality and the following day portions are taken to friends and relatives who have not attended the gathering at the house. Recipients of christening cake tend to be confined to those who, earlier, have given gifts to the child. Because of this, the giving of a piece of cake may be seen as symbolising the child's first act of reciprocity, whereby he/she begins to engage in relations of mutuality in the village. Significantly, the process of rites relating to birth concludes with the main participants coming together in a ritual meal. The meal suggests both celebration, through conviviality and toasting, and also aggregation or incorporation, through the communal consumption of food. The meal is underscored by a sense of unity which signifies the resolution of the liminality of both mother and child and successfully brings to a close the ritual observations surrounding childbirth.

Death

Like birth, death too demands social recognition in the form of ritualised action and belief. Theoretically and methodologically the dominant approach to the understanding of such religious elements has again been that of structural functionalism. Functionalist writers have consequently stressed the disintegrating effect of death upon communal existence, especially in primitive and traditional societies, and the efficacy of mortuary ritual as a restitutive force (Herz 1960; Malinowski 1954). Commentators on attitudes and beliefs relating to death in contemporary society have taken a different view, however. The central task of writers such as Gorer (1965), Kübler-Ross (1970), MacIntyre (1968) and Mitford (1963) has therefore been to show how in highly differentiated and segmental societies, responses to death do not manifest themselves collectively. Death, it has been argued, represents one of the most virulent taboos of contemporary culture and has been reduced, in MacIntyre's phrase, to a 'private matter' (1968: 719). Attenuated funerary rituals, along with an impoverished framework of beliefs for coping with bereavement are characteristic manifestations of this 'denial of death' which contrasts so markedly with the ostentatious funerals and protracted mourning injunctions of the Victorian period. In the United States, where the denial has reached its zenith, Jessica Mitford has argued that 'The American Way of Death' represents a set of attitudes and practices which seemingly refuse to acknowledge mortality at all, in a situation where even the funeral has become a celebration of American consumerism (1963). This assault on the notion of death, perpetrated largely by funeral directors, has not pervaded the British situation to the same extent. British society, Gorer (1965) and MacIntyre (1968) have argued, is marked rather by confusion and lack of norms relating to death. The subject has become an embarrassing source of unease, epitomised, for example, in the cremation ritual which is impersonal, efficient and highly mechanised, but which remains ritually and emotionally unsatisfying for mourners.

Yet such broad brush strokes fail to come to grips with concrete situations and, as we have argued earlier, frequently neglect heterogeneous elements existing in specific social settings. It will become clear that the themes put forward by current writers are not entirely borne out by the evidence from Staithes, where mortuary ritual is very much in evidence and where clearly defined rules continue to regulate individual and collective responses to death. This is not to say that the forces of social change have left Staithes untouched, and by contrasting the contemporary situation in the village with that existing at the beginning of the century we shall try to show just how beliefs and practices relating to death have changed as external structural factors have impinged ever stronger on communal norms and values.

Death in Staithes in the early twentieth century

With the exception of accidental fatalities, death in Staithes in the early part of the century almost invariably took place in the home, where the sick and the dying were the immediate responsibility of the family, to whom also befell the task of laying the dead to rest in an adequate and befitting manner. In the midst of their bereavement, therefore, the kinsfolk were kept busy by funeral preparations and various related tasks. The first duty was that of laying-out the body, known in Staithes as 'the lying-out'. As one old man put it, 'When a person passed away the first thing they did was go for the board – the lying-out board.' This board, upon which the corpse was stretched out – it was known in Northumberland as the 'streaking board' (Henderson 1866: 53) – was kept in the workshop of the village joiner, who also performed the duties of undertaker. 'Lying-out', however, was the charge of a handful of women who were recognised in the village as qualified to carry out the work and who, from their painstaking attention to detail, appear to have taken considerable pride in their task. The process began with the washing of the body and the tying-up of the jaw; the corpse was then wrapped in a white sheet and layed on the board in the centre of a double bed. White woollen stockings were used to cover the feet, a pillow was placed on each side of the head and another sheet, meticulously folded in a series of horizontal pleats which ran down its entire length, was laid over the body. Finally, a large white handkerchief covered the face. The linen used in the laying-out was of the finest quality and that edged with Maltese lace was particularly popular. In common with the practice in many other areas and classes of society, the material was usually purchased well in advance.

The attention paid to the body at this point, if seen in terms of the van Gennep triad, constitutes a ritualised counterpart to the separation which death induces between individual and group. The preparation of the body therefore underscores its disconnection from the community through various rites which ensure that its contagion may not spread to the living. As if to confirm this, the body was watched over in the period leading up to the funeral in the manner of a wake, where members of the family took it in turns to sit by the body throughout the day and night. Thus laid out, the corpse became the object of formalised visits on the part of kin and friends, who upon calling at the house would be invited to go upstairs to see the dead person for the last time. 'Would you like to have a look at him?', was the usual question asked of visitors, who would then be escorted upstairs. The person watching over the corpse would then lift the face cloth for a few moments to allow a final view of the deceased, at which point the visitor was expected to touch the body as an expression of sympathy or, as one man put it, 'to show that they always held out goodwill while the person was alive'. Following a few moments of silence the visitor would return below to the other members of the family.

After the initial separation of the dead person, the stage leading up to the burial had all the aspects of liminality associated with the middle phase of the rite of passage; we see therefore the suspension, not only of normal conventions and patterns of behaviour, but also, one feels, of time itself. The progression of day and night became meaningless as clocks were stopped and members of the family sat up throughout the night, dozing in chairs and taking it in turns to go to sit by the body. Mirrors and pictures were carefully covered over with white napkins and curtains remained drawn.

Meanwhile, funeral preparations continued to occupy various individuals – the joiner, in the construction of the coffin, and the women, in the baking of the special funerary foods. One woman, known as the 'bidder', was specially employed at this time to announce the day and time of the funeral throughout the village. Her task took her to every house in Staithes, at each of which she would knock at the door and 'bid', or invite, the household to attend. Sunday was the preferred day for funerals, despite the charging of double burial fees. Since sabbatarian observance prohibited working on the Sabbath, all who wished to attend were free to do so. The preference for Sunday funerals seems to be linked, in turn, to the belief still found in the village that 'if a body lays over a Sunday, there will be two more to follow'. Such a belief clearly points to the potency of the corpse as a source of contagion which, if allowed to remain unburied throughout the Sabbath, must bring about further death and misfortune. Another essential task was the choosing of coffin bearers and women to serve tea to the mourners after the funeral. Coffin bearers were usually recruited from close kin; as one old lady put it, the rule was that 'you always went as near as you could' (i.e. in degrees of kinship). The bearers were always of the same sex as the deceased. The servers at the funeral tea, known locally as 'waitresses', were usually neighbours, although one woman told me that it had been known on occasions for a dying person to leave a note, indicating the hymns to be sung at the funeral, and also the choice of 'waitresses'.

On the day of the funeral itself, and at the appointed hour, a group of villagers would congregate outside the house of the deceased. Inside, when all members of the immediate family were present they would gather around the open coffin (or 'box' as Staithes people habitually refer to it), whereupon the minister or priest placed one hand upon it, and delivered a short extempore prayer of thanks for the life of the dead person and the comfort of the mourners. One Methodist lay-preacher who had worked in the area for fifty years remarked, 'The first time I went down for a funeral they told me "make sure you put a hand on the coffin", they used to like that.' At the conclusion of the prayer the coffin lid was fixed in position and at this point special sweet 'funeral biscuits', along with glasses of port, or occasionally spirits, were taken to the people outside. Clay pipes and tobacco were passed around among the men on a special black patterned funeral plate which each family kept for such occasions. The bearers also received food and drink for, as one man put it, 'they used to like a glass before the lifting'. Vallee points out that such a 'lifting' custom is also prevalent in some Scottish communities, where it is an occasion 'not only for solemn ritual but also for mild feasting' (Vallee 1955: 124, n.1). When the food and drink had been consumed the coffin was carried out of the house and placed on two chairs in the street or alleyway. This rite clearly indicates the extension of the liminal period and conforms closely to van Gennep's notion of a transition rite. As members of the family left the house, care was taken to leave the door open in the belief that this facilitated the departure of the dead person's soul. Then, with the coffin resting on the chairs, all present would sing the first verse of a funeral hymn.

Still singing, the bearers took the coffin and began moving away in the direction of the chapel. There appear to have been two methods of carrying the coffin; on some occasions it would be carried shoulder high, whilst on others it was placed on wooden poles which were carried at waist height. No-one I spoke to could offer any explanation for the existence of the two methods but a likely solution to the problem appears in the writings of a local folklorist. Thus, Gutch, referring to the nearby fishing village of Flamborough, states that, 'The coffins of the fishermen and sailors drowned at sea are carried shoulder high by their fellow seamen. Those of landsfolk are carried, like those of women, underhand and close to the level of the ground' (1912: 135). If, as seems likely, this was the practice in Staithes, an interesting structural opposition is revealed between the social position of seafarers and landsfolk. It is significant that women appear to have been placed in the latter and less honorific category, so that the structurally 'inferior' were carried lower and closer to the ground in contrast to their social 'superiors', who were raised up high in the funerary ritual. As we saw in our discussion of both New Year and birth rites, folk religion appears to be no respecter of feminist principles.

Behind the bearers in the funeral procession came the women who would later serve at the tea. Six or eight in number, they wore black hats with white crocheted shawls and black silk sashes. With characteristic meticulousness, the women walked in pairs, one wearing her sash diagonally from the left shoulder and the other wearing hers from her right in order to form an inverted V pattern. The minister followed, then came a separate group made up of the bereaved family and finally the rest of the company. Such careful attention to detail is indicative of the great concern expressed for correct ritual behaviour which is further emphasised by the fact that the practices in question were essentially folk customs having no basis in any formal liturgy. After the service had taken place in the chapel it was necessary to carry the coffin some one and a half miles to the graveyard of the parish church at Hinderwell. Even today Staithes has no cemetery of its own. In the days before motor transport this meant a steep climb out of the village followed by a tiring walk along the cliffs; in later years the coffin was carried up to the main road and thence by horse-drawn cart to the graveyard. This was not without its difficulties, and one man recalled a funeral in heavy snow in which he and his fellow bearers had been faced with the daunting prospect of carrying the coffin up the hill in treacherous conditions.

At the foot of the hill, and before returning to prepare the funeral tea, the serving women stepped to one side and watched as the others left the village. The processions were evidently a spectacular sight. Male coffin bearers wore small white bows or rosettes in their lapels – three men with them on the right side and three on the left side. The bows had to be worn on the side nearest to the coffin.[7] Women bearers wore black skirts, white shawls and white hats. Behind the bearers came the men, wearing seal-skin caps or bowler hats, dark blue jerseys and serge trousers. Then came the women, all in black. The singing would sometimes continue all the way to the graveyard and as the walk was a long one it was necessary to have six bearers instead of the customary four. This enabled two to rest at any one time and then relieve another two. Women bearers seem only to have carried the coffin to the chapel before the men took over for the walk to Hinderwell. Vallee describes how in Barra, where similar processions are found at funerals, considerable pains are taken to ensure that on the journey from home to church *all* of the men in the cortège are able to take a turn at carrying the coffin, and indeed, where the distance is short, a circuitous route is deliberately chosen (1955: 124).

At the committal it was the duty of the gravedigger to throw soil down onto the coffin during the final obsequies and when the prayers were completed a hymn would be sung at the graveside; 'Gather at the River' was a popular choice. The company then set off back to the village where they were met at the top of the bank by the serving women who divided them into small groups for the funeral tea. Once again, we are able to see at this point the careful planning and organisation which went into the funeral preparations. Large attendances at funerals, coupled with the smallness of the fishermen's cottages, made a collective meal impossible and gave rise to the practice of holding the meal in several different households. Very often a neighbour having a slightly larger house would offer assistance by putting it at the disposal of the waitresses. In later years the problem was overcome by holding the funeral tea in the relevant chapel Sunday Schoolroom. Smoked ham, fruit cake (known as 'funeral bread') and Madeira cake were the traditional foods for the tea, which was manifestly an expensive affair. During one funeral I attended, I was told by a man in his early seventies that in the past, 'the poorer class o' person often had to spend his last penny paying for everything', whilst in an interview another man remarked, 'nearly everyone had a small insurance out to cover the cost of the fees and the funeral tea'. There were also funeral clubs into which weekly subscriptions were paid. J. Fairfax-Blakeborough, writing in a local weekly paper, notes that,

Up to half-a-century ago most villagers [in the area] made provision for the cost of 'siding by' a member of the family who died . . . They paid a few coppers a week to 'the club' (Shepherds, Oddfellows, Foresters or Buffs). When occasion came they were able to draw 'benefit' which was most helpful. I remember a villager (crippled financially by funeral expenses), saying 'we should have been in a queer spot if it hadn't been for t'club'.   (*Whitby Gazette* 11 April 1975)

Nevertheless, the clubs seem to have existed to provide far more than an ability to meet the basic expenses. They enabled members to buy not only an expensive oak coffin, handsomely finished with brass handles and plate, but also to finance the vast and lavish funeral tea. Threats of financial ruin accruing from the enormous expense of a funeral seem in fact to have heightened the sense of having given the deceased a 'good send-off'.

The funeral tea may be seen as the first in a series of rites of incorporation, bringing the group together in a final acknowledgement of the death, whilst at the same time preparing the bereaved for their return from the fraught liminal phase and their subsequent re-entry into the regulated pattern of group life. Consequently, when the family returned to their home after the funeral, the white napkins would be removed from the mirrors and pictures and the curtains partially opened. While it was true that the bereaved family had to follow a host of mourning rules and injunctions for many weeks, there was a steady divestment and relaxation of sanctions, which progressively admitted the re-entry of the mourner into a normal role in the community. The emphasis throughout this re-admission, however, was on a *gradual* progression. I was told, for example, how in some families window blinds would be slowly raised, inch by inch, day by day.[8] For women in particular, mourning represented a protracted period wherein onerous restrictions on movement and dress were only gradually removed during subsequent months. For example, women frequently ceased to attend chapel for as much as a whole year; indeed one old lady told me that 'some never went for five or six years – they used to think it wasn't reverent'. Not only attendance at chapel, but any appearance outdoors in the early weeks and months after the death was considered improper and gave rise to unfavourable comment – 'They used to say, "bye, she's soon come out, they can't have much respect".' Added to this was the duty of wearing black at all times. Some widows remained in black for the rest of their lives. Many old photographs still to be seen today in homes in the village show women, clearly in mourning, wearing black versions of the Staithes bonnet and black aprons. The widow's weeds were not quickly abandoned and it might be several years before a woman went into a period of 'second mourning' where grey and mauve were considered permissible colours. For the men, sartorial mourning does not appear to have existed; they did, however, acknowledge death within the family in one highly distinctive custom. This was the practice known as 'putting a coble into mourning', whereby each spring, when the fishing boats were repainted, any vessel belonging to a family. which had suffered a bereavement during the previous year was given a single maroon stripe or listing, signifying the death, which would remain there for twelve months before its removal the following year.

More permanent reminders of the death were kept in the house for years to come. Throughout the Victorian period and on into the early twentieth century it was common to have special mourning cards printed to commemorate the death of a member of the family. The cards were solemnly funereal in design and style and contained various biographical details of the dead person.[9] In particular, explicit references were made on the cards to the cause of death, especially when this involved drowning at sea. Religious texts of various sorts were included on the cards, such as verses from psalms and hymns or quotations from the bible; in other cases lines of verse appear. One typical example which I was shown consisted of a printed centrepiece surrounded by heavy card relief in black, depicting angels set among trellis work and sombre pillars, accompanied by the verse,

> He felt not the tomb's devouring breath,
> Nor thought of the woe of tomorrow,
> Till suddenly called from his kindred dear,
> Though none at that moment bent o'er him,
> 'Twas then he beheld his last enemy near,
> And eternity all before him.

Another, in remembrance of a fisherman and his thirteen-year-old son who died in 1865, whilst attempting to put into Hartlepool during a storm, reads,

> There is a port, a peaceful port,
> A safe and happy shore,
> Where weary mariners do resort,
> When life's rough voyage is o'er.

Large cards such as this (some seven inches by nine) were framed and hung on the walls, whilst small ones were often tucked behind picture frames or mirrors. Grim reminders they must have been to a community where death was such a frequent and untimely visitor.

Death in Staithes today

Whilst listening to old people talking of the beliefs and rituals surrounding death in the early part of the century I was continually impressed by their detailed and highly specific accounts. These displayed a remarkable internal consistency and few differences appear to have existed between funerals taking place at the different religious institutions in the village. Even funerals at the parish church differed from those in the chapels only in so far as the company had to walk to the church at Hinderwell beforehand. When we turn to the subject of death in the contemporary situation, however, a number of important changes are immediately apparent and various traditional practices appear to have been abandoned or modified. I could find no evidence, for example for the continuance of the custom of covering up mirrors and pictures in the death house. Similarly, bearers are no longer of the same sex as the dead person; in fact, to have bearers at all is now rather exceptional, since the duty frequently falls to the undertaker's staff. Curtains are still drawn in the house of the dead, but now only on the day that death occurs and then again immediately before the funeral. The practice of printing special death cards ended in the 1940s. Perhaps the most significant innovation is the emergence of a number of specialist organisations which increasingly concern themselves with the processes of death and dying. It is a transformation which has stripped the family of one of its traditional functions, so that some of the familial and communal rituals previously associated with the death of a villager have disappeared beneath a general trend towards standardisation. Today, significant differences are also apparent between churches and chapels in terms of funerary rituals, and the introduction of cremation during the course of the century has resulted in further variation.[10]

For analytical purposes it is possible to distinguish five separate types of ritual by pairing the means of disposal with the setting in which a particular funeral service is held. These are: chapel/burial, chapel/cremation, church/burial, church/cremation and crematorium/cremation (i.e. the entire service takes place in the crematorium). On the basis of this typology we shall be concerned, firstly, with the fundamental distinction between cremation and burial, and secondly, with church funerals followed by cremation and, finally, chapel funerals followed by burial. In taking the examples of church/cremation and chapel/burial we thereby hope to demonstrate the ways in which church and chapel have become increasingly dissimilar in the form and content of their respective funerary rites. Initially, however, we turn to discussion of a process which has come to effect all aspects of funerary ritual in Staithes.

The professionalisation of death

In Staithes today, and in contrast to the situation in the early part of the century, the immediacy of death as a communal event has been considerably attenuated. For most villagers contact with death takes place at a distance or through intermediaries, in the form of bureaucratically organised agencies which perform the duties and tasks once held to be the responsibility of the family or community. We may call this process the professionalisation of death since it perpetrates the notion that competence to deal with the practical matters associated with death is vested solely in specially trained professionals, who in conducting their work seek to emphasise the ascendancy of their skills in this matter over any related ones held by the family. Professionalisation has thereby resulted in a vastly different set of responses to the problem of death.

First of all, it is important we recognise that the home is no longer the only setting in which death is likely to take place. Other alternatives exist, such as hospitals, residential homes and geriatric units, which in assuming responsibility for care of the dying have taken death not only out of the home, but also out of the village. At the same time the duties of the undertaker, transferred from village joiner to local Co-operative Society and then aggrandised in the role of 'funeral director', have been made to include many of the responsibilities formerly borne by relatives and neighbours. Thus, when death occurs in one of these institutions it is common for the body to be removed to the funeral director's memorial house rather than to the individual's home, and for the preparation of the corpse and laying-out to be done by the funeral director rather than by the traditional female specialists in the village. While some villagers remain strongly in favour of keeping the body at home, others have been persuaded, often on grounds of convenience and hygiene, to leave matters to the funeral director. Other indirect consequences result from this trend; for example, since the memorial house is some four miles from the village, the likelihood of a person going there to make the traditional last visit to the laid-out corpse is considerably diminished. The familiar circumstances of the final visit in a friend or relative's cottage now gone, only the more zealous are likely to avail themselves of the 'service' which the funeral director provides. Elsewhere, other members of the village are no longer required to carry out their former duties. Formal announcement of the death and notification of the date and time of the funeral have ceased to be jobs for the 'bidder' and whilst news of the death still travels quickly, it is usual for the funeral director to arrange for publication of details in the death and obituary column of the local evening newspaper. Face-to-face social relations therefore disappear and are replaced by the dispassionate newspaper announcement. Similarly, making the coffin, once a task for the local joiner, is now arranged by the funeral director, who in addition to ordering flowers and wreaths also makes provision for the preparation of the funeral tea by outside caterers. One woman summed the changes up thus, 'Now the Co-op has it all – tea, flowers, box – he'll put it in t' paper and everything.' Even the laying-out board itself has become the property of the North Eastern Co-operative Society, and hangs on a gate next to the village store.

Burial and cremation

Perhaps the greatest innovation coming from those professional agencies who now concern themselves with death has been the introduction of cremation as an alternative form of disposal of the dead. Its implications for any analysis of death in the village are considerable. During the period of fieldwork in Staithes there were thirty-five funerals. Three of these took place entirely at the crematorium and two were at the Roman Catholic Church. Of the remaining thirty, twenty-two were held in one or other of the three chapels and eight took place in the parish church. Six out of ten funerals were burials, whilst the remainder were cremations. These figures almost reverse those for the country as a whole, which show that in 1974 approximately 60% of all deaths in Britain were followed by cremation.[11] What interpretation can we give to this local phenomenon? Two possibilities exist. The first is that, in common with the situation in many other areas, a considerable distance must be travelled to the nearest crematorium, thereby creating undue expense and making the funeral itself a lengthy and tiring affair. Practical considerations may therefore militate against the choice of cremation among villagers. Alternatively we might consider whether or not there are to be found in the village any indication of values and attitudes *vis-à-vis* cremation which might prevent it from being regarded as an acceptable means of disposal of the dead.

Let us consider these alternative explanations more carefully. The nearest crematorium is situated in Middlesbrough, about twenty-two miles from Staithes. Another exists in Scarborough, a little further away, though in my experience this has never been utilised by people from the village. The journey from Staithes to the crematorium at Middlesbrough takes about fifty minutes, taxis have to be hired to transport members of the family and time may be at a premium for those who should be at work. Inconvenience might seem a feasible enough explanation for the low incidence of cremations; surprisingly though, on only one occasion did I hear this cited as a reason. In fact a far more satisfactory explanation can be found. As should become increasingly apparent, the people of Staithes have never allowed considerations of time or cost to interfere with what they consider to be the right and proper way of bidding farewell to the dead. Popular though the notion of the parsimonious Yorkshireman may be, it is not confirmed here; indeed cremation, which requires no grave-plot or headstone, is cheaper than interment. The high figures for burial are rather, we suggest, the product of a particular aversion to cremation, combined with a deep-seated preference for the traditional ritual.

Chief protagonists in what amounts to an anti-cremation faction are those women who are still usually called in to lay-out a body. The bodies are prepared in like fashion both for cremation and burial and since the women are not paid for this work, their views cannot be attributed to mere self-interest. During the course of a long conversation on the subject one of them remarked, 'I don't want cremating . . . I've never been to one [i.e. a cremation] and I don't wish to go. They reckon [the] body goes through that hatch and they keep it for days.' Another woman claimed that bodies were kept at the crematorium 'in cold storage', whilst one other, the forty-year-old daughter of one of the laying-out specialists, said, 'They only have a burning day once a week', and expressed some doubts about the authenticity of the ashes saying, 'You get a few ashes back, you don't know if they belong to you or not.' This aversion to cremation is further attested by the funeral director, who told me, 'When I came here, ten years ago, they never talked about cremation, they practically shuddered when you mentioned it. Today it's not quite as bad, but the vast majority don't like it.' In fact this last statement is corroborated by the few records available. The register for the parish church of Hinderwell shows that during the first three years (1961–3) in which the crematorium at Middlesbrough was open, no cremation of a Staithes person took place there. In 1964 four Staithes funerals were held at the parish church and one was followed by cremation. The same occurred in 1965. In the following ten years just under a half of deceased Staithes Anglicans have been cremated. There is no sign of an increase. National cremation figures show a rise of about 2% per annum between 1970 and 1975,[12] yet this does not seem to have been mirrored in Staithes where, after an initial reluctance to accept cremation at all, some six out of ten funerals continue to involve interment.

Specific religious values and ritual practices can be used to explain this continued preference for the burial of the dead. The graveyard of the parish church at Hinderwell and the council cemetery which lies adjacent to it are places of great importance to the people of Staithes. It is here that the dead of the village have been taken for three centuries. Enormous gravestones adorned with capstans, ropes, anchors and other symbols of the sea mark the graves of dozens of drowned fishermen and sailors. Visiting and tending graves constitutes the most important way in which the memory of the dead is perpetuated. Every Saturday and Sunday afternoon, especially in summer, people can be seen walking from the village to the cemetery carrying flowers. After one funeral which I observed, the gravedigger remarked sardonically,

Staithes people are terrible for funerals. In fact I think they think more of them when they're dead than when they're alive. If you look round here at all the graves with flowers on, you can bet your bottom dollar that nine out of ten are for Staithes people. If ever a sheep gets into the cemetery they're always up in arms, though I wish there were a hundred sheep in, it would help keep the grass down.

This concern with the graves of the departed, similar in certain respects to that found in some Roman Catholic countries, is not merely an activity confined to special occasions such as birthdays, anniversaries or even Sundays. For example, one woman described to me how, after a visit to the chemist's shop at Hinderwell, she had thought to herself 'I'll just pop into the cemetery and then walk back to Steeas.' In similar fashion people going out for a walk may leave the village heading in the general direction of Hinderwell and end up by visiting the graveyard and the grave of a deceased relation. One man, while recommending me to go to see the elaborate gravestone of a former coxswain of the lifeboat, situated near the back of the cemetery, was able to pin-point its position with remarkable accuracy, thereby revealing an intimate acquaintance with the layout of the graveyard. I was told by another that his elderly maiden aunt, a woman often called in to do the laying-out and a particularly vehement critic of funeral homes and cremation, had already purchased her grave-plot; moreover when visiting the grave of her sister, she would usually stop to have a look at the spot where she herself would ultimately be laid to rest. Such practices have also been noted in other rural areas. Williams quotes a man in the West-Country village of Ashworthy: 'Families here like to be buried in the same ground. A lot buy a piece of land and when the first one's buried they dig the grave eight feet instead of six. It can be opened then for the other one [i.e. spouse]' (Williams 1963: 187–8). The purchase of family graves is also a common practice in Staithes and on several occasions I heard people refer to having bought 'two deep', i.e. had the first entry in the grave, a spouse, for example, buried at a sufficient depth to allow another coffin to be placed in at a later date. In the case of the accidental death of a boy in the village, such was the shock and distress of the parents that in making the provisions for burial they had neglected to get 'three deep'. When the funeral was over, however, they lost no time in purchasing the adjacent grave plot for themselves in order that they might eventually be buried next to their son.

After each of the burials observed at Hinderwell it was possible to see men and women dispersing to various parts of the cemetery in order to visit particular graves. On occasion some people stayed behind to weed the graves of deceased relatives. In this way every funeral takes on a wider significance. Transformed from a rite of passage for one individual, it becomes a remembrance of the entire collectivity of the dead. A powerful bond is thus created between the world of the living and the world of the dead. The graves are set apart, they must be visited regularly, they must be tended, protected and adorned with flowers. These ritualistic acts take on a quasi-religious significance wherein two separate social worlds come into contact with one another. Furthermore, the situation is a *familiar* one; villagers know that following their own death they will ultimately be surrounded by other men and women from Staithes. By contrast, cremation takes place in strange surroundings in a large town. In the crematorium the coffin disappears from view into some hidden room, where, for the villager, who knows what takes place? Even the ashes, which can be retained if desired, may not be those of the person concerned. Above all, no lasting memorial exists except the illuminated entry in the Book of Remembrance, displayed annually at the crematorium on the anniversay of the death.

It appears then that while family and community responses to death have been eroded and undermined by the forces of professionalisation, certain elements of *traditional* belief and ritual are still retained. This is most strongly highlighted in the case of interment, which shows no signs of decline. However, given the existence of a certain percentage of funerals which do culminate in cremation, we may select from our continuum two of the pairs of variables mentioned earlier in order to illustrate and contrast typical styles of funerary ritual occurring today. The variables of church/ cremation, on the one hand, and chapel/burial on the other, are the most useful in providing a representative view of the contemporary range of responses to death in the village.

Church/cremations

We turn first of all to a discussion of funerals falling into the category church/cremation, i.e. those taking place at the parish church at Hinderwell which are followed by cremation at Middlesbrough. There were four of these during fieldwork. Perhaps the first thing that can be said about them is that essentially they are not village events at all, since the funeral service takes place in the next village and is then followed by a forty-five minute interval whilst the coffin is transferred to Middlesbrough, where the rite concludes in the committal of the body at the crematorium. Little of the ritual actually takes place in the village, which is perhaps a reason for the low incidence of such funerals.

At the appointed time the hearse and taxis arrive at the house of the deceased; if the body has been retained it will be carried out to the hearse, but if not, it is simply a matter of seeing the 'mourners', as the close kin are known, into the waiting taxis. The cortège then drives to Hinderwell. If the deceased was a well known person in the village the family may have arranged for a coach to be available to transport those who wish to attend the funeral. The same local bus company is invariably hired to perform this service, which is more often provided after chapel funerals in the village, and the bus driver usually acknowledges the gravity of the occasion by wearing a black tie. The atmosphere on the bus during the short ride to Hinderwell is relaxed and friendly, with conversation usually focussing on the weather rather than the deceased. Many of the women dress in dark blue or black and although the men normally wear black ties, their sartorial solemnity contrasts starkly with the informal ambience which prevails.

At the church, early arrivals who have travelled independently go in and take their seats, being careful to leave the front pews vacant for the mourners. Usually the bus from Staithes arrives at about the same time as the taxis. The parish priest waiting at the churchyard gate then meets the coffin, turns, and, reading from the prayer book, leads the procession into the church. At the funerals observed, processions divided themselves into three distinct groups; first came priest, coffin and mourners; then women; followed by men at the rear. Coffin bearers are usually the taxi drivers employed by the funeral director. In fact, 'bearer' is a grossly inaccurate term by which to describe their role, as the coffin is not carried at all but simply lifted onto a small collapsible trolley, which is then wheeled into the church. At one funeral, that of a man who had previously been the village policeman, four police officers acted as bearers, but even they made use of the trolley. Inside the church, the mourners sit in a separate group at the front, and the funeral director normally sits with them. The taxi men, having brought in the coffin, vacate the building.

In all cases observed the standard Anglican liturgy was employed, consisting of one or two hymns, prayers and a brief address. On completion of this part of the rite of passage the coffin is taken from the church back to the road where the company stand and watch as it is loaded once again into the hearse. For most people this is the end of the funeral, although the committal has not yet taken place. On no occasion was a coach provided to take people to the crematorium and the few people who witnessed the final obsequies were those members of the immediate family who travelled in the taxis. The bus journey back to Staithes is, if anything, rather more light-hearted than the out-going one. Certainly no mention is likely to be made either of the deceased or the funeral. Indeed, on one occasion some of the passengers joked with the driver and tried to persuade him to take them off directly on an outing to the Lake District. Another distinctive feature of these funerals is that no tea is held after the cremation. The funeral therefore ends prematurely for the majority of people who attend, since the rite does not reach its natural resolution through a ritual of incorporation. Clearly, the response to death set in this framework is in sharp contrast to the situation described for the earlier period. Accordingly, it is rarely the choice of villagers, who readily classify it as the funerary style of the 'foreigner' who has settled locally.

Chapel/burials

In contrast to the church/cremation funeral, the category which we have labelled chapel/burial contains many more of the elements which were described in the historical material. All of the funerals in this group were of people born in the village, the majority of whom lived in 'Steeas' rather than 'Lane End'. This is reflected in the attendances, which even in the middle of the week never fell below fifty and which for the funeral of a village fisherman held on a Sunday afternoon, in November 1975, rose to over 200.

Once again, at the appointed time, members of the family gather at the house of the dead person. If the body has been kept at the memorial home, the hearse containing the coffin will stand outside, awaiting the appearance of the family members. It is usual for the officiating minister to call at about this time and say a short prayer with the relatives. Then, if the coffin is in the house, it is removed to the hearse and the mourners get into the taxi. The first time I saw this happen I was struck by the apparent ridiculousness of it, as the house from which the people were leaving was only about 150 yards away from the chapel. Wherever possible, this appears to be the normal procedure. Taxis have to be hired to take the mourners to Hinderwell for the interment and the apparent rationale on the part of the funeral director is one of rendering the full service at all costs. In many cases, however, the narrow passages and alleyways which characterise the village effectively prevent the use of vehicles and the coffin must be transported by means of the aforementioned trolley. Whilst singing around the coffin outdoors last took place in the early 1970s and the distribution of food and drink before leaving for the chapel only rarely occurs, funeral waitresses are still employed. Usually two in number, though four at larger funerals, they are traditionally dressed in white shawls and black sash. They accompany the coffin from the house to the chapel and, shunning the use of motor transport, they insist on walking immediately behind the hearse. The role of coffin bearers, as we have seen, is now usually assumed by the taxi men and a special request must be made by families who wish to choose their own bearers; but as it is a case of contracting-in to such an arrangement, most people tend to acquiesce to the standardised procedure set down by the funeral director. In exceptional circumstances though, the bearers may still be especially appointed; for example, in the case of the funeral of a fisherman which I observed, the four bearers were all men from the village, and even wore the traditional white bows in their lapels. However, the selection procedure for bearers does seem to have been modified. Whereas formerly it was the practice to choose close kin, or perhaps a friend of the deceased, today the emphasis seems to have shifted towards representation of specific groups or organisations with which the deceased was associated. Thus, in the example referred to, the bearers consisted of one fisherman, a village publican, a fellow-member of the deceased's pigeon fancier's club, and a trustee of the Wesleyan Methodist chapel, at which the funeral took place. An unlikely combination, one might feel.

When the funeral procession arrives at the chapel, the minister enters first, the coffin is brought in behind him, then come the waitresses and last of all, the mourners. Inside, the rest of the company have already taken their places. None of the chapels have a centre aisle, so the coffin is set down parallel to the first row of seats, grimly confronting the mourners at eye level. Above them, the minister's lectern is draped with a black tasselled cloth. To their left or right sit the funeral waitresses who always locate themselves apart from the rest of the congregation. Chapel funerals can be extremely impressive events and attendances are often greater even than those for the popular Harvest Festivals and Anniversaries. The minister's address tends on the whole to be longer than that of the rector in the parish church and it is more likely that he will have been well acquainted with the deceased – a fact which the congregation are quick to appreciate. When the service is concluded the minister descends from the pulpit, pauses briefly by the coffin, and then goes out. The coffin is wheeled or carried behind him, after which come the mourners, followed by the waitresses. When all of these have gone, the rest of the congregation leave the building. As the coffin is put into the hearse, the funeral waitresses walk to the foot of the bank which leads out of the old village; mourners get into the taxis and the rest make their way up the hill to the waiting coach. Some old people, deterred by the climb, may quietly go home at this point. The coach ride to Hinderwell is similar in atmosphere to that described for Anglican funerals. On several journeys I noticed men whom we passed on the road stop and remove their caps as the hearse went by.

On arrival at the cemetery the procession is reformulated and makes its way to the grave. Once there the coffin is lowered into the ground and the mourners ushered to the graveside. Artificial grass masks the bare earth. The moment of committal is the climax to the whole funeral and is usually the most distressing for the family. At the reference 'ashes to ashes', the gravedigger throws a handful of soil down onto the coffin. This often gives rise to loud weeping and vocalisations from the bereaved. These appear to have a cathartic effect and mark the beginning of a process of readjustment among the most distressed mourners. As if to emphasise this, a member of the assembly may, on the conclusion of the prayers, strike up one of the old funeral hymns. This practice of singing round the grave, I was told by the gravedigger, is quite peculiar to chapel funerals from Staithes; none of the other villagers in the parish ever do it, nor do Staithes Anglicans. In recent years though, since a man and a woman who had both led the singing have died, it has not been so common. When this final hymn is ended, all of the people solemnly file past the grave, each pausing to read the details recorded on the coffin plate.

Everyone is then transported back to the village where all who wish may go to the funeral tea, which is now usually held in the Sunday Schoolroom of the chapel concerned. Large quantities of food are spread out on trestle tables and the assembled company sits down to eat with gusto. The traditional ham sandwiches and fruitcake, or 'funeral bread', are invariably provided and the waitresses are always on hand to replenish supplies and serve more tea. This ritual meal concludes the funeral but in the weeks after the death the closest female kin of the deceased may continue to wear black, especially on Sundays. A widow will probably remain indoors for about ten days after her husband's funeral. In the past, ritualised avoidance of attendance at chapel was the accepted practice, but today, by contrast, it is normal for a whole family to go to chapel on the first Sunday morning after the funeral. No other mourning injunctions now prevail.

Summary

This is not the place to begin an extended discussion of anthropological theories of ritual and the various problems of interpretation and analysis which they raise. Nevertheless, by way of conclusion to our description of birth and death rites, it may be useful to make a few general comments.

An obvious criticism of the account, which we might anticipate at this point before discussing further in Chapter 9, is that it appears to represent the people of Staithes in an antique light, clinging to customs which have apparently disappeared elsewhere, but nevertheless doomed, as older villagers die off, to come into line with more generally observed practices. Such a view is rejected here for two reasons.

Firstly, the responses to birth and death are demonstrably subject to modification, accretion and reconstruction. We have therefore contrasted the situation in the village at the beginning of the century with the present, in order to highlight the forms which change may take and identify the mechanisms which precipitate it. In general, we have argued that certain communal aspects of both sets of rituals have been usurped by professional and bureaucratic agencies. Health administrators, funeral directors, clergy and ministry have all in turn helped to erode certain communal obligations and duties and, with them, a sense of control over life-critical events. Villagers certainly sense this, and, as we have suggested, in some cases bemoan the changes. Yet while change has taken place, it has not always obliterated ritual, and, as some of the birth rites reveal, new folk elements continue to emerge; for example the surrogate rite of churching, developed in response to the abandonment of the official rite.

Secondly, it is clear that contemporary ritual in the village cannot be dismissed as the vestigial remains of some more overtly religious past. It is both too extensive and too carefully prescribed for this to be the case. In trying to make sense of it, we should therefore adopt the viewpoint of Ortner, who argues that rituals 'dramatize basic assumptions of fact and value in the culture' (1978: 2).

The question then becomes one of disentangling what the rituals are 'saying'. It has, of course, often been argued that what they 'say' is less important than what they 'do': i.e. do they achieve 'group equilibrium'? But such a viewpoint overlooks an important dimension of the rites and is certainly unconcerned with their content and meaning. The processual approach, on the other hand, allows us to observe rites of passage, which for sociologists otherwise mean little more than formal events in a church or chapel, within their broader social and interpretive context. As Ortner correctly points out, 'Rituals do not begin with the eternal verities, but arrive at them' (1978: 2–3). In so doing they tell us something about the 'fundamental cultural assumptions' (*ibid.*: 3) of the society in which they occur. In Staithes they appear to be bound up with a concern for communal identity. In discussing chapel life and the annual cycle it has been clear that villagers frequently capitalise on opportunities for presenting stylised self-images to a wider audience. The displays therefore serve to mark off village life from that in the wider society. In the observances of birth and death, however, there is less emphasis upon this than upon a shared contribution to village culture and continuity. Birth and death are essential for a society to continue; the rituals which attend them can in turn be powerful expressions of the *type* of persistence which is valued. In Staithes they interweave individual uncertainty with the 'facticity' of the community. They are therefore powerful representations of the ways in which men and women create their society.

8

Occupational beliefs

The economic life of Staithes has been dominated historically by two industries – fishing and mining; both serve to expose the worker to extreme and hostile environments and carry particularly high risks of accident or injury. As we saw in Chapter 2, stories of fishing disasters abound in the village. Indeed, in the past losses at sea and drownings were so frequent that it was customary for every item of the fisherman's clothing to be embroidered with his initials to facilitate identification of the body, even after prolonged immersion in seawater had produced its worst effects. Equally numerous are tales of accidents as well as serious and often gruesome injuries in the ironstone mines, where cramped conditions and an alien environment seemed to compound misfortune. Today, though fewer in number, fishing accidents persist and even the high technology of the potash mine has not succeeded in eliminating the risk of injury or fatality.[1]

We are concerned here with the particular consequences which these dangers might have in the realm of folk religion, namely the tendency for them to give rise to a set of occupational observances which come to constitute the 'superstitions' of fishing and mining. In such occupational contexts, where uncertainty forms a part of the individual's everyday work experience, it is possible that certain coping mechanisms will be generated which serve to mitigate the threat of unfortunate events. Malinowski, who expounded such an anxiety-ritual theory at length, makes his position clear in an oft-quoted passage on Trobriand fishing.

While in the villages on the inner lagoon fishing is done in an easy and absolutely reliable manner by the method of poisoning, yielding abundant results without danger and uncertainty, there are on the shores of the open sea dangerous modes of fishing and also types in which the yield greatly varies according to whether shoals of fish appear beforehand or not. It is most significant that in the lagoon fishing, where man can rely completely upon his knowledge and skill, magic does not exist, while in the open-sea fishing, full of danger and uncertainties, there is extensive magical ritual to ensure safety and good results. (Malinowski 1954: 30–1)

Malinowski's final sentence indicates the dual dangers of fishing. These are, as Poggie *et al.* have stated, 'risk related to "production" and risk related to "person" ' (Poggie *et al.* 1976: 258). Not only is the good catch a matter of

uncertain outcome but the physical well-being of the fisherman is also
threatened. Magic is therefore invoked in order to secure the success of the
enterprise at two levels. When both types of danger are absent and a relative
mastery of the situation is possible, we find, as in the case of the inner lagoon
fishing, that magical strategies disappear.

Whilst Malinowski is particularly concerned with the relationship
between uncertainty and magical *acts*, other writers have pointed to the
connection with various forms of *belief*. Gouldner, in his study of a North
American gypsum mine, writes,

Miners handled their anxieties in several ways, one of which was the fatalistic
acceptance of danger as ultimately unavoidable; 'it will get you in the end'. Yet this
attitude of resignation was only one side of an ambivalent response to the dangers of
the mine, for they adhered also to a set of beliefs which focussed upon adjustment
possibilities, and strengthened their hopes of coming out uninjured. Their beliefs
were expressed in time-worn stories, passed down by word of mouth through
generations of miners.   (Gouldner 1955: 117)

Such beliefs and practices are best seen in relation to other occupational
factors. It is well known, for example, that extreme occupations like fishing
and mining tend to be accompanied by highly developed subcultures.
Accordingly, members of groups like the Hull fishermen (Tunstall 1962)
and the Ashton miners (Dennis *et al.* 1969) were inclined to spend most of
their leisure-time with workmates, where in each case subcultural and
occupational norms and values had grown up around the work-group. This
inward orientation frequently results in certain stereotypical societal
reactions to the group in question, such as in the popular conception,
reported by Tunstall, that fishermen are 'a race apart' (1962: 166) or the
belief among Gouldner's gypsum miners that they were considered by the
rest of society to be 'a strange lot' (1955: 122). Members of such
occupations may therefore come to be regarded as deviant by the wider
society, in so far as they adhere to a set of values which is in some way in
conflict with the normative order. As writers in the sociology of deviance
have shown, it is precisely this situation which provides the structural
conditions wherein incipiently deviant behaviour and values may flourish –
a process usually referred to as 'deviancy-amplification' (Wilkins 1964).
This point should be kept in mind when considering the occupational beliefs
found in Staithes today and may help us to explain the anachronistic
persistence of various subcultural superstitious elements within what is
more generally deemed a 'secular' society.

Methodism and superstition

We saw in Chapter 4 that the early Methodists had often sought for outright
confrontation with the beliefs, attitudes and way of life of the men and

women along the coast. Yet while nonconformity did establish itself as the predominant form of religious expression in the village, the popular culture was not simply obliterated in the process. The early Methodists certainly condemned the local culture which they found, but subsequently, during the period of consolidation and in relation to the denominationalising tendencies taking place in the movement as a whole, the new culture began to establish a different relationship with the old. Popular ideas, beliefs and practices were gradually *infused* by the influence of Methodism and there is even a sense in which the old culture found itself invigorated by the inclusion of new elements that served to highlight its rich and varied textures. Village Methodism, as we have seen, was then able to take on a highly idiosyncratic cast in which aspects of belief and practice otherwise holding no brief in official theology gained a central importance in the minds of villagers and indeed in some cases became indistinguishable from chapel religion itself. Methodism could not eradicate these elements; it could, however, exist alongside them in some measure.

Occupational beliefs are a case in point. The evangelists had clearly launched a full-blown attack on the superstitiousness and Sabbath-breaking of the local fishermen, but it is apparent that their achievements were only partial. Indeed, if we 'triangulate' our earlier account of nonconformist growth and the establishment of a sacred culture by means of reference to the writings of local historians and commentators in the nineteenth century, we see that these authors, whose bias is essentially Anglican and middle class, not only make little reference to the 'civilising' influences which the Methodists are so eager to attribute to their faith, but they frequently draw attention to the persistence of superstitious beliefs among the fishermen, well into the period when nonconformity had become entrenched locally. The following passages illustrate how these writers wasted no opportunity to both romanticise and belittle the 'quaint' habits of the fisherfolk.

The fishermen are a stalwart race; blunt, rude and with a strong dash of superstition . . . The fishermen regard Good Fridays, Christmas Days, and Sundays with so much veneration, or more properly perhaps, superstition, that they will on no account put to sea on one of them, as that would be 'unlucky'.

(Gordon 1869: 111 and 112)

The fishermen, although hardy, brave, and adventurous, are nevertheless, strongly tinctured with superstition, to an extent scarcely credible in these days of enlightenment. (Ord 1846: 299)

Or as a correspondent of *The Times* noted, 'The Staithes folk are imbued with all manner of quaint superstitions, which, whatever their origin, convey today no meaning and have no reason for their observance' (*The Times* 22 Sept. 1885). Equally baffled, it seems, were the local magistrates. On one occasion they were called upon to hear the case of a young couple

12. Abraham footbridge. Note the cliff path to Hinderwell, top right. *Photograph by Tom Watson, early 1900s.*

from Staithes who were charged with assaulting a woman whom they claimed had 'witched' the house they were building. The female defendant described how 'on the day she carried the first stone for building the house, the prosecutor [i.e. the alleged 'witch'] fell down on her knees and prayed the house might fall, and she (the defendant) might be carried out of it in baskets. On that day twelve months the house fell' (*Whitby Gazette* 12 June 1858). Even their 'witchcraft', however, was adjudged to be of inferior quality.

They have a firm belief in witchcraft, but a debased form of witchcraft of the *jettatura* order, the witch being wholly unconscious of his or her power of evil. Until quite recently – and I am informed that by some of the older inhabitants the custom is secretly maintained – it was customary, when a smack or coble had had a protracted run of ill-fortune, for the wives of the crew and owners of the boat to assemble at midnight and, in deep silence, to slay a pigeon whose heart they extracted, stuck full of pins, and burned over a charcoal fire. Whilst this operation was in process the unconscious witch would come to the door, dragged thither unwittingly by the irresistible potency of the charm, and the conspirators would then make her some propitiatory present. (*The Times* 22 Sept. 1885)

Notwithstanding the ideological bias of these accounts, they must be

13. The beck continues to provide shelter for the cobles during bad weather.
Photograph by Richard Cale, 1981.

taken into consideration as another perspective on religious culture in the village during the middle decades of the nineteenth century. They suggest that a number of items of superstitious belief continued to retain a legitimatory presence in local society, throughout a period which, outwardly at least, seems to be characterised by the achievements of Methodism. How could the beliefs persist in the midst of such an apparently unsuitable religious climate? The answer to this question is probably related to the ways in which hazardous occupations give rise not only to magical observances, but also to entire subcultures, having their own symbols, imagery, metaphor and sense of history.

In Staithes, the task of gaining a livelihood through fishing and seafaring has generated an important cultural heritage which, as we suggested in Chapter 2, has persisted even though the industry which inspired it has diminished in size and influence. In the nineteenth century, when for a time the village was entirely given over to the industry, it was the constraints and experience of the fishing trade which shaped the hopes, aspirations and fears of the populace. Nellie Erichsen, an artist who visited Staithes in the 1880s, gives us something of the flavour of this in her description of the fishing family's living-room.

The seafaring life of the family is everywhere evident; the pictures are all nautical, several prints of shipwrecks, a large oleograph, *The Fisherman's Return*, and, the gem of the collection, a real oil painting of a full rigged vessel. Texts are scattered here and there, all having reference to the sea, and what is known as a gospel compass hangs conspicuously above the fire.   (Erichsen 1886: 468)

Erichsen's description gives us some insight into one particular setting where the old beliefs and the new were strikingly juxtaposed. Contrary to what we might have expected, there is little evidence to suggest that after the arrival of Methodism, and in deference to some more abstract notion of God's providential care, the fisherfolk abandoned their traditional beliefs in luck and fate. Instead, they appear to have spontaneously invoked particular aspects of the sacred culture as protection against suffering or accident. This is nicely illustrated in the names with which they chose to endow their cobles. Thus in the pre-Methodist period we see a predominance of names reflecting family loyalties or the economic realities of the fishing: for example, *The Brothers, Nancy, Hopewell Success* and *Happy Return*.[2] Later, however, the names draw heavily on Methodist sources of inspiration such as *Pilot Me, Myzpah, Good Samaritan* and *Kindly Light*. It proved difficult to obtain information on ministerial attitudes to such appellations in the past. On the one hand, we might expect criticism and disapproval, based on a sense of vulgarisation of things sacred; alternatively, ministers may have actively encouraged the practices and exploited any opportunity to further implant the sacred culture. For the fishermen, who according to one writer were also in the habit of carrying ring-shaped 'luck stones' fastened into their cobles (Leonard 1976), the names would seem to have had a protective purpose as much magical as Methodist. Indeed, I was told by one minister in the area that the fisherfolk had actually regarded it as unlucky to 'take a preacher off in a coble', a belief which strikes at the heart of the ambivalent relationship between the two cultures. Likewise, in the case of Sabbath observance, which the evangelists fought so hard to secure, an unintended consequence seems to have been the belief that to fish on Sunday was not only morally reprehensible, but might also be 'unlucky' as well.

In similar fashion, many of the hymns and sacred songs of Methodism resonated with meaning for the fisherfolk. Again, the ministry may have consciously exploited the content of the *Methodist Hymn Book*, as well as *Moodey and Sankey* and *Redemption* in a bid to find material relevant to local experience. Methodism was, of course, 'born in song' and in Staithes the singing of pieces containing stirring sea-going images appears to have exercised a powerful influence over the fisherfolk. An important example of this may be found in the circumstances surrounding the Staithes lifeboat disaster of 27 November 1888, described in the *Primitive Methodist Magazine* as follows: 'the Staithes lifeboat capsized and the crew were given up for lost. They were miraculously saved by the crew of a passing steamer, who heard them singing hymns' (*Primitive Methodist Magazine* 1932: 126). On several occasions I was told this story by members of the chapels, who placed great emphasis on the hymn-singing; yet the *Whitby Gazette* account, published just three days after the incident occurred, whilst devoting a whole page to a detailed description of the event, is notable for a complete absence of any reference to the singing whatsoever.

By such careful editing and embellishment of historical accounts, the safeguarding powers of the sacred culture were established; yet the popular culture showed few signs of capitulation before the incoming faith. Instead, the most unlikely alliances occurred. For example, considerable emphasis had been placed in Methodist teaching on the evils of drink and alcoholic dissipation and great stress had been laid on 'pub' and 'chapel' as diametrically opposed centres of village life. Yet, as we have seen, one popular aspect of nonconformity, the hymn-singing, actually found a comfortable niche within the smoky pub atmosphere. With the notable addition of a 'juke box' containing numerous recordings of popular religious tunes, the 'custom' continues today. To the outsider, the phenomenon might appear anachronistic and it has certainly provoked the scorn of numerous ministers who have persistently attacked the idiosyncracies of Staithes Methodism, but for villagers, no distinction is made between two cultures which present themselves as quite capable of coexistence. If commensal relations of this type are possible and the members of a particular community are capable of subscribing selectively to discrete aspects of otherwise counterposed belief systems, then the continuance of quasi-magical occupational beliefs in the village today begins to look more explicable. Indeed, these unofficial beliefs may exhibit a resilience which allows them to persist long after the 'official' doctrines of nonconformity have lost their conversionist edge. If they do so, it is because they continue to have some relevance to practical, everyday life experiences.

Occupational beliefs today

During the period of fieldwork, observations, interviews and informal conversations of various kinds all served to reveal a rich underlife of occupational beliefs which appear to predict, control or otherwise influence the fickle forces of luck, fate and chance. A variety of words, situations and actions were therefore deemed 'bad luck'.

1   Do not launch a boat on a Friday.
2   Do not put new gear on a boat or start any new type of fishing on a Friday.
3   Do not utter the word 'pig', especially in any situation connected with

fishing, e.g. when baiting lines or when at sea. The word 'grecian' should always be substituted.[3]

4   [Women] do not wind wool after dark as this is winding fishermen to their graves.

5   Do not put to sea after meeting a woman on the way to the boat (also applicable to miners on their way to the pit).

6   Do not whistle at sea.

7   Do not put anything white on board a boat.

The beliefs and taboos are, of course, subject to varying degrees of observance, and few would readily admit to taking them seriously or submitting to their injunctions. However, this should not necessarily lead us to suppose that the beliefs no longer have any genuine social significance and the subject of superstition, indeed, remains the source of some embarrassment. Moreover, as we pointed out in our introductory and methodological chapters, the study of folk religion is plagued with difficulties arising from the inchoate nature of the beliefs and practices. The subjective feelings which surround them are also ambivalent. Accordingly, respondents often adopt strategies of personal avoidance when identifying particular observances, for example, by referring to a particular incident in the past as illustrative of a set of beliefs and practices which are now extinct. In other cases, the part played by the respondent in the narrative might be that of the rational debunker of the myths and their fallacious reasoning. Consider the following statements, the first of which was made by an eighty-year-old retired fisherman.

1   There was some [who were] very superstitious, they didn't like to hear you talk about foxes when they were baiting a line. If you went in when the [fishermen] were baiting a line and you said, 'fox hounds is out today', oh! they'd play 'Hamlet', you know. They didn't like pigs either, fishermen didn't like to hear you talk about pigs.

Or a retired miner:

2   The miners were superstitious on pigs. Now I was going to work one morning... I went to Grinkle for a few weeks... and there was a lad called —, his father had pigs and the sow had got out and he was chasing it at 'Lane End'... kicking it and doing, and I says, 'Eh! what are you doing man?' Oh, he starts to swear about this sow, you know, and I said to him, 'Have you had your breakfast?' He says, 'Yes.' I says, 'What have you had?' He says, 'I've had bacon and egg.' 'Why', I says, 'what's the difference between the bacon that you've eaten and that then? Leave the thing alone.'

A retired fisherman:

3   Some used to be very superstitious about pigs or a woman, meeting a woman when they were going to work...
Q. What was this about pigs?

They were very superstitious, they didn't like to see a pig or hear about a pig, or foxes, all different things, they were terrible about such as that.

Another retired fisherman:

4 If someone mentioned a pig while the fishermen were baiting the lines, they'd stand up and walk away . . . and if you mentioned it at sea you did it at your peril.

Another ex-miner:

5 Aye, there used to be some people very superstitious here, they didn't like to meet a woman before they went to work. We were going to work one morning and we met a lady called — and she said, 'Well lads, I'm sorry I've had to pass you, but I can't help it, it's one of those things, I've had to come down.' I said, 'You needn't bother as far as I'm concerned because I see my mother every morning . . . and it doesn't matter to me about seeing a woman.'

All of the above statements contain the implication that the speaker never took the observances seriously, that it was always 'fishermen' or 'miners' in general who believed in such things – this despite the fact that each respondent was himself a former fisherman or miner. Statements two and five go a stage further and reveal a self-consciously rational view and measure of scorn for the beliefs and practices. The implicit meaning of these two anecdotes is that the speaker remained aloof from superstition and tried to discourage it in others. We thus have two categories of statement: one which ascribes superstitiousness to others but not oneself and another which demonstrates a personal contempt for irrational beliefs. I could in fact find no-one who would freely admit to having been influenced personally by these beliefs or to have made a point of observing the taboos.

A similar situation prevailed when examining aspects of contemporary folk belief in the village, where individuals were equally reluctant to acknowledge personal observance. The following incident took place in the home of a retired couple along with their middle-aged and married daughter. Earlier that week the daughter, an habitué of salerooms, had seen a painting which she wanted to buy. Describing it, she said it depicted, 'Chickens, ducks, *grecians* and all sorts.' 'What are grecians?' I asked. 'They're pigs, but I don't like to call 'em that in front of my mam and dad', she replied. Whereupon her father interrupted, saying, 'We calls 'em pigs too.' An embarrassed silence followed and the subject was quickly changed. On another occasion I was in the house of a part-time fisherman, the television was switched on and a children's cartoon was showing. At one point a pig came on the screen and the man's daughter jumped up and shouted, 'piggy, piggy'. 'There', the man said, pointing to the child, 'the little 'un knows that pigs is unlucky, so she says it over again. If she says it [my wife] says, "that's it, your dad won't get any lobsters now", but it doesn't stop her.' When asked how much importance he attached to the notion of the pig as an

14. The wide scaurs, exposed at low tide, were an important source of bait for the fisherfolk. *Photograph by Tom Watson, early 1900s.*

unlucky animal, the man replied awkwardly, 'there's a lot gets upset if they hear it'. 'And what about you?' I asked. 'Oh, I never bother with it', was the self-contradictory reply.

In both of these incidents the participants, when questioned, had denied any personal identification with the superstition, yet each had spontaneously demonstrated an observance or recognition of the taboo. Similar responses are reported by Mullen in his study of folk beliefs among Texas fishermen (1969: 215) and also by Poggie *et al.* in their account of taboos among New England fishermen (1976: 260). The illustrations from Staithes suggest a felt tension on the part of respondents who are clearly reluctant to make explicit any personal identification with beliefs and practices which, to an outsider, might appear irrational or even slightly bizarre. On the other hand, in some cases there was clear evidence of superstitious observance which no degree of circumlocution on the part of villagers could conceal. In these instances a clear relationship begins to emerge between overt superstitiousness and experience of work in a dangerous environment. As far as it is possible to tell, the examples which follow were taken very seriously by those involved.

The first example concerns the arrival of a new fishing coble in the village. Shortly after the fieldwork began, two Staithes fishermen who had recently sold their old coble were awaiting the completion of a new boat, which was being built at Whitby. When the boat was finished it was given its sea trials. These were carried out one Thursday in April and upon successful completion the boat was passed ready for collection the following day. Despite their eagerness to obtain the new boat in order to commence fishing as soon as possible, the men absolutely refused to collect it on the following day, since Friday was regarded by all concerned as most inauspicious for taking possession of a coble and bringing it into the village for the first time. Collection was therefore postponed until the following day. The Friday concerned was in fact fine and sunny; about midday, shortly after the morning's catch had been landed, one of the fishermen from the new boat approached a group of men standing on the sea-front. 'You're missing a good day today', said one of the men. 'I don't care', the young man replied, 'we wouldn't bring her on a Friday.' His father, who was also present, added in concurrence, 'no, you're right, you can't bring her on a Friday'. The boat duly arrived the next day. Some time later I spoke to the owner of the new coble in his home and asked why he had refused to collect the boat on the appointed day.

Well, Friday's the Devil's day isn't it? I know it's superstitious but I would never forgive myself if anything happened. We never bend gear [i.e. put new equipment on the boat] on a Friday either . . . when I worked in the shipyards at Teesside and we had union meetings . . . the shop steward would never call them on a Friday, it's the Devil's day.

The remarks were put with seriousness, tinged with embarrassment. The man clearly recognised the apparent irrationality of his actions but was nevertheless not prepared to take the risk of beginning a new enterprise on a day when such activity is considered to be threatened by the forces of ill luck.

Observance of Friday as an unlucky day was further borne out by other fishermen. The day after the new coble's sea trials was, as we have seen, one of good weather; in fact, it was the first really fine day for several weeks. For some while the part-time fishermen of the village had been awaiting the opportunity to commence fishing with their crab and lobster pots. Yet none of them took advantage of the fine day, preferring instead to wait until a 'safer' day – the following morning – when, ironically, conditions were far less suitable. When I remarked on this observance to a member of one of the Methodist chapels, he confessed to being mystified by it. 'I can't understand it', he said, 'it's not as if they come to chapel or 'owt.' For him the avoidance would have been intelligible if the men concerned had been 'overtly' religious in practice; yet to the observer, the occupational belief appeared as one having no referent within nonconformity. But in the mind of the villager, the two seemed inextricably intertwined and no distinction between 'folk' and 'official' religion could ever have seemed appropriate.

Some of the taboos which have been described are clearly related to the uncertainties surrounding the fishing trade, and fishermen observe the injunctions in the belief that they may thereby secure good catches. In other circumstances some fishermen seek to explain unfortunate events through a theodicy grounded in terms of avarice. Thus one man suggested to me that the drowning of a fellow-fisherman, some years earlier, had resulted from the dead man's over-eagerness to go off to his pots, even though conditions were unsuitable. In another case, a part-time fisherman lost several lobster pots when they became badly tangled during a spell of rough weather. Explaining to me that after much effort he had finally managed to recover nine of the twenty pots, he added that in previous years he had only worked sixteen pots in each 'fleet'. He therefore felt that in putting four extra pots on he had been 'greedy': 'and that's it you see, that's what you get when you're greedy'.

The character of such statements as theodicies is clearly apparent. They assume the existence of a moral universe which is somehow homeostatically regulated and in which evil, in this case greed, is rewarded with evil, so that those who seek more than their fair share must run the risk of restitutive sanctions. In common with other theodicies from the folk realm, these beliefs can be invoked *post hoc* in a manner which enables them to serve as rationalisations of unfortunate events. If explanations for such events *are* sought, if individuals do experience, as Berger claims, a congenital compulsion to impose order and meaning on reality (1973: 31), then in countless situations it is folk religion which provides a repository of acceptable solutions. The inability of the institutional church to bridge the gap between ideal and real experience was made clear on a number of occasions in Staithes when these and similar beliefs served to mitigate encounters with misfortune. A final illustration will suffice; it concerns an occasion when I visited a worker from the potash mine, who was also a part-time fisherman, and found him soaking a badly swollen ankle in a bowl of water. He explained that he had had an accident that morning in his boat when jumping down from the engine box. His explanation of the event bears the typical hallmarks of folk religion.

It's funny, some of the blokes at work had been asking me about pigs – I'd say, 'don't mention those bloody things' – and since then they've been on about it all the time. Then just yesterday a bloke came up and said, 'hey, I've got a book about superstitions and it mentions pigs'. And then today this goes and happens.

Summary

We have shown that occupational beliefs and practices continue to exist in Staithes and have suggested that their prevalence seems to be, at least in

15. The old village is regularly pounded by high seas. *Photograph by Richard Cale, 1981.*

part, related to the high risks involved in fishing and mining. Such an explanation could entail unwelcome overtones of psychological reductionism, however, and it is preferable that we go beyond it to show how folk elements are able to reproduce themselves and persist in a specific social context. It appears that folk religion derives considerable supportive benefit from the presence of certain structural conditions, such as closely knit communal and kinship networks. Moreover, the occupational subculture not only gives expression to the beliefs, but also acts as an insulator against the dominant belief systems of the wider society. Parkin (1967) has argued that so-called 'deviant voters' (in his view all Labour voters) are often sustained in their deviance through membership of subcultures such as traditional working class communities or work place groups, which act as 'buffers' against the prevailing and largely conservative values of society in general. Where these subcultures are well developed, political deviance, i.e. a rejection of conservative attitudes, can be sustained; where, on the other hand, the individual is not the member of such a subculture, then deviant political behaviour is less likely to emerge. Similarly, in the case of religion, when those in the wider society are, as Wilson puts it 'for most of their time, in most of their activities . . . very little touched – if they are touched at all – by any direct religious intimations' (1976: 6), then we would expect seemingly irrational behaviour, such as that embodied in superstitious practices, to disappear. Conversely, religious deviance might persist where an effective 'buffer' is present to keep out burgeoning rational tendencies.

The theory would help to explain the embarrassment and lack of personal involvement which surround respondents' accounts of occupational taboos. When villagers recognise that modern society has an ever-diminishing place for religion and traditional values, adherence to superstitions, and their recounting to an outsider, would make them appear naive and foolish. Indeed, the very act of telling must have brought their incongruity with the values and mores of the wider society sharply into focus. In the village itself, however, and particularly within the tightly knit occupational subculture, superstitions retain credibility and enjoy free expression. This ability to resist the forces of secularisation seems rather less surprising if we reconsider for a moment their earlier survival in the face of evangelical opposition. The tension which existed between the two belief systems, as we have seen, was reduced in time and resolved in a form of mutual interdependence whereby Methodism both reinvigorated some of the occupational beliefs and was in turn moulded by them.

Brief comment should also be made on the content of some of the beliefs which have been described. The superstition which holds that it is unlucky to meet a woman on the way to work seems, for example, to lend itself to sociological explanation. If we consider the sexual division of labour which existed in the village during the period when fishing and mining were the dominant industries, it is apparent that in both cases it was men who figured as primary breadwinners. The catchers of fish and hewers of ironstone were men, and whilst, particularly in the fishing, women provided vital ancillary labour, a rigid division between 'men's' and 'women's' work was in force. Women never went out in the cobles and only in exceptional wartime circumstances did they go down the mines.

At the same time differences existed in the conjugal roles of husband and wife and a similar division of labour was present within the family, with certain tasks – collecting, drying and chopping firewood, tending the allotment – seen as the duties of a husband, and others – cooking, knitting, repairing clothes – equally clearly those of a wife. Elizabeth Bott (1971) in *Family and Social Network* shows how this type of familial organisation, which she describes as incorporating a 'segregated conjugal role relationship' (1971: 53), usually occurs where the family is part of a 'close-knit' social network (*ibid.*: 59). This form of social network was highly developed in Staithes in the nineteenth and early twentieth centuries. Gluckman, in the preface to the second edition of Bott's work, points out how her theory casts considerable light on relationships in traditional societies. He refers, for example, to the way in which it helps to explain the rigid sexual division of labour which is found in societies where men's and women's work are clearly divided and kept apart by ritual injunctions. He quotes Arensberg, who describes the situation in rural Ireland, where,

> Immemorial folklore bolsters this division. The woman is unlucky to masculine enterprises, for instance: it is dangerous to see a woman on the road to the fair. Likewise, man is dangerous to woman's work. If he so much as takes his lighted pipe out of the house while she is churning, he may 'take the butter', through fairy magic...
>
> (Arensberg 1937, quoted in Gluckman 1971: xx)

The observation is obviously helpful in explaining the taboo on seeing a woman before work, which once existed in Staithes. Men setting off to their work, to a hazardous and dangerous world in which women had no place, feared the contagion which might result from meeting a member of the opposite sex. Women did vital work in the community, but this was essentially based on the home, which men left behind each day; consequently to meet a woman *en route* to the pit or boat represented an intrusion whereby the separateness of the two worlds was violated. Today the injunction is no longer observed. The disappearance of the superstition is probably related to a breakdown in the rigid sexual division of labour both within the family and elsewhere. If women are also going to work at the same time as men, if not actually in some cases to the same work, a purely practical difficulty places itself in the way of superstitious observance. The disappearance probably also signals some improvement in the status of women in the community.

We have seen that in the village certain animals, notably pigs and foxes, are the object of taboos. I was also told that further down the coast at Filey, the rabbit was regarded in similar fashion. Any reference to these animals, particularly in situations concerned with work, such as during the preparation of the lines, was strongly discouraged. Respondents explained the injunction in one of two ways. Some emphasised risk related to 'production' and explained how the mention of a pig could ruin the chance of a good catch on the next fishing trip; whilst others, speaking in terms of risk relating to 'person', believed that the word was in itself an augury of coming danger or misfortune. Accordingly, it was the usual practice to substitute the word 'grecian' for pig or alternatively to refer slightly contemptuously to 'the gentleman of the sty'. A similar practice is noted by Firth among the Malay fishermen, whose ritual injunctions include 'avoidance of animal terms while at sea and substitution for them of other more neutral and more honorific terms' (Firth 1966: 122). Poggie *et al.* also found the pig to be a taboo creature for the New England fishermen (1976: 260). Leach has considered the problems posed by the use of animal categories in taboos and verbal abuse and argues that where animals are the focus of ritual attitudes then 'one fact that is commonly relevant and needs to be taken into consideration is the edibility of the species in question' (1972: 43). This does not appear helpful here, however, for as Leach's own set of categories makes clear, the animals in question occupy quite different structural locations (*ibid.*: 58–9). Thus, pigs come into the category of edible farm animal whilst foxes and rabbits are both ambiguous; the former occupy 'the borderline between edible field and inedible wild animals' and the latter hover between 'game or vermin' (*ibid.*). The animals' significance in the present context does not appear to lie in this direction so much as in a common factor which they all share as *land* creatures. The crucial symbolism therefore seems to point to the opposition between land and sea. As we saw in Chapter 2, a strong rivalry still persists between the coastal and agricultural villages in the Cleveland and North Yorkshire area. Indeed, in Staithes itself the term 'farmer' is one of abuse, signifying a general stupidity, ignorance and incompetence. It is this animus towards things rural and agricultural which may give some clue to the taboos. Pigs and foxes are somehow central elements of a rural life which is abhorrent to the fisherfolk. Even today, many villagers are loath to be away from the sea for long periods and will often take their annual holidays in other Yorkshire coastal towns rather than go inland or further afield.[4] Interestingly, then, it is this deep love of the sea which has given rise to and shaped the content of occupational beliefs and also some of the unofficial elements within the local nonconformist culture, both of which, in certain settings, exude a quasi-magical and protective aura.

9

Conclusions

The purposes of this concluding chapter are two-fold. Firstly, we must attempt to draw together the empirical data which has been presented on religious life in Staithes in order that the reader may arrive at some final picture of folk religion in the community. Secondly, using this material as a basis, it is important that we offer some remarks on the implications of our findings for a broader understanding of religion in contemporary society. This is not to say that we wish to proceed inductively from the particular to the general, but some further comment is called for if our argument is to go beyond the social and temporal limits of the study area and point the way to an improved understanding of religion outside the institutional churches.

Perhaps the most obvious reaction to our description of folk religion in Staithes is that it seems at times to lean heavily in the direction of the folkloristic, in a manner which is uncharacteristic of the interests of contemporary sociology. Is the investigation of seemingly irrational, odd and fragmentary beliefs really within the domain of social science? Should the sociology of religion not address itself instead to ideas and actions which are recognisable to both actor and researcher alike as unambiguously religious? Should not a sociology of the churches, of sectarianism or even of theology be our subject matter? The reasoning implicit in these questions, that the sociologist should not waste time on a few scattered beliefs and practices which are ultimately beneath intellectual concern but concentrate instead on institutional religiosity of one sort or another, is rejected here. We have tried to argue that religion may not always conform to the limits set for it by religious organisations and that it may exist in a variety of forms – superstition, half-belief, local custom – all of which hang together as a heterogeneous complex of unofficial elements. However insignificant these may seem individually, when taken together they are demonstrably part of an intricate and varied folk religion. To set the limits for sociological enquiry purely by reference to what is 'obviously' religious, i.e. that which in a commonsense manner is accepted by both laity and clergy as religion, is not only difficult to do – the lay person, for example, is frequently unclear about what is 'true religion' and what is not – but is also to commit the error of overlooking a variety of unofficial religious forms. Moreover, it is a line of enquiry which has typically raised more questions than it has answered.

Secularisation, for example, seen in this light has generally been treated in terms of the decline of church affiliation, religious rites of passage, belief in God, etc., with little reference to the subjective dimension of religious worldviews (e.g. Wilson 1966; Glock and Stark 1965). Similarly, the sociological study of sectarianism, in developing numerous typologies, classifications and continua has sought to explain the proliferation of sects in a way which often fails to recount the sectarian world in terms of the meanings which it has for those who inhabit it (e.g. Beckford 1975; Whitworth 1975).

The present study has therefore attempted to offer an account of folk religion in a way which makes it intelligible within the frame of reference of those who adhere to its beliefs and practices. For, as Towler states, the sociology of religion ought to 'grasp the meanings attached to various situations strictly in terms of the components of the respective people's own mental worlds' (1974: 2). If the approach has produced accounts of what appear curious beliefs and practices, then this reflects upon a commitment to a particular methodological objective rather than any deliberate attempt to seek out quaint or exotic superstitions. That the beliefs and practices described may appear unusual to the sociologically 'informed' is as much a testimony to the blinkers imposed by the over-systematised, church-oriented and theologically constrained approach of much sociology of religion as to any quality inherent in the beliefs and practices themselves. 'Survivals' from an earlier and more primitive culture were, of course, the concern of nineteenth-century folklore (Tylor 1871). But to speak of 'survivals' is merely to beg the question of *why* the beliefs and practices have persisted. My contention is that they endure not as some functionless relic of earlier times – the appendix of the religious organism – but rather because they continue to have a legitimising relevance in everyday life. Whereas the folklorists were largely concerned with the collection and codification of a vast body of tales, superstitions, customs, songs, etc., a more overtly sociological task would be to offer an account of these within their social context.[1] The 'subterranean theologies' (Martin 1967: 74) of folk religion may be disparate, fragmentary and covert, but are nevertheless worthy of serious study. The point was recognised by Durkheim over eighty years ago: 'there are innumerable religious manifestations which do not belong to any properly recognised religion. In every society there are scattered beliefs and practices, be they individual or local, which are not integrated into a definite system' (1975: 74).

The vehicle for my investigation has been that of the community study, wherein we have attempted to elucidate the nature of religious life in a particular village. Some of the elements of folk religion described seem to be generated and sustained within the *gemeinschaftlich* setting which still persists in Staithes. Traditional practices and local customs and beliefs are in some ways the stuff of folk religion in that they express the sentiments which arise out of group life. In Staithes, folk religion is one of the agencies by which group membership is defined and renewed. We are therefore forced to offer some explanation of how this form of religion can persist in a broadly secular(ising) culture. As we saw in the last chapter, Parkin's (1967) notion of political deviance seems useful for the way in which it demonstrates how deviant values (in the present case religious) can be sustained given the presence of certain structural prerequisites. In other words, where suitable 'buffers' or insulators exist, which not only keep out the wider secularity but also keep in communal religion, then the persistence of superstition, allegiance to denominational labels abandoned elsewhere and a desire to maintain local customs are all greatly facilitated.

It would be wrong to place too much emphasis upon geographical isolation as an important 'buffer' in Staithes, though, as I suggested in Chapter 2, it is often the case that we overlook some of the differences which exist between rural and town life in terms of the availability of public services and amenities. None the less, life in 'Steeas' can frequently seem cut off and remote from the wider society; that is certainly a conception which villagers like to perpetrate. When listening to people in the village discuss some item of national or international news, one would often hear the disapproving comment – 'Ah! The world's turned upside down!' Indeed, many still want no part of 'the world' and are content to remain within what they perceive to be the secure and predictable round of village life. This sense of communal identity cannot be divorced from an understanding of folk religion in Staithes. Folk religion embodies beliefs and practices which deviate not only from institutional religion, but also from the wider secularity. It thereby establishes an important frame of reference for group identity.

It is interesting to note that the religious form around which many communal sympathies are now woven was once an alien and unwelcome intrusion. I have tried to show how nonconformity first imposed itself upon local life as a sacred culture rigidly counterposed to existing customs, values and beliefs. Some early resistance to the new faith did not prevent its establishment as the first active institutional religious presence in the village; despite its consolidation and entrenchment, however, nonconformity never completely swamped the popular culture which it manifestly opposed. Instead, a commensality ensued whereby official and unofficial religious elements could be sustained in a delicate balance – despite apparent contradictions. In time, the sacred culture was itself characterised by division. Consolidation served to highlight the tensions and rivalries existing between the chapels and respective ministries. At times, these divisions within nonconformity (specifically, Methodism) threatened to submerge the nuances of doctrine and belief. Folk items also found a way into the sacred culture and official elements were in their turn appropriated and deployed in unofficial contexts. Those aspects of folk religion which ensued often had a strong presence at times of crisis or personal misfortune, allowing some pragmatic means of coping with threatening and stressful events. Thus, elaborate ritual embellishments surrounded birth and death, fishing boats were given religious names and annual events were endowed with a variety of ritualistic observances.

In turn, 'chapel life' became the object of a deep-seated and powerful affection. Affiliation therefore came to symbolise far more than mere deference to a particular mode of denominational thinking and now rests on a love for the singing and the warmth and emotion of important annual events, like the Sunday School and Chapel Anniversaries and Harvest Festivals. Yet this affective involvement in the chapel and its traditions rarely extends to regular Sunday attendance and active participation. Sunday services are poorly supported and multiple office holding, whereby the major task of running the chapel falls onto the same few shoulders from one year to the next, is the general rule.[2]

To the casual observer, institutional religion in the village may appear as the ailing and moribund preserve of a faithful but ageing few, who struggle against insurmountable odds to keep their places of worship open and functioning. This view, which is also the one held by the Methodist Church at circuit and district level, is not totally inaccurate. Small memberships and low attendances, coupled with the rising costs of heating and maintaining the buildings and the practical difficulties of arranging preachers, constitute an enormous threat to the continuance of the three chapels in the village. Yet on the other hand, the chapels do continue to survive and to collect large sums of money at particular annual events; Sunday School membership figures are high and in the case of the Methodists, a well-developed 'Primitive' and 'Wesleyan' allegiance persists. To assume, therefore, that the chapels are in imminent danger of closure would be quite erroneous and would be to overlook the deeply rooted and still fertile underlife of chapel religion maintaining itself in Staithes which is able on occasion to call forth a considerable network of support and sympathy. When the Methodist District attempted to close down the Wesleyan chapel, for example, there was fierce local opposition. Moreover, the feasibility of keeping two Methodist chapels open in the village was strongly underlined by a sudden increase in levels of attendance when the joint system of worship was reintroduced.

The outward signs of religious stagnation in the village are therefore only relevant to those who persist in using the variables of church membership and attendance as indices of secularisation. Limited by its own institutional parameters, such an approach inevitably produces a uni-directional picture of the demise of piety and the rise of secularity. It fails however to come to grips with the meaning which religion has for the individual and is thereby unable to take account of a situation where, for example, infrequent attendance at a chapel on Sundays may be quite compatible with a set of sincerely felt beliefs about the chapel's importance in village and family life as well as a general sympathy with all that it symbolises – warmth, fraternalism, emotionalism, and so forth.

Sentiments of this kind we have chosen to designate a part of folk religion; it is important that they are not viewed merely as vestiges of a decaying communal existence or as part of a retrospective and romantic yearning for past times. The continuing rivalry between the Primitive and Wesleyan chapels in Staithes is clear evidence of sympathies which are neither dwindling nor content to remain implicit. This should not be underestimated: for the principal protagonists the conflict is the focus of considerable effort and emotional investment. The elaborate forms of inter-chapel rivalry – a continuous progression of fund-raising events, competition to obtain speakers and preachers, as well as the apocryphal stories and jokes depicting 'Prims.' and 'Wesleyans' – are all testimony to the degree of involvement in chapel life which is found in the village. They provide an interesting illustration of a more general point made by Cohen in his discussion of identity on Whalsay (1978). The tensions between chapel supporters are never allowed to dominate social relations entirely, for they are always secondary to a 'public identity' (*ibid.*: 461) (in this case a *joint* opposition to the Methodist heirarchy) which overrides and controls them. As Cohen puts it, the separate identities 'have idiomatic boundaries which preserve the essential cultural homogeneity of the community' (*ibid.*: 462).

Elements of this kind came to be seen during the course of the study as important aspects of folk religion, despite their unlikely origin within the institutional fabric of the church itself. It may be argued, of course, that attachment to the customs and beliefs associated with the local church does not in itself constitute an autonomous aspect of folk religion and that the rich variety of local practices might indeed be seen as evidence of the inclusiveness of official religion. Yet in Staithes the situation goes well beyond this to open disagreement between the chapels in the village and the denominational authorities at regional and national levels. These differences spring from the disjuncture between two genuinely conflicting positions: that of the official purveyors of religion, who seek to channel belief and practice into certain agreed institutional moulds, and that of the folk or community, for whom traditional practice is felt worthy of preservation even in the face of disapproval from the church. As Bryan Wilson, who throughout his work argues consistently for the notion of an increasingly secular society, is forced to admit: 'There is a general social phenomenon of institutional persistence, which is perhaps especially evident in the case of religious institutions, which, possibly because they are ultimate repositories of strong emotional commitment, however latent and traditional that commitment has become, manifest an especial durability' (Wilson 1966: 29–30). Our findings here suggest that this situation is particularly marked at a local level, where persistence is further supported by a variety of communal and familial ties. It is argued, therefore, that the religious setting where persistence is most clearly perceptible is the whole 'irregular institution' (Towler 1974) of folk religion itself.

Throughout the present work I have attempted to distinguish between folk religion and official religion. I have indicated that this distinction has a sociological reality since by peeling back the layers of meaning attached to religious items it is possible to identify elements stemming from quite different traditions. It should be made clear at this point, however, that such an analytical process is not engaged in by the typical villager during the course of everyday life. The highly complex inter-connections between the official and the folk reflect their symbiotic relationship. For the villager, however, they are woven inextricably together: they are all 'religion'. Needless to say no-one in Staithes (as far as I know) conceives of the religious realm in terms of folk and official elements; the individual is merely born into a social setting in which a rich variety of religious beliefs and practices are in existence, both inside and outside the church. To say, as I have done, that folk religion implies a repudiation, if only implicitly, of official religion, is not to suggest that the individual consciously rejects the church and the beliefs and practices purveyed by it (though this may happen in specific cases) but is rather to demonstrate how a range of alternative religious items exist and are capable of reproducing themselves. In so doing they constitute a readily available repository of belief and practice, which can be drawn upon as required. The outcome is a blend, a heterogeneous complex of folk and official religion. Unfortunately, sociology has almost completely failed to recognise this blend and has proceeded instead to the manifestly (i.e. institutionally) religious as the object of analysis. As I have argued repeatedly, to do this is to overlook a large and important aspect of religious culture.

The evidence from Staithes suggests that folk religion and the local community are interrelated phenomena. What can the analysis tell us about the nature of religion in the wider context? Do similar folk elements persist among those who live in the towns and industrial conurbations of a highly segmented and associational society? The first reply to this question must be a word of warning against adopting a viewpoint which equates society *in toto* with the conditions which prevail in the large centres of population. The breakdown of communal and familial networks (and hence the optimum location for folk religion) must not be assumed to be complete and a variety of enclaves still exist in which collective norms and values continue to impart a sense of belonging and communal identification. For the sociologists involved, the so-called 'end of community' remains an unresolved debate. We might point, for example, to the traditional working class communities, described extensively in the sociological literature (Dennis *et al.* 1969; Horobin 1957; Young and Willmott 1962) and to the rural areas which have been depicted in various other community studies (Emmett 1964; Frankenberg 1957; Littlejohn 1964; Rees 1950; Williams 1958). In such settings it is still possible to identify the *gemeinschaftlich* tendencies of mutual aid and support, common identity and extensive inter-personal contact.

Recent sociological theories of religion are guilty of a similar tendency to over-generalise from a limited base. The writings of both Berger and Luckmann, for example, may prove far more relevant to the situation of socially and geographically mobile members of the white American middle classes than to the English fisherman, miner, East-Ender, or North Yorkshire villager. Religious beliefs and practices only become intelligible within their social context and it is for this reason that more empirical studies are required which depict religion in particular localities. It is only through such studies that the heterogeneous range of regional and social variations in religious belief and practice which *seems* to be in existence can be adequately demonstrated and explained.

With these provisos firmly in mind we must nevertheless work on the assumption that for the majority of individuals in contemporary society, everday life experiences do not tend to take place within the context of a highly inter-related social and kinship network, still less in a frame of reference made meaningful by the beliefs and doctrines of the churches. Given the important relationship between folk religion and community, this may be of crucial importance when assessing the persistence of folk belief and practice. From its earliest days, sociology has pointed to the special characteristics which distinguish the modern world from traditional society – individualism, a complex and differentiated system of social stratification, the rise of rationally conceived bureaucracies, of scientific and technological ideologies and, above all, an inexorable process of secularisation, whereby religious elements are gradually filtered out of the social fabric. Such structural conditions seem essentially hostile to the maintenance of religious belief and practice. In particular, folk elements based upon local and regional variations would appear incapable of withstanding the force and power of a burgeoning tide of massification whereby communications and media break down cultural enclaves and replace them with the standardised items of mass society. Whether or not folk religion can persist in this context, where the structural prerequisites necessary to maintain it appear almost completely absent, must remain a matter for speculation since no empirical study has yet been carried out which attempts to understand folk religion in the modern urban context. Yet on the basis of our present findings, we can offer some tentative suggestions concerning the content and place of folk religion in contemporary society.

In my introductory chapter I discussed various forms of individual and social experience likely to engender or initiate unofficial religious responses. Whilst these forms of experience, grounded in the human existential condition itself, are common to individuals in the entire spectrum of social settings, it has been argued that they are most likely to result in folk religion where social-structural support mechanisms are also present. This is largely a question of degree rather than kind, however, and it is clear that some of the factors which typically stimulate folk religion – the problems of theodicy, mortality and the succession of temporal cycles – are aspects of the social experience of those inhabiting all social milieux. Thus we might expect to find the same *underlying* patterns, in superstition, for example, wherever it is found.[3]

But are the problems encountered through the experience of suffering and misfortune, the crises of the life cycle and the progression of annual events sufficient in themselves to sustain unofficial beliefs and practices? It *is* conceivable that such life experiences will continue to call for explanations among those who seek to locate their own personal biography within some kind of meaningful framework. Even a world habitually taken for granted will produce consternation when its routine and predictable qualities are interrupted, as through death, sickness or economic hardship. In such cases, especially when the ideas of official religion are not invoked in mitigation, minimal concepts like good and bad luck may prove supportive. The chief problem posed by the predominance of individualism, however, is the decline of adequate agents of transmission. Folk religion clearly remains viable where traditional attitudes predominate and where items can be confidently invoked on appropriate occasions. When, on the other hand, the body of tradition is eroded and the individual becomes the sole arbiter on religious matters, then the confidence which previously characterised folk practices and beliefs disappears. We have seen how in Staithes the older women especially are the holders of an extensive body of knowledge concerning folk religion. It is they who are seen as particularly authoritative on such matters as the 'correct' way to deal with a birth or death or the celebration of the New Year. In a social setting which has no place for such repositories of traditional wisdom it seems less likely that folk religion can be successfully transmitted over time.

An essential feature of folk religion is that it has neither formal creed nor liturgy; its beliefs and practices may be highly localised and subject to extensive geographical and social variation. It is therefore heterogeneous in the extreme. Folk belief and practice are fundamentally non-institutional; they have little or no dependence on either the thoughts of theologians or the ministrations of priests. These qualities reach their most overt expression when we see how folk religion has insinuated itself into the very life of the churches, where it remains a constant irritant to clergy and ministers. Yet such is its tenacity that for centuries it has frustrated all attempts at expurgation. The limited amount of historical and sociological evidence reviewed in Chapter 1 suggests that folk religion should be seen as both prior to and independent of the churches. As such it presents considerable problems for recent theories of secularisation – a process which sociologists have typically regarded, according to Luckmann, as one of 'religious pathology to be measured by the shrinking reach of the churches' (1967: 23). When religion and the church are equated then the 'decline' of religion may be easily measured by reference to specific institutional indices. But when religion also exists outside the church, institutionally bound explanations of secularisation cease to be viable. The possibility then exists of a folk religion which is not index-linked to fluctuations in the fortunes of the churches and denominations. Indeed, the persistence of a set of folk elements in a society which is officially underpinned by *secular* legitimations becomes increasingly likely. If we are to avoid making inferences which are far removed from the actual experiences of large sectors of the population, we must beware of over-emphasising the spread of rationalising tendencies. The 'demystification of the world' remains incomplete and has advanced further in certain social configurations than in others. In many cases transcendent elements may continue to perform legitimating tasks. Where institutional religion has experienced a decline, these are likely to be folk religious in character.

The evidence from Staithes alone does not allow us to judge whether folk religion merely represents the last vestiges of a formerly rich religious life. Could it be, for example, that folk religion is simply less vulnerable to secularising influences than its institutional counterpart but that it must, nevertheless, ultimately succumb to forces greater than itself? In this case some concept of a non-transcendent 'invisible' religion would seem a more plausible account of contemporary religiosity. On the other hand, might folk religion have the capacity to recreate itself in new items of belief and practice which will continue to legitimate social existence? At this stage these questions must remain unanswered, but it is clear that they remain important for a fuller understanding of the place of religion in contemporary society.

Notes

1. Introduction: some preliminaries concerning folk religion

1 See Berger and Luckmann (1963).
2 Limited evidence is available in Machalek and Martin (1976) and Cottrell (1980).
3 Other writers have briefly referred to such a form of religiosity but have not developed their concerns to any extent. See, for example, Martin (1967: 74ff) and Budd (1973: 9).
4 The term has been used differently by other writers. Mensching sees it as the religion of the *folk* or a particular 'vital community' (1964: 254), against which he contrasts 'universal religion', in which the individual is perceived subjectively as separate from the group – a form of self-consciousness which results in the problem of determining the meaning of personal existence (*ibid.*). Hegel's notion of folk religion is described by Plant as 'a means of providing some non-divisive cultural form in Germany, a cultural form which would unite the powers of the human mind into one society' (Plant 1973: 42). Both Mensching and Hegel see folk religion as part of a unified and integrated moral community whose social solidarity is attenuated with the onset of universal religion (viz. Christianity).
5 The dilemma is vividly illustrated in Evans-Pritchard's (1937) classic study of witchcraft among the Azande. Thus in one particular case, we read of a Zande who *knows* that his house falls down because termites eat away the legs which support it, but who is nevertheless compelled to question why it should actually collapse when he is inside. The Zande may not be so far removed in his quandary from the westerner dying of a terminal disease who likewise knows that the condition is attributable to physiological processes, but who still demands, 'why me?'.
6 These are explored in more detail in Chapter 3.

2. The village

1 In fact, some thirty-five households, on Cowbar Bank and at the top of the cliff, are administratively and fiscally within Cleveland County, though culturally they remain a part of Staithes.
2 O.P.C.S., *Small Area Statistics*, 1971, Whitby Rural District, Hinderwell, B 32/B; B 33/B; 34.
3 A drop of 530 persons.

4 This part of the village – the sea-front – is still known locally as 'the staith'.
5 A carucate consists of 'A measure of land, varying with the nature of the soil etc., being as much as could be tilled with one plough (with its team of eight oxen) in a year' (*O.E.D.*, 1961).
6 John Howard, personal communication.
7 See Peter Frank's (1976) discussion of women's work in the Yorkshire inshore fishing trade.
8 I am grateful to Stephanie Jones, of the University of London, for drawing this to my attention.
9 Steve Cornish at the Teesside Polytechnic is currently working on a sociological and historical study of the Cleveland ironstone miners.
10 The economic recession of the late 1970s and early 1980s may result in some redundancies at the mine.
11 Even today, the nature of the local topography makes the installation of a mains gas supply extremely unlikely.
12 From an article in the Middlesbrough *Evening Gazette*, Friday 12 September 1975.

3. Studying folk religion

1 For a review of these see Bell and Newby (1971: Chapter 3).
2 Some examples can be read in Bell and Newby (1977), Busfield and Paddon (1977), and Leonard (1980).
3 Staithes and the adjacent coastline are frequently visited by parties of geologists.
4 As we shall see in Chapter 5, the frequent presence in the village in earlier years of recently or still unordained ministers provided a ready category into which I could be inserted.
5 I was able to observe only two weddings.
6 The sociology of courtship and marriage in Britain has until recently been largely ignored by researchers. Leonard's recent Swansea study (1980) has gone a long way towards redressing this imbalance, though from a theoretical perspective very different to my own. While her work was published too late to be fully discussed here, her account is undoubtedly complementary to the present one. Indeed, she recognises the persistence of 'folk religion' in the marriage rituals and is critical of sociologists of religion who have dismissed the folk elements as 'well nigh meaningless' (1980: 211–13). The absence of any discussion of marriage here is therefore more than adequately compensated.
7 This was found to be the earliest period which my respondents could recall.
8 See Clark 1978a.
9 Despite a new research job which took me into the field of divorce and remarriage.

4. Institutional religion

1 Archbishop Herring's Visitation Returns (1743).
2 N. Yorks. Archives R/M/STY 1/1/1.
3 *Ibid.*

4 Public Record Office HO 129/531 X/K 6572.
5 A 'gracious revival' was said to have taken place among the Primitive Methodists in Staithes during the early 1850s (*Primitive Methodist Magazine* 1854: 633).
6 Public Record Office HO 129/53 X/K 6572.

5. Chapel life and chapel folk

1 If I might add my own observation to the list, it concerns the only reference to organised co-operation between the chapels which I was able to uncover in any of the records, albeit one probably inspired by wartime stringency. The Primitive Methodist Trustees Meeting Minutes for 5 December 1916 (Cleveland Archives R/M/LOF 2/10/2) include reference to the following suggestion: 'That the secretary make some arrangements along with the other chapels for buying a truck of coke amongst them.'
2 We shall see in Chapter 8 that a certain animus towards the local agricultural communities still persists in Staithes.
3 Cleveland Archives R/M/LOF 2/10/2.
4 North Yorkshire Archives R/I/WH 4/4.
5 *Ibid.*
6 *Ibid.*
7 This quotation is taken from a newspaper cutting from the *Whitby Gazette* found in a scrapbook in the library of the Whitby Literary and Philosophical Society. The cutting is undated, though entries adjacent to it in the scrapbook indicate a date somewhere in the late 1880s.
8 Conflict between ministry and laity has been examined in the Australian context by Dempsey (1969).
9 The man had not yet completed his full course of lay preacher examinations.
10 Cleveland Archives R/M/LOF 1/1/7.
11 *Ibid.*
12 *Ibid.*
13 Cleveland Archives R/M/LOF 1/41.
14 One of these, the Newton Memorial Chapel, as we noted in Chapter 3, was subsequently bombed in 1941.
15 Cleveland Archives R/M/LOF 4/4/28.
16 Cleveland Archives R/M/LOF 1/41.
17 Cleveland Archives R/M/LOF 1/4/1.
18 *Ibid.*
19 Cleveland Archives R/M/LOF 1/42.
20 The minutes of this meeting and of the Commissioners' report were kindly made available to me during fieldwork.
21 Information from account books.
22 This is, of course, a distinction which raises certain difficulties, since in failing to offer any empirical evidence on the nature of Methodism in the towns and cities, Moore can only provide us with half of the picture; the rest we must fill in by way of unsubstantiated inference.

6. The annual cycle

1 This is the usual local interpretation of the symbolism of salt (see Chapter 7 for its significance in birth rites), though elsewhere it is frequently seen as a symbol of preservation.

2 The point is illustrated further by the tremendous popularity of brass fire-side decorations, which are often the object of considerable attention and always kept highly polished.

3 On one occasion shortly after Christmas in 1975 I was in the house of a member of the Wesleyan chapel who was busy drilling his four-year-old son in the catechism. The scene was not without its amusing qualities as the young boy, plainly more interested in his newly acquired toys, was demanded gruffly by his father: 'Who is God?'

4 Pickering has referred to the *entertainment* value of the Sunday School Anniversary (Pickering 1958: xv, 27).

5 In 1976 the figures for the respective chapels were: Wesley, £152; High Street, £156; Bethel, £145.

6 See, for example, the rowdy football game which takes place each Shrove Tuesday, despite magisterial objection, in the streets of Sedgefield, Co. Durham.

7 A similar belief has been noted for nineteenth-century Lincolnshire by Obelkevich (1976: 267).

8 Similar Hallowe'en activities are noted for Gosforth by Williams (1958: 188).

9 Elsewhere in the country 'mischief night' may take place on 4 November.

10 Gallaher, in his re-study of Plainville, reports much wilder activities on the part of male youths in the Missouri village (1961: 271, n. 17).

7. Birth and death

1 The liminality of mother and child is also found in primitive societies, e.g. amongst the Konso of Ethiopia. Hallpike states, 'When a woman has given birth, she remains secluded in her homestead with the baby until some time in the third month . . . the baby is also regarded as still mystically tied to the mother until the coming out ceremony' (1972: 296). Similarly, Mead, writing of the Manus of New Guinea, tells us, '[Intercourse] is forbidden for thirty days after birth, but as the wife is not allowed even to see her husband during this period, this prohibition follows naturally' (1942: 238). Examples such as these indicate that in different societies women are required to pass through a liminal period after childbirth, before they can re-enter social life.

2 See also Hallpike (1972: 296) for a similar practice among the Konso of Ethiopia.

3 Records for the Methodist chapels were unavailable.

4 Wylie reports similar findings from the French village of Chanzeaux, in Anjou, a region of strong Catholic allegiance. 'It used to be that baptisms were held within a week of the birth because of the high infant mortality rate. Now that danger of death before baptism is all but removed, the ceremony is usually postponed until the mother is well enough recovered to attend' (Wylie 1966: 287).

5 I am grateful to Maurice Staton for our various conversations on the subject of churching and would refer the reader to his extensive historical and sociological study of the rite (Staton 1980).

6 J.S. La Fontaine describes a similar practice among the Gisu: 'The baby is formally greeted by members of the village, each household offering a small gift, usually a few small coins . . . the payment of which averts evil from the child, by demonstrating the goodwill of the giver. We can see it also as the first act of hospitality to the child, symbolizing his social relation with the giver' (1974: 176).

7 Faris also notes the practice of bearers wearing white ribbons in Cat Harbour Newfoundland (1972: 156).

8 A process also described by Faris (1972).

9 Similar cards were used by Roman Catholics, especially on the Continent.

10 The first crematorium to be opened in Britain was at Woking, in 1885. The first in the north-east of England was at Darlington in 1901.

11 From *Resurgam* – the Journal of the Federation of British Cremation Authorities 1975: 19–22.

12 *Ibid.*

8. Occupational beliefs

1 As recently as 1972, a Staithes fisherman was drowned when his boat overturned just outside the harbour, and during the fieldwork period itself a worker from a nearby town was killed in the mine. *The Sunday Times* of 23 April 1978 reported two more fatalities at the mine. The Holland-Martin *Report* found that in England and Wales 'Fishermen are alarmingly more at risk than the average male worker', having a chance of fatal, work-associated accident seventeen times greater than that for the population as a whole (Holland-Martin 1969: 11).

2 My thanks to Stephanie Jones for this information.

3 The word 'grecian' probably derives from the Scandinavian *gris*, meaning pig.

4 In one case which came to my attention, a man's wife and children took a holiday without him, since he did not wish to leave the village at a time when the lobster fishing was particularly good. On a number of occasions I heard him describe how they were going to the country 'to stay in a cottage in the middle of a field!'. Each time the man would roar with laughter at the thought of this 'holiday' which was so remote from his own concerns. Cohen makes a similar point in relation to Whalsaymen (1978: 458).

9. Conclusions

1 Obelkevich (1976) provides an excellent example of the profitable use which the modern historian can make of nineteenth-century folkloristic writings.

2 Similar forms of allegiance to the local chapel have been described by Moore (1974: Chapter 9) and Pickering 1958 (Chapter 15).

3 Peter Jarvis has elaborated this idea in a recent article (1980).

References

Abercrombie, N., Baker, J., Brett, S. and Foster, J. 1970. Superstition and religion: the god of the gaps. In *A Sociological Yearbook of Religion in Britain*, ed. D. Martin, pp. 93–129. London, S.C.M. Press.

Archbishop Herring's Visitation Return. 1743. In *Yorkshire Archaeological Society Record Series*, eds. S.L. Ollard and P.C. Walker, LXXI, LXXII, LXXV, LXXVIII and LXXIX, 1929–31.

Arensberg, C.M. 1937. *The Irish Countryman*, New York, Macmillan.

Atkinson, J.C. 1874. *History of Cleveland Ancient and Modern*, Barrow-in-Furness, Joseph Richardson.

Bailey, E.I.B. 1976. The religion of a secular society. Ph.D. thesis, University of Bristol.

Baines, E. 1823. *History, Directory and Gazetteer of the County of York*, 2 vols., Leeds. (1969 edn, London, David and Charles.)

Baker, J. 1975. Who is it believes in luck? *New Society*, 34: 199–200.

Barker, D. 1972. The confetti ritual. *New Society*, 20: 614–17.

Beattie, J. 1965. *Understanding an African Kingdom*, New York, Holt, Rinehart and Winston.

Becker, H.S. 1970. Problems of inference and proof in participant observation. In *Sociological Methods*, N.K. Denzin, pp. 398–412. London, Butterworths.

Beckford, J.A. 1975. *The Trumpet of Prophecy*, Oxford, Blackwell.

Bell, C. and Newby, H. 1971. *Community Studies*, London, George Allen and Unwin.

1977. *Doing Sociological Research*, London, George Allen and Unwin.

Bell, D. 1977. The return of the sacred? The argument on the future of religion. *British Journal of Sociology*, 28: 419–49.

Berger, P.L. 1973. *The Social Reality of Religion*, Harmondsworth, Penguin.

1974. Some second thoughts on substantive versus functional definitions of religion. *Journal for the Scientific Study of Religion*, 13: 125–33.

Berger, P.L. and Luckmann, T. 1963. Sociology of religion and sociology of knowledge. *Sociology and Social Research*, 47: 417–27.

1971. *The Social Construction of Reality*, Harmondsworth, Penguin.

Binnall, P.B.G. 1941. Correspondence. *Folklore*, 52: 75.

Bock, W.E. 1966. Symbols in conflict: official versus folk religion. *Journal for the Scientific Study of Religion*, 5: 204–12.

Bocock, R. 1974. *Ritual in Industrial Society*, London, George Allen and Unwin.

Bott, E. 1971. *Family and Social Network*, 2nd edn, London, Tavistock.

Budd, S. 1973. *Sociologists and Religion*, London, Collier-Macmillan.

Bulmer, T. 1890. *History, Topography and Directory of North Yorkshire*, Preston, Bulmer and Co.

Busfield, J. and Paddon, M. 1977. *Thinking about Children*, London, Cambridge University Press.

Cameron, D. 1974. Infant baptism. *Parish News of Eston and Normanby*, November.

Castenada, C. 1970. *The Teachings of Don Juan*, Harmondsworth, Penguin.

Chadwick, O. 1976. *The Secularisation of the European Mind in the Nineteenth Century*, London, Cambridge University Press.

Chamberlain, A. 1976a. Planning versus fatalism. *Journal of Biosocial Science*, 8: 1–16.

1976b. Gin and hot baths. *New Society*, 37: 112–14.

Chapman, S.K. 1976. *Gazetteer of Cleveland Ironstone Mines*, Guisborough, Langbaurgh Museum Service.

Cicourel, A.V. 1964. *Method and Measurement in Sociology*, New York, Free Press of Glencoe.

Clark, D. 1978a. Folk religion in a North Yorkshire fishing village. M.A. thesis, University of Newcastle-upon-Tyne.

1978b. Religion and superstition in a fishing community. *Research Bulletin*, pp. 56–69. Institute for the Study of Worship and Religious Architecture, University of Birmingham.

Cohen, A.P. 1978. 'The same – but different': the allocation of identity on Whalsay, Shetland. *Sociological Review*, 26: 449–469.

Cottrell, M. 1980. Invisible religion and the middle class. *Paper presented to the Third Consultation on Implicit Religion*, Ilkley.

Cuming, G.J. 1969. *A History of Anglican Liturgy*, London, Macmillan.

Currie, R. 1968. *Methodism Divided*, London, Faber and Faber.

Dalton, M. 1959. *Men Who Manage*, New York, Wiley.

Davies, R.E. 1961. The nature of modern Methodism. In *Anglican–Methodist Relations*, ed. W.S.F. Pickering, pp. 58–82. London, Darton, Longman and Todd.

Dempsey, K.C. 1969. Conflict in minister/lay relations. In *A Sociological Yearbook of Religion in Britain*, ed. D. Martin, pp. 58–74. London, S.C.M. Press.

Dennis, N., Henriques, F.M. and Slaughter, C. 1969. *Coal is Our Life*, London, Tavistock.

Denzin, N.K. 1970. *The Research Act in Sociology*, London, Butterworths.

Dickens, A.G. 1959. *Lollards and Protestants in the Diocese of York 1509–1558*, London, University of Hull.

Douglas, M. 1970. *Natural Symbols*, London, Barrie and Rockcliff.

Durkheim, E. 1975. Concerning the definition of religious phenomena. In *Durkheim on Religion*, ed. W.S.F. Pickering, pp. 74–9. London, Routledge and Kegan Paul.

Edwards, W. 1906. Cleveland and its Congregational Churches. *Paper presented to the members of the Yorkshire Congregational Union*, Middlesbrough.

Eliade, M. 1959. *The Sacred and the Profane*, New York, Harvest.

Emmet, I. 1964. *A North Wales Parish*, London, Routledge and Kegan Paul.

Erichsen, N. 1886. A north country fishing town. *The English Illustrated Magazine,* 31: 462–9.

Evans-Pritchard, E.E. 1937. *Witchcraft, Oracles and Magic among the Azande,* Oxford, Clarendon Press.

Faris, J.C. 1972. *Cat Harbour: a Newfoundland Fishing Settlement,* Institute of Social and Economic Research, Memorial University of Newfoundland.

Field, C.D. 1977. The social structure of English Methodism. *British Journal of Sociology,* 28: 199–225.

Firth, R. 1966. *Malay Fishermen,* London, Routledge and Kegan Paul.

Fox, G. 1952. *The Journal of George Fox,* London, Cambridge University Press.

Frank, P. 1976. Women's work in the Yorkshire inshore fishing industry. *Oral History,* 4: 57–71.

Frankenberg, R. 1957. *Village on the Border,* London, Cohen and West.
1969. *Communities in Britain,* Harmondsworth, Penguin.

Gallaher, A. 1961. *Plainville Fifteen Years Later,* New York, Columbia University Press.

Gaskin, R.T. 1863. *The Rise of (Whitby) Methodism,* London, Whittaker.

Geertz, C. 1966. Religion as a cultural system. In *Anthropological Approaches to the Study of Religion,* ed. M. Banton, pp. 1–46. London, Tavistock.

Gennep, A. van. 1960. *The Rites of Passage,* London, Routledge and Kegan Paul.

Gilbert, A.D. 1976. *Religion and Society in Industrial England,* London, Longman.

Glass, R. 1966. Conflict in cities. In *Conflict in Society,* eds. A. de Reuck and J. Knight, pp. 141–64. London, Churchill.

Glock, C.Y. and Stark, R. 1965. *Religion and Society in Tension,* Chicago, Rand McNally.

Gluckman, M. 1956. *Custom and Conflict in Africa,* Oxford, Blackwell.
1971. Preface. In *Family and Social Network,* E. Bott, London, Tavistock.

Goldthorpe, J., Lockwood, D., Bechofer, F. and Platt, J. 1969. *The Affluent Worker in the Class Structure.* London, Cambridge University Press.

Goody, J. 1962. *Death, Property and the Ancestors,* London, Tavistock.

Gordon, S. 1869. *The Watering Places of Cleveland,* Redcar, J.H. Webster.

Gorer, G. 1955. *Exploring English Character,* New York, Criterion Books.
1965. *Death, Grief and Mourning in Contemporary Britain,* London, Cresset Press.

Gouldner, A.W. 1955. *Patterns of Industrial Bureaucracy,* London, Routledge and Kegan Paul.

Gowland, D.A. 1978. *Methodist Secessions,* Manchester, Manchester University Press.

Gowling, A. 1973. The place of luck in the professional footballer's life. In *Men and Work in Modern Britain,* ed. D. Weir, pp. 139–43. Bungay, Fontana.

Graves, J. 1808. *The History of Cleveland,* Stockton-on-Tees, Patrick and Stotton (reprinted, 1972).

Gutch, Mrs. 1912. *County Folk-Lore,* VI, London, Folk-Lore Society.

Halevy, E. 1971. *The Birth of Methodism in England,* Chicago, University of Chicago Press.

Hallpike, C.R. 1972. *The Konso of Ethiopia*, Oxford, Clarendon Press.

Harris, C. 1974. *Hennage*, New York, Holt, Rinehart and Winston.

Harrison, M. 1973. *Parish of Hinderwell*, Whitby, Horne and Son.

Henderson, W. 1866. *Notes on the Folk-Lore of the Northern Counties of England and the Borders*, London, Longmans, Green and Co.

Herz, R. 1960. *Death and the Right Hand*, Aberdeen, Cohen and West.

Hick, J. 1966. *Evil and the God of Love*, London, Macmillan.

Hobsbawm, E.J. 1957. Methodism and the threat of revolution in Britain. *History Today*, 7: 115–24.

Hoggart, R. 1958. *The Uses of Literacy*, Harmondsworth, Penguin.

Holland-Martin, Sir D. 1969. *Final Report of the Committee of Enquiry into Trawler Safety*, London, H.M.S.O. Cmnd 4114.

Homans, G.C. 1941. Anxiety and ritual: the theories of Malinowski and Radcliffe-Brown. *American Anthropologist*, 43: 163–72.

Horner, J.P. 1971. The influence of Methodism on the social structure and culture of rural Northumberland from 1820 to 1914. M.A. thesis, University of Newcastle-upon-Tyne.

Horobin, G.W. 1957. Community and occupation in the Hull fishing industry. *British Journal of Sociology*, 8: 343–55.

Howard, J. 1966. *A History of Wesleyan Methodism in Staithes*, Guisborough, J.T. Stokeld.

Jahoda, G. 1970. *The Psychology of Superstition*, Harmondsworth, Penguin.

Jarvis, P. 1980. Towards a sociological understanding of superstition. *Social Compass*, 27: 285–95.

Kendall, H.B. 1889. *History of the Primitive Methodist Connexion*, London, Joseph Toulson.

Kimball, S.T. 1960. Introduction to English edition of *The Rites of Passage*, A. van Gennep, pp. v–xx. London, Routledge and Kegan Paul.

Knight, L. 1965. *The Magic of a Line*, London, Wm Kimber.

Kübler-Ross, E. 1970. *On Death and Dying*, London, Tavistock.

La Fontaine, J.S. 1974. Ritualization of women's life-crises in Bugisu. in *The Interpretation of Ritual*, ed. J.S. La Fontaine, pp. 159–86. London, Tavistock.

Lasch, C. 1978. *The Culture of Narcissism*, New York, W.W. Norton.

Lawson, M.S. 1948. The dialect of Staithes in the North Riding of Yorkshire. *Transactions of the Yorkshire Dialect Society*, 8–9: 24–8.

1949. An account of the dialect of Staithes in the North Riding of Yorkshire. M.A. thesis, University of Leeds.

Leach, E. 1972. Anthropological aspects of language: animal categories and verbal abuse. In *Mythology*, ed. P. Maranda, pp. 39–67. Harmondsworth, Penguin.

Leonard, D. 1980. *Sex and Generation*, London, Tavistock.

Leonard, T. 1976. *Cleveland Customs and Superstitions*, Guisborough, Tom Leonard.

Lévi-Strauss, C. 1969. *The Elementary Structures of Kinship*, London, Eyre and Spottiswoode.

Littlejohn, J. 1964. *Westrigg*, London, Routledge and Kegan Paul.

Lomas, P. 1964. Childbirth ritual. *New Society*, 4: 13–14.

Luckmann, T. 1967. *The Invisible Religion*, New York, Macmillan.

Lummis, T. 1977. The occupational community of East Anglian fishermen: an historical dimension through oral evidence. *British Journal of Sociology,* 28: 51–74.

Machalek, R. and Martin, M. 1976. 'Invisible' religions: some preliminary evidence. *Journal for the Scientific Study of Religion,* 15: 311–21.

MacIntyre, A. 1968. Death and the English. *The Listener,* 79: 719–20.

Malinowski, B. 1922. *Argonauts of the Western Pacific,* London, Routledge. 1954. *Magic, Science and Religion,* Illinois, Glencoe.

Marchant, R.A. 1960. *The Puritans and the Church Courts in the Diocese of York, 1560–1642,* London, Longmans.

Martin, D.A. 1967. *A Sociology of English Religion,* London, Heinemann. 1969. *The Religious and the Secular,* London, Routledge and Kegan Paul. 1978. *The Dilemmas of Contemporary Religion,* Oxford, Blackwell.

Mauss, M. 1970. *The Gift,* London, Cohen and West.

Maybury-Lewis, D. 1967. *Akwê-Shavante Society,* Oxford, Clarendon Press.

Mead, M. 1942. *Growing Up in New Guinea,* Harmondsworth, Penguin.

Mensching, G. 1964. Folk and universal religion. In *Religion, Culture and Society,* ed. L. Schneider, pp. 254–73. New York, Wiley.

Miall, J.G. 1868. *Congregationalism in Yorkshire,* London, John Snow.

Mitford, J. 1963. *The American Way of Death,* London, Hutchinson.

Moore, R. 1974. *Pit-men, Preachers and Politics,* London, Cambridge University Press.

Mullen, P.B. 1969. The function of magic folk belief among Texas coastal fishermen. *Journal of American Folklore,* 82: 214–25.

Niebuhr, H.R. 1929. *The Social Sources of Denominationalism,* New York, Holt and Co.

Obelkevich, J. 1976. *Religion and Rural Society,* Oxford, Clarendon Press.

Office of Population Censuses and Surveys. 1971. *Small Area Statistics.* Whitby Rural District, Hinderwell. B 32/B; B 33/B; 34.

Ord, J.W. 1846. *The History and Antiquities of Cleveland,* Stockton-on-Tees, Patrick and Shotton (reprinted 1972).

Ortner, S.B. 1978. *Sherpas Through Their Rituals,* London, Cambridge University Press.

Parkin, F. 1967. Working class conservatives. *British Journal of Sociology,* 18: 278–90.

Parsons, T. 1965. Introduction. *The Sociology of Religion,* M. Weber, pp. xix–lxvii. London, Methuen.

Patterson, W.M. 1909. *Northern Primitive Methodism,* London, Dalton.

Pickering, W.S.F. 1958. The place of religion in the social structure of two English industrial towns. Ph.D. thesis, University of London.

1961. The present position of the Anglican and Methodist churches in the light of available statistics. In *Anglican-Methodist Relations,* ed. W.S.F. Pickering, pp. 1–36. London, Darton, Longman and Todd.

1967. The 1851 religious census – a useless experiment? *British Journal of Sociology,* 18: 382–407.

1968. Religion – a leisure-time pursuit? In *A Sociological Yearbook of Religion in Britain,* ed. D. Martin, pp. 77–93. London, S.C.M. Press.

1974. The persistence of rites of passage: towards an explanation. *British Journal of Sociology,* 25: 63–78.

1975. *Durkheim on Religion,* London, Routledge and Kegan Paul.

Plant, R. 1973. *Hegel,* London, George Allen and Unwin.

Poggie, J. and Gersuny, C. 1972. Risk and ritual: an interpretation of fishermen's folklore in a New England community. *Journal of American Folklore,* 85: 66–72.

Poggie, J., Pollnac, R.B. and Gersuny, C. 1976. Risk as a basis for taboos among fishermen in Southern New England. *Journal for the Scientific Study of Religion,* 15: 257–62.

Probert, J.C.C. 1971. *The Sociology of Cornish Methodism,* Cornish Methodist Historical Association.

Radin, P. 1957. *Primitive Religion,* New York, Dover.

Raistrick, A. 1950. The alum trade of East Yorkshire. *The Dalesman,* April, May, June.

Rees, A.D. 1950. *Life in a Welsh Countryside,* Cardiff, University of Wales Press.

Resurgam. 1975. The Journal of the Federation of British Cremation Authorities, 18, 1.

Ritson, J. 1909. *The Romance of Primitive Methodism,* London, Edwin Dalton.

Robertson, R. 1978. *Meaning and Change,* Oxford, Blackwell.

Rogers, J. 1872. In *The Lives of Early Methodist Preachers,* 6 vols., ed. T. Jackson. London, Wesleyan Conference Office.

Rural Methodism, 1958. *Commision's Report to the 1958 Conference,* London, Epworth.

Russell, A. 1923. Hinderwell. In *A History of Yorkshire North Riding,* ed. W. Page, II, pp. 365–71. University of London Institute of Historical Research (reprinted 1968).

Semmel, B. 1974. *The Methodist Revolution,* London, Heinemann.

Sennett, R. 1977. *The Fall of Public Man,* London, Cambridge University Press.

Staton, M. 1980. The rite of churching: a sociological analysis with special reference to an urban area in Newcastle. M.A. thesis, University of Newcastle-upon-Tyne.

Steel, D.A. 1979. *A Lincolnshire Village,* London, Longman.

Thomas, K. 1973. *Religion and the Decline of Magic,* Harmondsworth, Penguin.

Thompson, E.P. 1968. *The Making of the English Working Class,* Harmondsworth, Penguin.

1976. On history, sociology and historical relevance. *British Journal of Sociology,* 27: 387–402.

Thompson, P. 1978. *The Voice of the Past,* Oxford, Oxford University Press.

Towler, R. 1974. *Homo Religiosus,* London, Constable.

Towler, R. and Chamberlain, A. 1973. Common religion. In *A Sociological Yearbook of Religion in Britain,* ed. M. Hill, pp. 1–28. London, S.C.M. Press.

Tunstall, J. 1962. *The Fishermen,* London, McGibbon and Kee.

Turner, V.W. 1974. *The Ritual Process,* Harmondsworth, Penguin.

Turton, R.B. 1938. *The Alum Farm.* Whitby, Horne and Son.

Tylor, E.B. 1871. *Primitive Culture,* 2 vols. London.

Umpleby, A.S. 1934. T' white hoss. In *A Cleveland Anthology*, ed. B. Cowley (1963), pp. 42–7. Yorkshire Dialect Society.

Vallee, F.G. 1955. Burial and mourning customs in a Hebridean community. *Journal of the Royal Anthropological Institute*, 85: 119–30.

Vasey, G. 1861. *Short History of the Introduction and Rise of Wesleyan Methodism in Whitby Circuit for 100 Years*, Whitby, Horne.

Wallis, R. 1977. The moral career of a research project. In *Doing Sociological Research*, ed. C. Bell and H. Newby, pp. 149–69. London, George Allen and Unwin.

Walmsley, L. 1932. *Three Fevers*, Harmondsworth, Penguin edn (1944).

1948. *Master Mariner*, London, Collins.

Weber, M. 1965. *The Sociology of Religion*, London, Methuen.

Weigart, A.J. 1974. Whose invisible religion? Luckmann revisited. *Sociological Analysis* (Los Angeles, California), 35: 181–8.

West, J. 1945. *Plainville, U.S.A.*, New York, Columbia University Press.

Whitworth, J.M. 1975. *God's Blueprints*, London, Routledge and Kegan Paul.

Whyte, W.F. 1943. *Street Corner Society*, Chicago, University of Chicago Press.

Wickham, E.R. 1957. *Church and People in an Industrial City*, London, Lutterworth.

Wilkins, L.T. 1964. *Social Deviance*, London, Tavistock.

Williams, W.M. 1958. *The Sociology of an English Village: Gosforth*, London, Routledge and Kegan Paul.

1963. *A West Country Village, Ashworthy*, London, Routledge and Kegan Paul.

Wilson, B.R. 1966. *Religion in Secular Society*, London, Watts and Co.

1976. *Contemporary Transformations of Religion*, Oxford, Oxford University Press.

Woodcock, H. 1889. *Sketches of Primitive Methodism on the Yorkshire Wolds*, London, Joseph Toulson.

Wylie, L. (ed.) 1966. *Chanzeaux*, Cambridge, Mass., Harvard University Press.

Yinger, J.M. 1970. *The Scientific Study of Religion*, New York, Macmillan.

Young, G. 1817. *A History of Whitby*, Whitby, Clark and Medd.

Young, M. and Willmott, P. 1962. *Family and Kinship in East London*, Harmondsworth, Penguin.

Magazines and newspapers

Evening Gazette (Middlesbrough)
Methodist Recorder
Primitive Methodist Magazine
The Sunday Times
The Times
Wesleyan Methodist Magazine
Whitby Gazette

Other sources

Borthwick Institute, York
Parish of Hinderwell, Tithe Map and Apportionment

Cleveland County Archives Department, Middlesbrough

Circuit Records
Loftus and Staithes (W.M.)
  Trust-Property Schedule: 1872–91
  Circuit Missionary Account Book: 1871–87
  Sunday School Union Quarterly Meeting Minute Book: 1879–1904
  Circuit Sunday School Schedule: 1899–1905, 1906–9
  Quarterly Meeting Minute Book: 1910–21, 1922–41
  Local Preachers' Meeting Minute Book: 1877–1912, 1912–32
  Circuit Temperance Schedule: 1883–7, 1888–92, 1896–8, 1898–9, 1904–5
  Schedule of Deeds and Papers in Circuit Safe: 1904
  Visitation of Classes Quarterly Schedule: 1908–25, 1945–8, 1949–52
Staithes (P.M.)
  Quarterly Meeting Minute Book: 1888–1910, 1910–20
  Annual Reports: 1865–78, 1880–9, 1890–1900, 1902–11, 1911–21, 1922–8
  Account Book: 1865–89, 1889–1909
  Sunday School Union Quarterly Meeting Minute Book: 1875–93
  Schedule of Deeds and Papers in Circuit Safe: 1925
Loftus and Staithes (M.)
  Quarterly Meeting Minute Book: 1959–66
  Quarterly Meeting Account Book: 1951–65, 1965–9
  Local Preachers' Meeting Minute Book: 1933–47, 1948–63
  Circuit Missionary Minute Book: 1957–73
  Trust Property Schedule: 1962–9
  Correspondence File: 1951–6

Chapel Records
Staithes (P.M.)
  Trustees Treasurer's Account Book: 1890–8
  Trustees Meeting Minute Book: 1915–24
Staithes (W.M.)
  Missionary Box Register: 1964–9

Baptism Registers
Staithes (P.M.) becoming Loftus and Staithes (M.) from 1941: 1878–1947
Brotton (P.M.) becoming Loftus and Staithes (M.) from 1941: 1908–50

Circuit Plans
Loftus and Staithes (W.M.): Jul. 1892–Oct. 1910; Oct. 1910–Apr. 1918; Apr.
  1918–Jun. 1921; Apr. 1910–Jul. 1910; Oct. 1913–Dec. 1917; Apr. 1918–
  Oct. 1919; Jul. 1922–Sep. 1922; Oct. 1928–Oct. 1932

Staithes (P.M.): Oct. 1891–Jan. 1892; Oct. 1892–Jan. 1893; Apr. 1893–Dec. 1893; Apr. 1894–Apr. 1898; Oct. 1902–Dec. 1902; Jul. 1906–Sep. 1906; Apr. 1907–Jun. 1907; Jan. 1908–Dec. 1909; Oct. 1912–Dec. 1912; Apr. 1913–Jun. 1913; Oct. 1913–Dec. 1913; Apr. 1914–Sep. 1915; Jan. 1916–Dec. 1916; Apr. 1917–Jun. 1919; Apr. 1920–Jun. 1920; Jan. 1921–Jun. 1921; Oct. 1921–Jun. 1923; Jan. 1926–Dec. 1926; Apr. 1927–Dec. 1929; Jan. 1932–Sep. 1932

Loftus and Staithes (M.): Oct. 1932–Apr. 1938; Jul. 1938–Dec. 1941; Oct. 1941–Sep. 1943; Apr. 1944–Dec. 1944; Apr. 1945–Dec. 1945; Jul. 1946–Sep. 1946; Jul. 1947–Sep. 1947; Feb. 1949–Jul. 1949; May 1950–Jan. 1951; Feb. 1952–Jan. 1965; Feb. 1967–Oct. 1968

Staithes (M.): Jan. 1933–Jul. 1935; Oct. 1937–Dec. 1939; Apr. 1940–Sep. 1941

John Rylands University Library, Methodist Archives, Manchester

Circuit Plans
Guisborough (W.M.): 1870–1
Stokesley (W.M.): 1834
Whitby (W.M.): 1804
Whitby and Guisborough (W.M.): 1824–5

North Yorkshire County Archives Department, Northallerton

Circuit Records
Guisborough (later Stokesley) Circuit Book: 1815–37
Miscellaneous papers: 1835
Visitors' Reports; Scarborough, Whitby and Middlesbrough District of the Yorkshire Congregational Union (Bethel Chapel): 1887

Public Record Office
1851 Religious Census Returns, Parish of Hinderwell

Index

Lightning Source UK Ltd.
Milton Keynes UK
29 December 2009

147967UK00002B/6/P